AF091206

The New Workplace

Radostina Purvanova · Alanah Mitchell

The New Workplace

Employee Alignment in Remote-First, Office-Forward, and Hybrid Work Organizations

Radostina Purvanova
Zimpleman College of Business
Drake University
Des Moines, IA, USA

Alanah Mitchell
Zimpleman College of Business
Drake University
Des Moines, IA, USA

ISBN 978-3-031-86045-4   ISBN 978-3-031-86046-1   (eBook)
https://doi.org/10.1007/978-3-031-86046-1

© The Editor(s) (if applicable) and The Author(s), under exclusive license to Springer Nature Switzerland AG 2025

This work is subject to copyright. All rights are solely and exclusively licensed by the Publisher, whether the whole or part of the material is concerned, specifically the rights of translation, reprinting, reuse of illustrations, recitation, broadcasting, reproduction on microfilms or in any other physical way, and transmission or information storage and retrieval, electronic adaptation, computer software, or by similar or dissimilar methodology now known or hereafter developed.
The use of general descriptive names, registered names, trademarks, service marks, etc. in this publication does not imply, even in the absence of a specific statement, that such names are exempt from the relevant protective laws and regulations and therefore free for general use.
The publisher, the authors and the editors are safe to assume that the advice and information in this book are believed to be true and accurate at the date of publication. Neither the publisher nor the authors or the editors give a warranty, expressed or implied, with respect to the material contained herein or for any errors or omissions that may have been made. The publisher remains neutral with regard to jurisdictional claims in published maps and institutional affiliations.

This Palgrave Macmillan imprint is published by the registered company Springer Nature Switzerland AG
The registered company address is: Gewerbestrasse 11, 6330 Cham, Switzerland

If disposing of this product, please recycle the paper.

Acknowledgments

We want to thank Dr. Renee Cramer, former Associate Provost at Drake University (currently, Provost and Dean of the College, Dickinson College) for hosting a book writing workshop that got us on the path to writing this book. We would like to thank Anne Janzer, our book coach, for helping us through the early stages of this book. We would like to thank Marcus Ballenger, our editor, for his support and guidance. We would like to thank the Zimpleman College of Business at Drake University for research support. We would like to thank the organizations we studied as part of this work including each of the individuals who spent time with us to help us learn more. Finally, we would like to thank our families for their support while we focused our energy on this project.

PRAISE FOR *The New Workplace*

"In a sea of uninformed opinions about remote and hybrid work, this book is a life raft. Two experts examine what the evidence actually shows about flexible work arrangements—and explore what it takes to get people across levels on the same page."

—Adam Grant, *#1 New York Times bestselling author of THINK AGAIN and host of the TED podcast Re:Thinking*

"*The New Workplace* offers a fresh perspective on aligning workplace strategies with employee preferences to create a more effective and fulfilling work environment. Through their insightful research and compelling personas, Purvanova and Mitchell provide practical guidance for leaders and employees navigating the complexities of modern office, remote, and hybrid work models. This book is an invaluable resource for fostering alignment, engagement, and success in today's ever-evolving workplace."

—Johnny C. Taylor, Jr., *President and Chief Executive Officer, SHRM*

"*The New Workplace* is a comprehensive guide that delves into the evolving dynamics of the modern work environment. It offers invaluable insights into the diverse personas that populate today's workforce, providing a nuanced understanding of how different employees align with remote-first, office-forward, and hybrid strategies. Through detailed analyses and practical tactics, *The New Workplace* provides actionable strategies for aligning employee preferences with organizational goals, enabling companies to foster a more engaged and productive workforce. By implementing the book's recommendations, organizations can navigate the complexities of the new workplace, ultimately driving success and innovation in their operations."

—Hannah Jackson Foldes, Ph.D., *VP Talent and Performance, 3M*

"Fascinating, practical, myth-busting research to inform the evolving office/hybrid/home conversation that is continuing towards a new 'one-size-*does-not*-fit-all' workplace equilibrium that best matches and aligns corporate strategies with employee preferences."

—Bernard Tubiana, *Principal, Deloitte Consulting LLP*

"*The New Workplace* is an essential guide to understanding the dynamics of today's evolving work landscape. Through well-researched insights, it identifies the diverse personas within organizations and offers practical advice on aligning individual work preferences with company strategies. This book is a vital resource for leaders managing the complexities of remote, office, and hybrid work models."

—Jenni Hipwell, *Vice President of People and Culture, Zirous*

"In today's rapidly shifting workplace landscape, success hinges on understanding the distinct strengths of remote, hybrid, and in-office models. Each approach brings unique opportunities and challenges, and when thoughtfully leveraged, they can drive innovation and strengthen organizational culture. *The New Workplace* provides leaders with the research and insights needed to strategically design virtual and physical experiences that empower their teams and position their organizations to thrive. As with many business decisions, there's no universal solution—only the right one for your organization to sustain and sharpen its competitive edge."

—Paul Hlivko, *EVP Chief Information and Digital Officer, Wellmark Blue Cross and Blue Shield*

"Purvanova and Mitchell have written what will become the definitive guide for organizations, managers, and employees in navigating the modern workplace. They dispel the notion of any one best way of organizing work, focusing instead on costs and benefits of remote, hybrid, and traditional workplaces. This engaging and practical guide serves as a valuable tool for organizational leaders looking to create the best work environment, for managers who face this new aspect of workforce diversity, and for employees looking to understand their own best workplace fit. It also provides a unique resource for college and university career resource centers as they work with companies and graduates to maximize success in finding employees and jobs that fit."

—Joyce E. Bono, Ph.D., *W. A. McGriff Professor of Management, University of Florida*

"Practical, insightful, and grounded in real-world experience, *The New Workplace* cuts through the myths surrounding remote, hybrid, and office work, bringing clarity to one of the most challenging debates of our time. With creative strategies and critical tips, it equips leaders and teams to build truly aligned and adaptable organizations in any setting—remote, hybrid, or in-office."

—Mollie Ross, *Vice President of Operations, Technology Association of Iowa*

"*The New Workplace* hits on a central aspect of modern society: how where we work affects organizations, leaders and employees. It is a deft distillation of timely research into the impact of in-office, remote and hybrid working environments on us and the institutions that make up society. More importantly, it offers a set of considerations and tools for us to use when determining how to align organizations and ourselves to maximize our potential and our happiness."

—Alejandro Hernandez, *Dean, Zimpleman College of Business, Drake University*

"The authors offer a well-researched exploration of remote, hybrid, and in-office environments to answer the question, 'Where do people do their best work?' By analyzing employee personas and their alignment within different organizational strategies, Purvanova and Mitchell provide a nuanced framework for understanding the intersection between work preferences and productivity. Grounded in data, this book is an important resource for business leaders seeking to understand modern workplace alignment and its implications for organizational success."

—Christina Trombley, Ph.D., *Associate Dean, Graduate and Professional Studies Chicago School*

"*The New Workplace* provides a fascinating look into the ways that employees and organizations are impacted by today's work strategies, along with actionable insights for managing these dynamics. As organizations have increasingly shifted to work-from-home and hybrid strategies, people have speculated about the impact of these strategies on organizations and employees. Purvanova and Mitchell bring evidence to this conversation. An in-depth study of three organizations provides insights about what happens when employee preferences align with the organization's work strategy, and what can be done when they don't. Leaders in charge of organizational work strategies, managers who are helping their teams adapt to new work strategies, and employees who want to understand their own preferences will all find ways to maximize engagement and satisfaction in these pages."

—Amy E. Colbert, Ph.D., *Professor and Distinguished Chair, University of Iowa*

"This book shows how important it is to understand the diversity of employee preferences and how those intersect with company policy. The three basic options (office-forward, remote-forward, and hybrid) balloon into nine different scenarios once employee desires are considered. The authors explain how each company can optimize their arrangement through office design, social events, selection criteria, and other key activities and tactics."

—Connie Noonan Hadley, Ph.D., *Founder, Institute for Life at Work*

Contents

Part I The New Workplace

1 Introduction	3
Introduction	3
Our Research	4
What's "The New Workplace" All About?	6
2 Where We Prefer to Work	11
Who Are the @Home Employees?	11
The Role of Gender	11
The Role of Executive Status	13
The Role of Parental Status	15
The Role of Marital Status	17
The Role of Race	20
Who Are the @Office Employees?	22
The Role of Executive Status	22
The Role of Being Single	25
Who Are the @Hybrid Employees?	31

Part II Personas in Remote-First Companies

3 Meet the Avatar, the Centrist, and the Community-Seeker	39
Introduction	39
Nudged or Pushed to Remote Work	39
Virtual Reality Versus "Real" Reality	43
What's a Cost and What's a Benefit?	50
4 Aligned and Misaligned Personas: Same Remote-First Company, Different Work Experiences	55
Aligned Personas: How Avatars Experience Work	55

	Half-Aligned Personas: How Centrists Experience Work	59
	Misaligned Personas: How Community-Seekers Experience Work	61
Part III	**Personas in Office-Forward Companies**	
5	**Meet the Officer, the Progressive, and the Producer**	71
	Introduction	71
	Disparate Access to Flexible Work	71
	Just a Work Space or My Place	73
	The Mitchells Versus The Machines	75
6	**Aligned and Misaligned Personas: Same Office-Forward Company, Different Work Experiences**	81
	Aligned Personas: How Officers Experience Work	81
	Half-Aligned Personas: How Progressives Experience Work	86
	Misaligned Personas: How Producers Experience Work	89
Part IV	**Personas in Hybrid Companies**	
7	**Meet the Integrator, the Traditionalist, and the Rebel**	99
	The Mystery of Who's In	99
	What You Say and What You Do	104
	Task-Location Fit	108
8	**Aligned and Misaligned Personas: Same Hybrid Company, Different Work Experiences**	115
	Aligned Personas: How Integrators Experience Work	115
	Half-Aligned Personas: How Traditionalists Experience Work	119
	Half-Aligned Personas: How Rebels Experience Work	121
Part V	**Finding Alignment**	
9	**How Do Organizations Align Their Workplace Strategy to Employee Work Location Preferences**	131
	Building Your New Workplace with a Remote-First Strategy	132
	Why Do Remote-First: The Good and The Bad	132
	How To Do Remote-First: Aligning Your People to Your Strategy	133
	Building Your New Workplace with an Office-Forward Strategy	138
	Why Do Office-Forward: The Good and The Bad	138
	How To Do Office-Forward: Aligning Your People to Your Strategy	139
	Building Your New Workplace with a Hybrid Strategy	144
	Why Do Hybrid: The Good and The Bad	144
	How to Do Hybrid: Aligning Your People to Your Strategy	145
	A Note on Clarity	150
	A Note on Productivity	151

10	**How Do Leaders Align Their Teams**	157
	Awareness Raising Primer: Myths Versus Facts	158
	Finding Common Ground: A Team-Building Activity	165
	Step One: A General Discussion	166
	Step Two: Dispel Myths and Raise Awareness	169
	Step Three: Team Alignment	173
11	**How Do You Grow into the Persona You Wish to Be**	183
	What Persona Am I?	184
	How Alignment Impacts the Home-Preferring Personas	187
	How Alignment Impacts the Office-Preferring Personas	190
	How Alignment Impacts the Hybrid-Preferring Personas	192
	I am a Half-Aligned Persona. How Do I Find Better Alignment?	195
	Centrists (Hybrid-Preferring Employees in Remote-First Companies)	195
	Progressives (Hybrid-Preferring Employees in Office-Forward Companies)	196
	Traditionalists (Office-Preferring Employees in Hybrid Companies)	197
	Rebels (Home-Preferring Employees in Hybrid Companies)	199
	I am a Misaligned Persona. How Do I Find Better Alignment?	200
	Community-Seekers (Office-Preferring Employees in Remote-First Companies)	201
	Producers (Home-Preferring Employees in Office-Forward Companies)	202
	I Am a Fully Aligned Persona. How Do I Refine My Perfect Alignment?	203
	Avatars (Home-Preferring Employees in Remote-First Companies)	203
	Officers (Office-Preferring Employees in Office-Forward Companies)	205
	Integrators (Hybrid-Preferring Employees in Hybrid Companies)	207
	A Note on Persona Change	210
12	**Alignment and the New Workplace**	213
	Not One New Normal	213
	Finding Alignment	215
	The Missing Piece in the Remote-First Strategy	218
	The Missing Piece in the Office-Forward Strategy	218
	The Missing Piece in the Hybrid Strategy	219
	In Closing	220
Appendix		221
Index		223

About the Authors

Dr. Radostina (Ina) Purvanova is a Professor of Management and Organizational Leadership in the Zimpleman College of Business at Drake University. Her research interests lie in the area of virtual work, flexible (virtual and hybrid) work practices, and leadership processes in virtual teams. Dr. Purvanova's research has been published in prestigious management journals, including *Academy of Management Journal*, *Personnel Psychology*, *The Leadership Quarterly*, and *Group & Organization Management*. As an educator, Dr. Purvanova teaches undergraduate and MBA classes in organizational behavior, leadership, and human capital development. Prior to entering academia, Ina worked in the non-governmental sector, leading multinational project teams focused on ushering local government reform in Eastern European countries. Presently, Ina continues her engagement with the non-profit sector via her consulting work. She also works with for-profit companies, providing training and development around virtual work, leadership, and women-in-leadership. Dr. Purvanova frequently speaks at industry conferences and events (e.g., Deloitte's Group Insurance Presidents' Forum; The Insurance Industry Charitable Foundation), participates in podcasts (e.g., All Things Work by The Society for Human Resource Management), and offers her expertise to the media (e.g., *BBC*, *Business Insider*, *Forbes*).

Dr. Alanah Mitchell is the Aliber Distinguished Professor of Information Systems, and Associate Dean of Academic Affairs in the Zimpleman College of Business at Drake University. For more than two decades, she has worked as a researcher, educator, and consultant in relation to the design, implementation, and use of information and communication technologies for collaboration, specifically in global virtual teams. Alanah's research and teaching experience extends to executive education as well as speaking and other consulting projects. Dr. Mitchell has worked with the U.S. Strategic Command Center, Principal Financial Group, General Mills, and a number of other Fortune 500 companies, educational institutions, and non-profit organizations. She also serves as an expert for news media outlets in print, radio/podcasts, and television, including the *Business Insider*, *Forbes*, *TIME*, *the Wall Street Journal*, and *the Washington Post*. For more information, please visit her website: https://www.alanahmitchell.com/.

List of Figures

Fig. 1.1	Personas Arising at the Intersections of Company Strategy and Employee Preference	7
Fig. 2.1	Employees are generally equally likely to prefer @home, @hybrid, or @office	12
Fig. 2.2	Men and women are equally likely to prefer @home, @hybrid, or @office	12
Fig. 2.3	Executive status explains @home preference for men, not women	13
Fig. 2.4	Parental status explains @home preference for women, not men	16
Fig. 2.5	Marital status explains @home preference for men and women	18
Fig. 2.6	Race explains @home preference	21
Fig. 2.7	Men and women are equally likely to prefer @home, @hybrid, or @office	23
Fig. 2.8	Executive status explains @office preference for women, not men	23
Fig. 2.9	Being single explains @office preference for men, not women	25
Fig. 2.10	Being single with no parental obligations explains @office preference for men and women	26
Fig. 2.11	Men and women are equally likely to prefer @home, @hybrid, or @office	31
Fig. 3.1	Personas in remote-first companies include Avatars, Centrists, and Community-seekers	40
Fig. 4.1	Avatars are fully aligned in remote-first organizations while Centrists are half-aligned and Community-seekers are misaligned	56
Fig. 5.1	Personas in Office-Forward Companies include Officers, Progressives, and Producers	72
Fig. 6.1	Officers are fully aligned in office-forward organizations while Progressives are half-aligned and Producers are misaligned	82
Fig. 7.1	Personas in hybrid companies include Integrators, Traditionalists, and Rebels	100
Fig. 8.1	Integrators are fully aligned in hybrid organizations while Traditionalists and Rebels are only partially aligned	116

Fig. 11.1	Personas arising at the intersections of company strategy and employee preference	187
Fig. 12.1	The new workplace	216
Fig. A.1	QR code for the new workplace book website with additional resources	221

List of Tables

Table 10.1	The home-preferring personas: Who are the @home preferers?	159
Table 10.2	The home-preferring personas: Why do they prefer @home?	159
Table 10.3	The home-preferring personas: New research-based findings about "why"	160
Table 10.4	The office-preferring personas: Who are the @office preferers?	161
Table 10.5	The office-preferring personas: Why do they prefer @office?	162
Table 10.6	The office-preferring personas: New research-based findings about "why"	162
Table 10.7	The hybrid-preferring personas: Who are the @hybrid preferers?	164
Table 10.8	The hybrid-preferring personas: Why do they prefer @hybrid?	164
Table 10.9	The hybrid-preferring personas: New research-based findings about "why"	164
Table 11.1	Workplace persona assessment	184

PART I

The New Workplace

This book is about finding alignment between company workplace strategy and employee work location preference. How do you get company strategy and employee preference to align—for yourself as a person, or for your company as a leader?

To really grasp the notion of alignment—and more importantly, the art of finding alignment, it is important to first understand the main work location preferences that employees have developed in the workplace of today. There are three of them: a preference for work-from-home (@home), a preference for work-from-office (@office), and a preference for hybrid work (@hybrid).

Strangely, though it's certainly a hot topic, our understanding of employees' work location preferences is quite anecdotal. Employees, and really, all of us, slipped into these preferences almost inadvertently. It is time to dig deeper and truly understand who these @home, @office, and @hybrid employees are.

In this section, we begin with an introduction to the research that informs our book (Chapter 1) You'll learn about the three companies we studied and the workplace strategy each had adopted: remote-first, office-forward, and hybrid. Then, you'll learn about the employees we studied (Chapter 2). We'll share our analysis of core demographic characteristics that predispose employees to develop an @home, @office, and @hybrid work preference. Who are the employees who prefer to work-from-home? Are they more likely to be men or women? Older or younger? More or less tenured? Who are the ones who prefer the office? And the ones who prefer hybrid—who are they?

CHAPTER 1

Introduction

INTRODUCTION

In modern folklore, the post-pandemic workplace is a war zone. On the battlefield are return-to-office-obsessed CEOs—think Elon Musk or Andy Jassy—on a quest to extinguish the troubles of remote work lingering on from the COVID-19 pandemic. Standing strong against them are recalcitrant work-from-home-loving employees, fighting to keep their love affair with remote work going.

That's catchy but inaccurate. Rather than a battlefield, we see the workplace as a testbed where organizations are trying different approaches to a "new normal." Some organizations are indeed throwing down the gauntlet via an office-forward strategy to preserve company culture. But others are embracing reinvention via a remote-first strategy to provide maximal employee flexibility. Still others are threading the needle via a hybrid strategy to synergize culture and flexibility. Workers too are experimenting. Some have indeed realized they never want to step foot in a corporate office again. But others have rediscovered the office as the place most conducive to work and career growth, and still others have found they prefer to switch scenery as they combine work-from-home with work-from-office.

As professors of management (Ina) and information systems (Alanah), we have studied virtuality and work technology for over two decades. When COVID-19 made virtual work mainstream, we were uniquely positioned to research emerging workplace practices and preferences. We spent months immersed in ethnographic study of several national work organizations, observing workplace reinvention as it unfolded, learning about the employee experience. As we visited these companies' offices, joined their

© The Author(s), under exclusive license to Springer Nature Switzerland AG 2025
R. Purvanova and A. Mitchell, *The New Workplace*,
https://doi.org/10.1007/978-3-031-86046-1_1

Zooms, hosted focus groups, and conducted in-depth interviews with executives and employees, we saw a disconnect. In each company, executives were crafting their post-pandemic workplace strategy: office-forward, remote-first, and hybrid. Meanwhile, employees were quietly settling into their own work location preference: the home, the office, or a combination of the two. At first, we bought into the popular narrative of a war zone. We feared that the workplace reinvention experiment was failing, that a unified solution to a new normal was slipping away. But then, it hit us. In the post-pandemic world of work, there is not one new normal, not one right way to be a worker, not one right approach to build a workplace. Sameness is out. Choice is in. The solution to a new normal is to find alignment. As an employee, how do you align your work location preference to the workplace options available to you? As a work organization, how do you align your workplace strategy to the mix of employees in the workforce? The idea that it is about alignment that works for you—not about fitting to some standard of "normal"—is liberating! We wrote this book to share this liberating epiphany with employees and business leaders alike. We want to help you—not to be right, but to be aligned.

Our Research

In this book, we draw on our ethnographic research with three professional organizations, each featuring a distinct post-pandemic workplace strategy: remote-first, office-forward, and hybrid.

We'll call our remote-first organization Promethean. With a meaning of "daringly original or creative," we thought that's a fitting name for a remote-first company.[1] Promethean is a large Fortune 500 company with Midwest U.S. headquarters and multiple satellite offices throughout the country. It employs over 25,000 employees, and is a *Fortune* magazine "100 Best Company to Work For." Since 2020, the company's revenue has exceeded $30 billion. post-pandemic, Promethean had engaged in major office renovations of its main headquarters as well as its secondary headquarters. However, as the company was charting its post-pandemic course, it realized its workforce had been just as productive—if not more productive—during lockdown when most everyone worked from home. It also realized that the investments the company had been making in technology had been almost prescient. Technology is now the lifeline that keeps employees connected and engaged. In contrast, the office is now secondary. Office presence is not expected (unless dictated by the nature of the position and certain local regulations). The company has aggressively downsized its real estate, selling some office properties and reducing others. Remaining offices have been converted to the hoteling system of office use; only full-time office users have personal workstations. As Promethean adopted its remote-first strategy, it completely reinvented its HR practices; for example, hiring is now based on expertise versus geographic location. However, to maintain a sense of connection and culture, the company hosts annual company-wide conferences where employees can meet up and interact in person.

We'll call our office-forward organization Apollonian. Apollonian means "measured and ordered;" we thought this captures the philosophy of an office-forward company.[2] Apollonian is a midsize, privately held company with headquarters in the Midwest and satellite offices across the U.S. It employs just over 1,000 employees, and is consistently rated a Best Company to Work For in industry-specific business publications. Since 2020, this company's revenue has exceeded $750 million. post-pandemic, Apollonian had engaged in major office renovations of its main headquarters and some of its satellite offices. At the same time, the company also invested in technology to expand its geographic reach in recruiting talent and to support employee flexibility. As the company charted its post-pandemic course, it realized that the office spaces it had created were inextricably linked to its DNA as an organization. So, the company has re-dedicated itself to making its offices a physical embodiment of its culture, intentionally bucking the hoteling office trend and doubling down on providing a personal workstation to each employee. However, as the company adopted its office-forward strategy, it realized that personal workstations and fancy office amenities like coffee bars and gyms are not what truly draw people in. Making the in-office experience worthwhile is what Apollonian believes matters most. Employees can expect some type of social event or activity on any given day and can also use the space to host their own events.

We'll call our hybrid organization Harmonium, inspired by the word "harmonic" or "having integrated nature."[3] The term Harmonium fits this hybrid company well. Harmonium is a multinational Fortune 500 company with headquarters in the Midwest and multiple satellite offices throughout the U.S., Asia, and South America. It employs approximately 20,000 employees globally; over 80% of its employees say it's a great place to work for. Since 2020, this organization's revenue has exceeded $13 billion. post-pandemic, Harmonium had engaged in major office renovations of its main headquarters, moving to a hoteling office arrangement. Teams sat in neighborhoods with no assigned seating; each employee was supplied with a laptop, bag, travel mug, and other necessities for a mobile workstyle. The underlying message was that flexibility in work location, whether on or off campus, was encouraged. The company's hybrid strategy post-pandemic was a natural outgrowth of its flexible pre-pandemic workplace. Under the hybrid strategy, employees are expected to be in the office two-to-three days per week. However, this varies widely by team, unit, and division. The company IT department actively monitors office occupancy and maximizes IT resources accordingly. This makes for a seamless work experience whether employees connect to company servers in-office or from home. Through employee surveys, Harmonium learned that employees had concerns about team connectedness and promotion pathways under hybrid. Harmonium now encourages more regular in-person team meetings, has re-opened its coffee shops and cafeterias, and has re-started hosting social events in-office.

For our research, we spent months immersed in each organization. This started pre-pandemic, extended into lockdown, and ended well into the new post-pandemic reality. Frankly, we are still pinching ourselves. The pre-pandemic work model had reigned supreme—with some small changes around the edges—since the days of the Industrial Revolution. That's two-and-a-half centuries ago! And here we were, observing it all unfold in real time: the shock of having to reinvent work overnight, the drinking from the fire hose during lockdown, the agonizing decisions about what's next, the oppositional, polarizing perspectives on what's best for the "new normal," and most importantly—the differing employee work experiences as each company implemented its own post-pandemic workplace strategy.

On the pages of the book, you will hear a lot from our interviewees (their names have been replaced with aliases). These 89 employees worked across functional areas: IT, finance, data analytics, accounting, marketing, learning and development, and others. Their tenure ranged from a few months to over 25 years. They were executives (17), team leaders (14), and team members (58). They were gender-balanced (44 women; 45 men); gender was also balanced across hierarchical levels. Employees were predominantly White (73) with fewer racial minority employees represented (16). Some were single (31), and some were married (58); some were parents of children living at home (40), and some were not parents or had grown children (49). Crucially to this book, these employees had developed specific work location preferences: some preferred working from home (35 employees), others preferred working from the office (27 employees), and still others—working from both the home and the office (27 employees). In our interviews, they told stories about their experiences at work under their company's remote-first, office-forward, or hybrid workplace strategy.

What's "The New Workplace" All About?

Here is the big discovery our research made: In the post-pandemic workplace, there's a wild mix of employee personas.[4] Nine personas, to be exact. These personas arise at the intersections of company workplace strategy (remote-first, office-forward, hybrid) and employee work location preference (the home, the office, a combination of the two). To help illustrate this idea, consider the visual below. It shows the nine personas that emerge when company workplace strategy and employee work location preference are considered at once (Fig. 1.1).[5]

1 INTRODUCTION   7

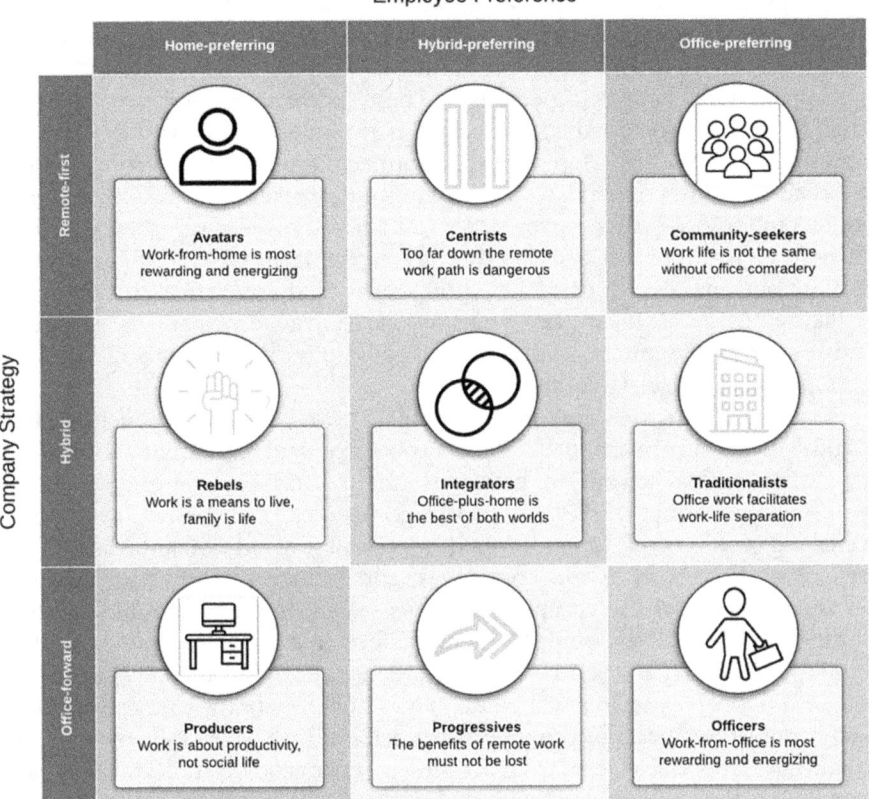

Fig. 1.1 Personas Arising at the Intersections of Company Strategy and Employee Preference

Our discovery of these nine personas is interesting. Is it game-changing? Probably not.

But here is what's game-changing, our big *Ah-ha!* Only three personas—that's three out of nine—are aligned to their company's workplace strategy. The other six personas exist at some degree of misalignment between their own work location preference and their company's strategy. Why does that matter? Because alignment is good. Misalignment—not so much.

See the three solid-black personas? They are the lucky ones. They reside at that sweet spot of alignment. Their personal work location preference perfectly aligns with their company's workplace strategy. So, Avatars are home-preferring workers in remote-first companies, Integrators are hybrid-preferring workers in hybrid companies, and Officers are office-preferring workers in office-forward companies. We will tell you more about these personas—who they are and how they experience work. We'll explain why they are fully supportive of their company's chosen workplace strategy. But if you are a company leader, be forewarned: these personas are not an overwhelming majority within your company. This means you have more alignment work to do, and we will help you figure out how.

See the two boxed-in personas? These personas experience complete misalignment. Unfortunately, they reside at two degrees of separation between strategy and personal preference. So, Producers are home-preferring workers in office-forward companies, and Community-seekers are office-preferring workers in remote-first companies. We will tell you more about these personas. Their story is important because they are suffering in silence. If you are one of these personas, we hope to help you realize that you can regain happiness by taking charge. You can, and you must, craft your own path to alignment. And if you are a company leader, we will offer ideas about how you can make these personas' (work) lives better.

Finally, see the four personas in gray? These personas are neither fully aligned, nor fully misaligned. They experience half-alignment: they reside at one degree of separation between strategy and preference. So, Rebels are home-preferring workers in hybrid companies, Progressives are hybrid-preferring workers in office-forward companies, Traditionalists are office-preferring workers in hybrid companies, and Centrists are hybrid-preferring workers in remote-first companies. These personas are a sizeable minority within their respective company. They believe that their company's strategy should move closer to their personal preference, not the other way around. If you are a people leader, we will guide you in how to work with these personas. This is important because these personas are loud, they are influencers. They should get a special role in your alignment efforts, or else, they could lead your workplace reinvention experiment astray.

Here's something else really important. In remote-first and in office-forward companies, personas range the gamut. There is the fully aligned persona (Avatars in remote-first and Officers in office-forward), the half-aligned persona (Centrists in remote-first and Progressives in office-forward), and the fully misaligned persona (Community-seekers in remote-first and Producers in office-forward). So, companies choosing a remote-first or an office-forward strategy have one thing in common: they each have to deal with extreme persona diversity. We will focus on this issue in later chapters.

In contrast, in hybrid companies, there are only fully aligned and half-aligned personas. These are the Integrators (fully aligned), and the Rebels and Traditionalists (half-aligned). No fully misaligned personas here. But think twice before you assume that hybrid companies have it easy. As we will show in later chapters, Integrators are on cloud nine, having found their fit. But Rebels and Traditionalists? They are pulling in exact opposite directions, each empowered by the fact that their company's strategy is only one degree of separation from their personal preference. This particular persona mix may make hybrid the hardest strategy to square.

We hope you are as excited to learn about these personas as we are to share their stories with you. If you are a leader—whether of a small, midsize, or large work organization—we hope this book helps you understand how you can craft the persona mix within your workforce that would best support your company's chosen path. And if you are an employee, we hope this book helps you understand how you can craft the persona that would most authentically fit your chosen career journey. In all, we hope this book helps YOU find alignment.

How Is "The New Workplace" Organized? The New Workplace opens with our systematic exploration—the first, to our knowledge—of employees' work location preferences: @home, @office, and @hybrid. We analyze what demographic characteristics differentiate employees with these general preferences (Chapter 2).

We then dive into the big discovery our research made: That employees with @home, @office, and @hybrid preferences come to inhabit a specific persona when they work for a remote-first company (Chapter 3 and Chapter 4), an office-forward company (Chapter 5 and Chapter 6), or a hybrid company (Chapter 7 and Chapter 8). We explore how a company's chosen workplace strategy pushes employees into these various personas, and we take a deep look at the vastly different work experiences of the personas.

In the last section of the book, we turn our attention to our big *Ah-ha*: It's about finding alignment. We zoom in on three layers here—macro (how to align your organizational strategy to your employees' preferences; Chapter 9), meso (how to align your team members; Chapter 10), and micro (how to align yourself; Chapter 11). Here, you'll also find our useful Workplace Persona Assessment, complete with instructions for how to use the assessment in support of your alignment efforts.

Read on!

NOTES

1. "Promethean," in *Merriam-Webster.Com Dictionary* (Merriam-Webster, n.d.), https://www.merriam-webster.com/dictionary/Promethean.
2. "Apollonian," in *Merriam-Webster.Com Dictionary* (Merriam-Webster, n.d.), https://www.merriam-webster.com/dictionary/Apollonian.
3. "Harmonic," in *Merriam-Webster.Com Dictionary* (Merriam-Webster, n.d.), https://www.merriam-webster.com/dictionary/harmonic.
4. R. Purvanova and A. Mitchell, "Where Companies Want Employees to Work—and Where People Actually Want to Work," *Harvard Business*

Review, November 2, 2023, https://hbr.org/2023/11/where-companies-want-employees-to-work-and-where-people-actually-want-to-work.
5. The Noun Project, *Icons Are from the Noun Project*, 2024, Icons, 2024, https://thenounproject.com/.

CHAPTER 2

Where We Prefer to Work

Modern myth holds that workers have developed a love affair with work-from-home. We'll have to dispel that myth. In our research, we learned that employees—executives and associates alike—are nearly evenly split across work location preferences. True, many employees do prefer to work-from-home. But surprisingly large numbers prefer to go to the office or prefer a mix (Fig. 2.1). See for yourself below:

So, opposite of modern myth, no work location preference reigns supreme (as others have also reported).[1]

But what drives employees to develop an @home, @hybrid, or @office work location preference? Let's start with demographics here. In later chapters, we'll dig deeper to reveal how employees with an @home, @office, and @hybrid work location preference develop into different personas when they work for remote-first, office-forward, or hybrid companies.

WHO ARE THE @HOME EMPLOYEES?

The Role of Gender

Who do you think most prefers to work-from-home? When you close your eyes and try to imagine an @home worker, are you seeing a woman? Well, rub your eyes and try again. Even though historically women utilized work flexibility policies more than men—think HR innovations such as compressed workweek, job sharing, telecommuting, or (gasp) parental leave—something about the pandemic changed that gender distribution dramatically.[2] In each company we studied, we saw equal numbers of men and women @home

© The Author(s), under exclusive license to Springer Nature
Switzerland AG 2025
R. Purvanova and A. Mitchell, *The New Workplace*,
https://doi.org/10.1007/978-3-031-86046-1_2

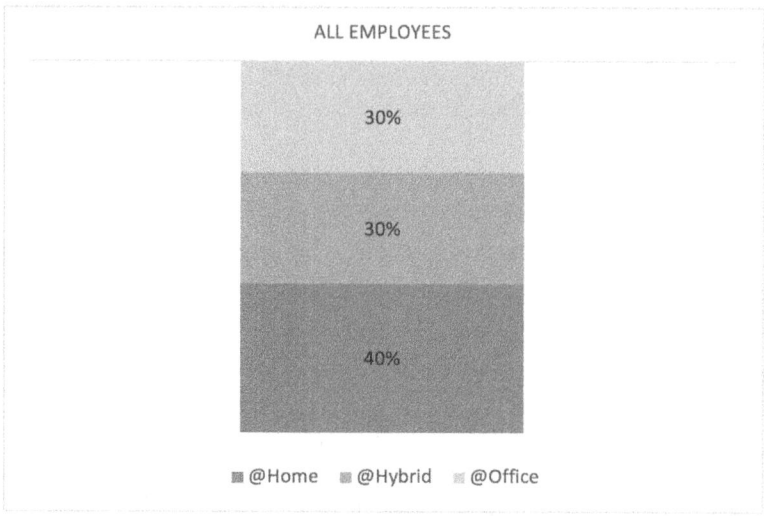

Fig. 2.1 Employees are generally equally likely to prefer @home, @hybrid, or @office

workers. Our finding that men may be just as likely as women to prefer to work-from-home is very important. It flies in the face of preexisting notions of who wants to set foot in the corporate office and who doesn't (Fig. 2.2).

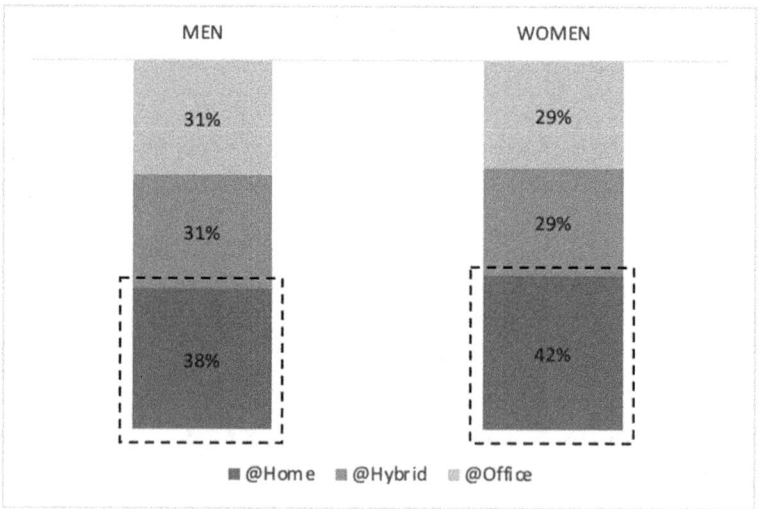

Fig. 2.2 Men and women are equally likely to prefer @home, @hybrid, or @office

The Role of Executive Status

To understand why men and women may have come to share a similar predilection to work-from-home, let's dig deeper. We bet you'll be shocked to learn what drives some men to become @home workers. Being a boss! In our data, almost a half of the male executives preferred @home; the other half preferred @hybrid, with one sole @office exception—the Elon Musk in our research. In contrast, only a third of the women executives preferred @home (but a whole half of them preferred @office). So, hierarchical status seems to be a big influence on employees' work-from-home preference for men. Men in power, men in high-ranking leadership positions, seem to be answering the beckoning call of the home, wanting to work-from-home always (@home) or at least some of the time (@hybrid). And, to complete the musical chairs game here, leadership status works in the exact opposite way for women: it is women in power who want to be in the office. We will let that sink in a little bit (Fig. 2.3).

While you are mulling over that revelation, let us share that we are not the only ones to observe that high-ranking corporate men want to work-from-home. Powerful men's conversion to the work-from-home (WFH) gospel has been noted in the press. Sometimes, you have to read between the lines to see this. Consider *Fortune's* proclamation that *Wall Street Keeps Pushing to End WFH, But Their Own Senior Staff Would Rather Quit Than Comply.*[3] Well, who is Wall Street's "senior staff" mostly comprised of? Why, men, of course. Other times, this unlikely development is much more clearly explained. For example, in *Boeing Eases Return to Office for TopBrass, The Wall Street*

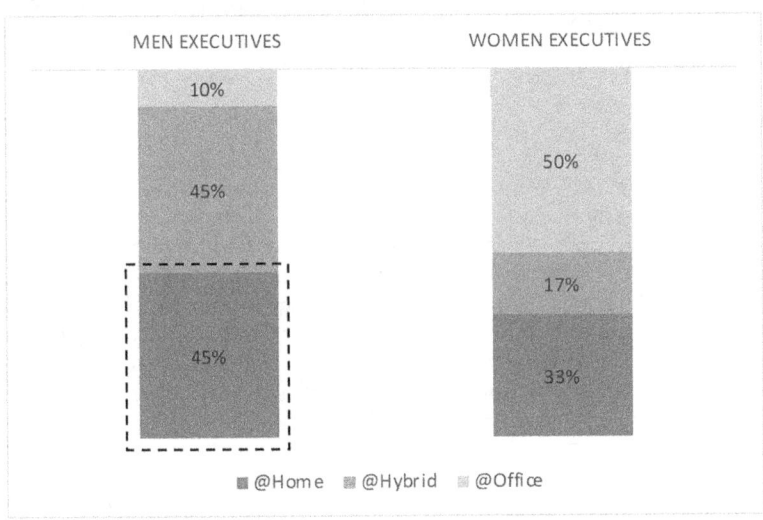

Fig. 2.3 Executive status explains @home preference for men, not women

Journal reported: *Chief Executive David Calhoun began running Boeing from home when the COVID-19 pandemic forced much of the country to avoid the workplace. Even after the pandemic, Calhoun has said he wouldn't be traveling much to visit his staff.*[4]

And the latest case of a senior man executive demanding work-from-home? It's Starbucks's new boss, Brian Niccol, who—in addition to the typical cash sign-on bonus and millions in stock-based compensation—requested an unusual perk: remote work.[5] Clearly, work-from-home is fast becoming a recruitment tool ... for senior male staff!

Apropos, we haven't run into media reports on women executives' remote work attachment ... and you know the press would have been all-over *that* story. But as our data reveal, there simply isn't such story. We'll come back to why women executives may be more likely to be @office workers later on.

Our interviews help shed light on why men executives are shuttering stereotypes with their newfound appreciation for work-from-home. Let's show you some of their thoughts. One male executive felt "enlightened":

> It's almost like a lot of people came up for air. We all had our noses down, and then it was like, You know what? It is nice to work from home! That is absolutely a perk that I find extremely valuable. I think work-from-home does, you know, enlighten, for lack of a better word. It does help reframe, you know, Okay, wow, am I just going to do this? Can you grind non-stop for the next 25 years? There's a lot more than just sitting in my office for 9 hours a day, and then drive home, get home at 6pm, make dinner, put the kids to bed, repeat times five. Now, we're getting a lot more out of our days from a non-work perspective. We get to experience a lot more, whether it's running over to my kids' elementary school to pick them up or to attend some school program. So, having that mix, you know, I think that has enlightened a lot of people. (Tom, product director)

Another male executive "changed perspective":

> I was at a VP level, and I've stepped down to a Director level. I've just changed my perspective on all that stuff. I want freedom and flexibility. I want to work in exciting companies and exciting roles where I think I add significant value. But I want to do that because that's my interest, not because I have to do it. I said, "I want to work on this thing," not "I need to stay at this hierarchical level." I don't really care about that anymore. And it's not like I'm not making a decent living here, too. But it's much less stress, and I'm only in this role because they were willing to hire me remotely. And so that's kind of the perspective that I have now. (Mike, product development director).

A third male executive gained a sense of self-determination:

> It's odd that I'd say this, but I feel like I get more done now, I get more accomplished now, working from home. From a work perspective, I have so much flexibility with when I start my day, when I end my day, or if I have to run an errand. It doesn't feel like I'm working as hard as I did when I was in an office. That'd be the big thing for me, I kind of felt like, you know, I was usually the first one in, the last one to leave. I felt like I was busy all day. But now, I feel like I get more done, more of the real important things done, and it doesn't seem as difficult for me. And maybe that's because I'm already home and I feel like--like I mentioned, if I wanna pop on my laptop and maybe do some work at night--it's kind of more like when I wanna do it, I don't feel like I have to do it. So it seems like I get more done today, but because I've got a lot more flexibility, it doesn't feel like I'm working harder than I was before. (Travis, division director)

Do you detect a theme here? Executive men seem to talk about a profound realization—that life is more than work. Having been through the corporate grinder for years—decades—of their life, you almost hear a sigh of relief from this group: they can come up for air, finally. And now that they are out, now that they've tasted another way of being, they see work from the office as stressful and subjugating. But work-from-home? That's fulfilling and liberating!

And, if you tried to take-away this "liberating" work arrangement, what would these "enlightened" male executives do? "If, you know, all of a sudden they told me to change, to go into the office now, I'll be like, well, okay, maybe I'll retire a little early then" (Jason, senior data analyst), said one. Another agreed: "If my work said, 'No, you're in the office 5 days a week,' I would have motivation to look elsewhere" (Tom, product director). And there you have it. *Fortune* magazine, *Wall Street Journal*, you got it right! Senior staff would rather quit than return to the office ... male senior staff, that is.

Interestingly, we did not detect such a theme in our conversations with the few women executives who preferred to work-from-home. These powerful women had fallen into the @home preference simply because they enjoyed working from home. No profound realization there. Except—we should note—these women were moms with children at home.

The Role of Parental Status

This brings us to the main reason why some women become @home workers—being a mom. Among all women in our data who were moms with children at home, two-thirds had an @home preference. In contrast, dads with children at home were equally likely to prefer @home, @office, or @hybrid. But there is another way to examine the role of parental status—look at its opposite: non-parental status. In our data, men and women who were not parents (or who's kids were grown and not living at home anymore) were roughly equally likely to prefer @home, @office, or @hybrid. So, moms want to work-from-home more than dads, more than non-parenting women, and more than non-parenting men. Parental status seems to be a big determinant of employees' work-from-home preference for women, not for men (Fig. 2.4).

What this all means is that when you don't have child-rearing obligations, your work location preference is just as likely to include the office as it is to include the home, whether you are a man or a woman. But when you gain family responsibilities, you stay away from the office *if* you are a woman. So much for the pandemic breaking down gender divisions in family roles. You see, for a short time—during the COVID-19 lockdowns when parents were stuck with children at home—it seemed that gender roles can change. "*Could The Coronavirus Pandemic Shift Gender Roles Once and For All?*"—asked *Forbes* with a measured dose of excitement.[6] "*Could the Pandemic Operate Like Exposure Therapy and Lead to Greater Gender Equality?*"—wondered *The Guardian* with restrained enthusiasm.[7] These and many other optimistic pieces in the popular press circa 2020 cited data on men's increased involvement in childcare. But fast-forward just one year ahead, to 2021, when offices started to open up. Citing emerging concerns about possible gender differences in return-to-office, the press began to sound an alarm. *Are Men-Dominated Offices the Future of the Workplace?*"—asked the *BBC*.[8] "*Is the 'Zoom Ceiling' the New Glass Ceiling?*"—wanted to know *CNBC*.[9] "*Experts Worry Remote Work Will Hold Women Back*"—piled on *The New York Times*.[10]

We see the reason to sound the alarm. The "mommy track"—the career and income rut that women get in when they have children and begin to take advantage of flexible work arrangements—could resurface in the modern,

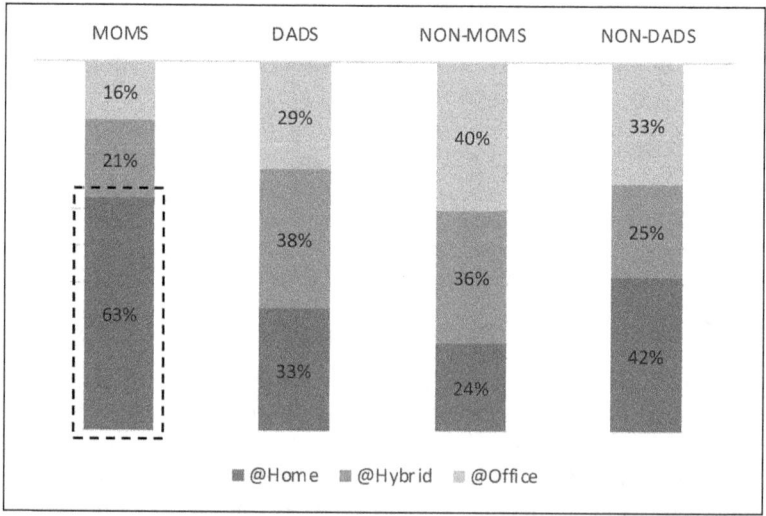

Fig. 2.4 Parental status explains @home preference for women, not men

"flexible" workplace. But our data suggest a super important reason to be optimistic that the "mommy track" may be a thing of the past. Yes, most moms prefer @home. But remember who else shares this @home preference? Male executives. That powerful men may have fallen for work-from-home is great news to anyone who wants to keep working from home, including moms. To wit, here's what one of these @office-turned-@home male executives told us:

> I was one of the people who really didn't want to work from home. If you had asked me pre-pandemic: 'What's your thoughts on letting your employees work from home?' I would have been flexible in the sense of, hey, if they have something going on a particular day and they need to work from home for that day, that'd be fine. But if someone would have said, 'Hey, can your team work 100% from home?' I probably would have been resistant to that idea just because we have this office here, we're all local, why can't we go into the office, it's not that big of a commute. Now, having seen both sides of it, I'm more a proponent of offering a lot of flexibility because I know there may be some companies that might be more rigid, and they want people to come in on a more set schedule. But we can offer a lot of flexibility to make sure that we're attracting good talent, keeping good talent. So I'm a big proponent of doing that. That's probably the one big difference with me and my leadership pre-pandemic to now. (Travis, division director)

In all, being a mom is a defining—albeit a disappointingly stereotypical—characteristic of an @home worker. But the good news is that work-from-home preferring moms have powerful new allies: work-from-home preferring male executives. So heads up, company leaders: Offer work-from-home options to recruit and retain moms...along with your top male brass.

The Role of Marital Status

Is there a unifying demographic characteristic among @home employees? We are glad you asked. When you close your eyes, feel free to imagine someone with a ring on their finger. Marital status was the single best driver of work location preference we uncovered, all else being equal. Almost half of all married people in our data had an @home preference (and another third—an @hybrid preference). This means that if you're married, you have a very, very strong proclivity to want to work-from-home all the time (@home), or at least some of the time (@hybrid). Not to spook you, but if YOU work-from-home, we almost certainly know something about you: you're married! (Fig. 2.5).

In our interviews, some married workers enjoyed working from home because they had a work-from-home spouse. These @home employees often sounded hooked on sharing the workday with their spouse. They enjoyed coffee in the morning together, lunch over the midday break together, a casual stroll in the neighborhood together, prepping dinner together. Picture this romantic scene from the life of a married @home worker:

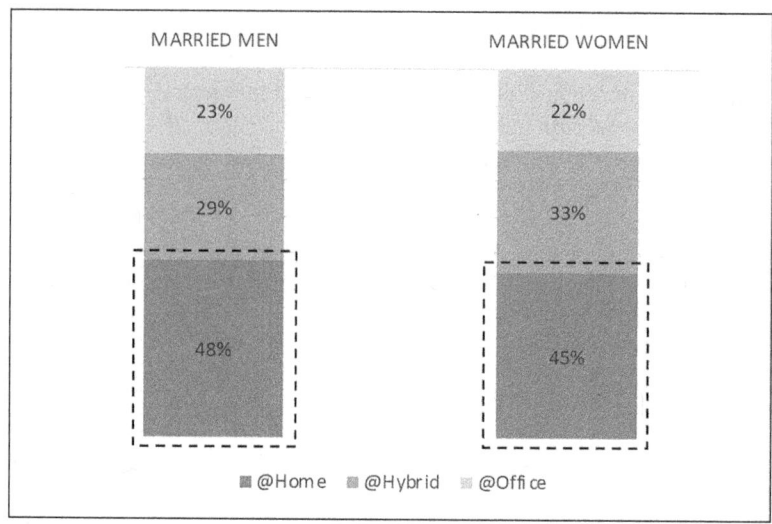

Fig. 2.5 Marital status explains @home preference for men and women

> My wife also works home, probably 50% of the time. We have a main floor office that she works in that has the same kind of setup as I do down here. So, if I need somebody to talk to, or something like that, she's up there, she's upstairs. And you know, my favorite memory is, it was spring, and it just felt like springing. Things were bright and cheery out. And I just remember turning some Jimmy Buffett on, like Margaritaville. It was like a Friday afternoon, and just, you know, Yup, we're done, we can go have our Margaritas now. And we didn't have to go anywhere, we could just have it at home. So, I just kind of opened the windows up, it felt like spring. (Tim, senior product consultant)

Idyllic, right? But not all married @home employees basked in marital bliss while working from home. Many worked from home alone because their spouse practiced an occupation that cannot be performed at home (policing, teaching, physical therapy), or worked full-time at the office. Our point is that being married did not necessarily guarantee a work-from-home buddy to be social with during the long, long workday. So, partner work-from-home status was not necessarily what pushed so many married people to develop an @home preference.

You might say, OK, then maybe it's life stage? Married people tend to be older (or shall we say, mature). Do they maybe feel more established at work, more embedded in their professional networks? Perhaps. Said one 50-yrs-young married @home worker:

I have all the relationships that I need for the most part. I've done a lot of face-to-face, you know, I've worked in [company name] for 18 years. I know a lot of people in the industry. I have worked at other companies. So, from that standpoint, I thought I was well-equipped to work from home versus somebody just starting out. (Jason, senior data analyst)

Or, perhaps married @home workers' social life revolves around the home, not around the office? Another 50-something married @home employee explained:

I've had these conversations with others. When I look back at that timeframe—being an early 20 something person—my colleagues, we did lots of social things together. I mean, they became our best friends because, partially, we moved to a new town, to a new job, and that was how you got to know people. But later when we had kids, we made friends in the neighborhood and through the school and through our kids' activities. So then work friends didn't matter as much. It still was there, but not as much. And so now, where I'm at now, my kids are in high school or college, but now we've got established relationships outside of the work. And so, work from a social aspect is not as important to me. (Theo, senior project manager)

Similarly, a third married @home worker commented: "At this stage in my career, I'm usually not looking to the office for a lot of socialization. So that's not a primary mode, but just occasionally, I guess" (Robbie, senior content strategist).

These thoughts—being established at work, having social connections outside of the office—make sense for the mature crowd of married @home employees. But, in a counterintuitive twist, almost fifty percent of our married home-preferring interviewees were under 30! These should be precisely the employees who should want to be in the office in order to develop those helpful work connections, to get under the wing of a powerful mentor, to learn the unspoken rules of how their organization and its hierarchy function. And yet, young married @home workers also wanted to work-from-home, just as their older (hmm, mature) married peers did. As one of them put it: "My wife and I are like, it's cool; as weird as it is, it's great, we don't mind it all, it works for us" (Mark, onboarding coordinator). So, life stage was also not what pushed so many of our married interviewees to develop an @home preference.

Why then was marital status such a strong driver of a work-from-home preference, regardless of partner work-from-home status or life stage? It seems that married @home workers—more so than any other demographic—had an epiphany. They realized: The relationships that matter to me, the relationships I should invest in, are my personal ones. Work-from-home sharpened married @home workers' homing instinct. It called them home, to the personal stuff, to the familial relationships that are rooted there. In fact, our interviews reveal that work-from-home became self-reinforcing for married @home employees. As they settled into their home office, they invested the time saved from going into the company office right back into their personal life. This felt rewarding and right, and it further fed into their work-from-home preference. Hear this married @home worker explain the self-reinforcing cycle that work-from-home creates:

> The personal family side of working from home just makes it so much easier, you know. I gain almost an hour in my day because I don't have the commute anymore, so I can prep dinner quick before I have to go get the kids. And you know, it's just, I have more me-time and more time for my family than I did going into the office every day. And knowing the perks that I have with the position that I'm in, I would struggle if I had to go into the office every single day. Just thinking through the amount of time that I would lose in my day… How would I make sure that I am compensated for that? (Patty, risk manager).

In the end, that prototypical @home employee we asked you to imagine—you know, the one with the ring on their finger? That home-preferring person is pointing to an undeniable shift in married workers' work location preference toward the home. One take-away for work organizations is to recognize that their married workers are most likely to appreciate and even demand a work-from-home option. Another is that organizations may need to be extra creative to pull married workers from the magnetic draw of the home. The revelation that marital status is the demographic characteristic to focus on is quite interesting. We've been doing research on work organizations for 20+ years. We can tell you, marital status has never been a thing. Academics and consultants have always advised organizations to focus on gender, or race, or LGBTQ identification, or socioeconomic status, or age … but never on marital status. So, this is uncharted territory for work organizations.[11] And yet, let us say it one more time: marital status was the single best demographic driver of work location preference we uncovered, all else being equal.

The Role of Race

There may be one more demographic factor that is true for @home workers. We are talking about race. Now, only 15% of the employees we interviewed identified as non-White (African American or Hispanic). Though this sample is small, it still suggests a large—and frankly, uncomfortable—story. You see, two-thirds of our minority employees preferred @home. That means that minority employees are more likely to prefer working from home than to prefer a hybrid or an in-office option. In contrast, White employees are equally likely to prefer @home, @office, or @hybrid. So racial identity does not push White employees into a specific work location preference, but it pushes non-White employees toward a work-from-home preference (Fig. 2.6).

Others have also noticed a tendency for non-White employees to lean toward the home. Research by Slack's Future Forum reports that a stunning 97% of Black knowledge workers want hybrid or fully remote work.[12]

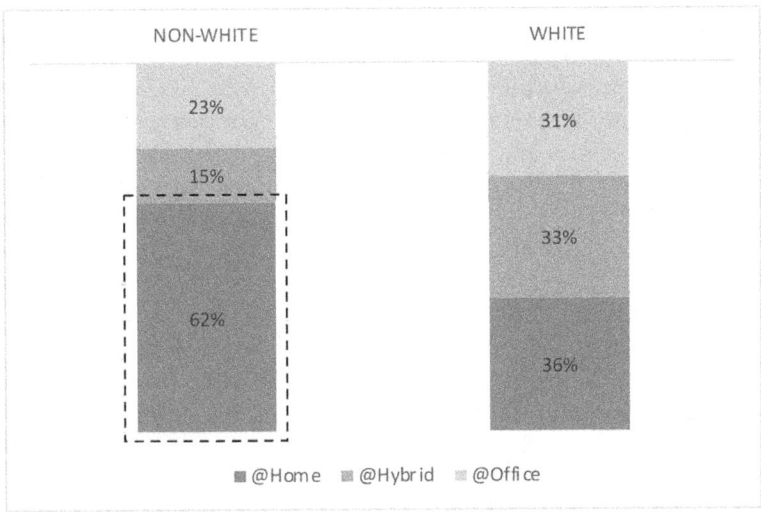

Fig. 2.6 Race explains @home preference

While Slack only focused on Black employees, other research has studied minority employees broadly defined. The conclusion is strikingly similar—minority workers overwhelmingly have an @home preference.[13] This likely is a testament to the poor work experience of employees of color who often face microaggressions and plain-out discrimination in the office.[14] So it seems like minority employees are taking their mental health and well-being into their own hands, and removing themselves from toxic offices. This should be a wake-up call to work organizations. At the same time, it is crucial that minority @home workers do not become an "out of sight, out of mind" phenomenon. Work organizations should use remote work as a tool to positively affect inclusion and belonging. How could you engage with your racial minority @home employees in a meaningful way?

Wrap-Up: Who Are the @Home Employees
So, who are the @home workers, demographically speaking? When you close your eyes and picture a home-preferring employee, who should you see? In terms of gender, it's complicated. Gender on its own does not describe @home employees. When picturing a man, you should see an executive; when picturing a woman, you should see a working mom. In contrast, in terms of marital status, it's quite straight-forward. You should see a married person. Any married person would do: a married person whose spouse also works from home…or not; a married person who is older…or younger; a married person who lives in a kids-filled house…or in a tranquil home. Again, the point is that this @home worker is married. Finally, in terms of race, you should see an outsized number of racial minority @home workers. To be clear, picturing these characteristics doesn't guarantee that you'll be right in every single case.

But it significantly increases your chance of being right in how you imagine a home-preferring employee.

Are you one of these @home workers? What is your reason to prefer homework? Are you a high-level male boss? Are you fed up with the corporate grind, and longing for freedom and for work on your own terms? Perhaps you are a working mom? Perhaps you find it easier to combine work and motherhood, two things you genuinely care about? Or are you married? Have you realized that you value personal and familial relationships most, and that those are rooted in the home, not in the office? Maybe you are a member of a minority? Maybe you are looking to escape toxic offices? If yes to any of the above, then being an @home worker is your thing.

But you could say, "Hold up! My demographics are just a tiny reason why I prefer to work-from-home. You're just scratching the surface here, authors." Guilty as charged! If you gave us another shot, we'll delve into much deeper reasons people prefer work-from-home in later chapters.

Who Are the @Office Employees?

Let's get to the @office workers now, and repeat the close your eyes exercise. Who do you see? We already shared that gender on its own is not a demographic characteristic that predicts work location preference. Just as men and women were about evenly split in the @home preference, so they are evenly split in the @office preference. That men and women equally want to be in the office is another reminder to check our preconceived notions about who is a "company man" and who's not. "Man" is not accurate. Here is that gender breakdown graph again (Fig. 2.7).

The Role of Executive Status

Remember how executive status predicted men's preference to work-from-home? And remember how it predicted women's preferences, but in the opposite direction? So, in contrast to men executives, women executives prefer to work from the office. In fact, half of the female executives in our dataset were office-preferring employees, compared to only a tenth of the male executives (Fig. 2.8).

If you're catching yourself fighting a deep-seated urge to imagine a power-hungry woman who had thrown away her chance at personal happiness by choosing to be single and childless in the name of corporate success—good! Keep on fighting this pre-programmed thought until you evict it out of your head. Our women @office executives were happily married, and all but one were moms of children living at home. These powerful women preferred the office for a variety of unique reasons, none of which included feeling pressure to be in the office to prove one's worth. One female executive simply enjoyed the camaraderie of being in the office:

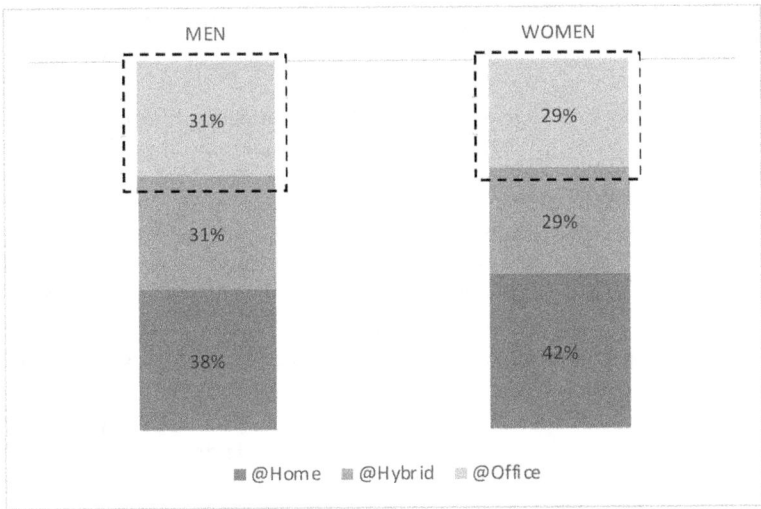

Fig. 2.7 Men and women are equally likely to prefer @home, @hybrid, or @office

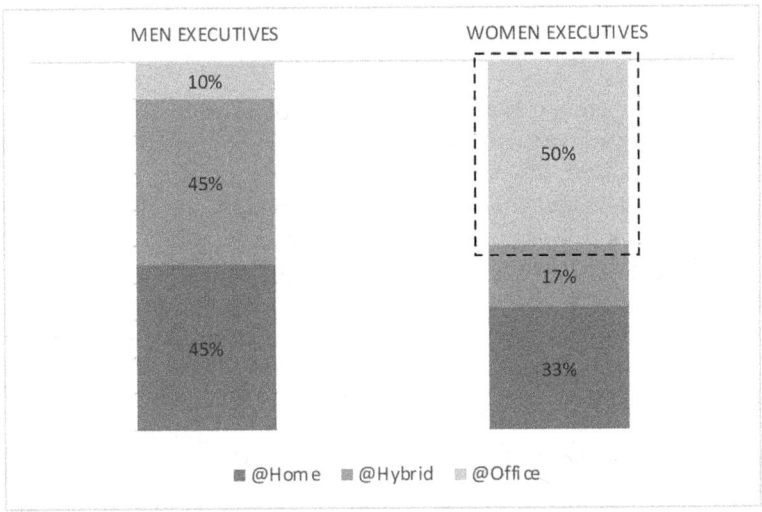

Fig. 2.8 Executive status explains @office preference for women, not men

I like coming into the office. I think, you know, even when I enter the office space, it gives me that collaborative feeling, belonging feeling. Having the receptionist there and her smiling and saying "Hello, Elena" actually makes your day a little bit. So that's nice. And also, when you come in, you'll see somebody, you'll run into somebody, so that's nice too. (Elena, division vice president)

Another was a segmentor who found it easier to do work at the office and life at home:

> Because of my working style and how my brain segments things, it's better for me to be here than to be at home. At home, I would find myself when I have 15 min, rather than diving into another project, I would go change the load from the washer to the dryer, I would go fold a little laundry versus getting into my work. I feel like that is stunting my growth as a leader and as a professional. So the positive of being here is that I can segment. Here, I can separate myself from home. (Jessica, area director)

Yet another felt it was easier to collaborate in-person, with the added bonus of less back pain in the office:

> Just being around people, I think is easier. For example, it's easier to work with [name; the CEO] in person. So today, I mean, I've been on the phone with him probably three hours today. And if I'm in the office, he doesn't seem to bother me as much [laughs]. But when I'm home, I get calls from him all the time. And you know, our office space here is great, and we love to use it. Plus, I also find that I'm sitting more if I'm at home, I'm just sitting working, and I don't get up much, so it's kind of hard on your back. (Maria, division vice president)

But while these women executives' reasons to prefer the office varied, what unified them and pushed them toward an @office preference was the love they shared for their company's culture, the urge they felt to restore it, and the belief that culture happens in the office. One said: "I would like to see the majority of our people in the office at some point, just because I think there's a deeper connection that grows when we're all together" (Jessica, area director). Another agreed: "It's a ghost town. I mean, you walk around and there is no one. And it's weird. Once we re-do the space, we hope that they will want to come back in, at least three days a week. This is our goal. That's what we're hoping" (Maria, division vice president). A third explained:

> We need more proactive thinking though. How do we keep employees as engaged and as connected to the company, how do we make sure that they don't, like [changes her voice] 'Oh, it's no big deal to leave here and go work for somebody else, I don't know anybody here anyway, I don't go to the office.' So the office space is important. I honestly don't see us staying that way, I don't see that for us. I do still see significant value of connection—of actual physical connection—with people. (Elena, division vice president)

Interesting... Who knew? In the post-pandemic workplace, women executives may become the new bearers of the office torch!

The Role of Being Single

And what about men? What pushes men to develop an @office work preference? At first glance, it looked like the answer was being single. Whereas single women had a small tendency to prefer @office (while over a third preferred @home), single men overwhelmingly preferred office (or hybrid), and only a tiny number preferred work-from-home (Fig. 2.9).

But something about this observation struck us as strange. Gender didn't matter for married employees. Married men *and* married women were equally likely to prefer @home. Why would gender matter for single employees? Why would single men be more driven to the office, and substantially less driven to the home, than single women?

To be honest, this question really got us stomped. We went down several paths. Perhaps "the office" is more a part of men's than women's identity? But this couldn't be true because remember, across all interviewees, men and women were equally likely to prefer @office. Perhaps men are more social and outgoing than women? But this also couldn't be true because research has well established that gender differences in Extraversion—the trait most related to being social and outgoing—are not that large at all.[15] Then, we asked the question in reverse. Instead of asking why single men are more driven to the office than single women, we asked: Why are single women less driven to the office and substantially more driven to the home than single men? And then it hit us! Looking at the single women in our dataset, we realized that some of them were single moms. And, of the single moms, all but one preferred … you guessed it—@home (the exception preferred @hybrid). Not

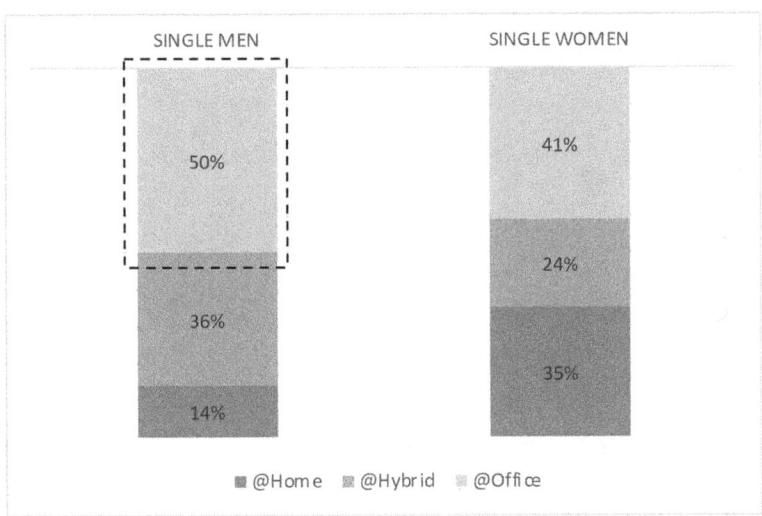

Fig. 2.9 Being single explains @office preference for men, not women

one single mom preferred @office. When we looked again at the work location preferences of single men and single women *with no parental obligations*, men's and women's preferences looked very, very similar. Clearly, most single non-parenting employees—whether men or women—want to work from the office all the time (@office) or most of the time (@hybrid). Only a minority of single non-parenting men *and* women want to work-from-home (@home) (Fig. 2.10).

Why does singlehood push employees toward an @office (or @hybrid) preference, and away from an @home preference? A simple explanation is that it's just about age, and by extension—work experience. Single employees with no parental obligations tend to be young. In our dataset, they were on average 25 years old—about 10 years younger than the average married and single-parent employee. Naturally, then, they don't have much work experience either. In our dataset, their work tenure was on average 3.5 years—about 5 years lower than the average married and single-parent employee. Arguably, their general lack of work experience sharpens single non-parenting employees' career growth instinct, pushing them toward the @office preference.

Indeed, single non-parenting @office workers talked about how they prioritize in-office work as a pathway to professional development. For one young @office worker, the office provided opportunities for networking and mentorship:

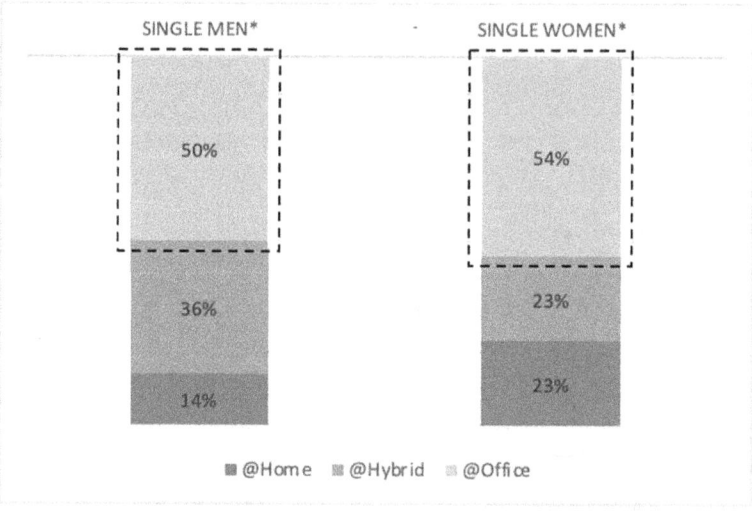

Fig. 2.10 Being single with no parental obligations explains @office preference for men and women

Once I joined the company that summer, I worked completely remote. About the fall time, I started to work in the office so I could kind of get some frequent touch bases with my boss. My superiors were in the office most of the time, and I thought it was good face time for me to be there, you know, moving in and out of these different roles. I find it easier to, you know, pick up and learn a little quicker when I'm in the office and ask those questions. You can overhear those conversations, too, and just, again, be able to ask questions. (Jake, client analyst)

For another single non-parenting @office worker, an intern, the office was a source of new ideas:

Something that I didn't even think about prior to this job—because all my internships had been previously remote—is that sometimes you might be working on a project, and then you might run into someone in the hallway, and then you talk to them about your project, and then they have ideas, and then, you know, you kind of get a lot of value from that. And that's something you really cannot do virtually. You can't just run into someone and then have that casual conversation on your project unless it's planned or scheduled already. (Sophia, intern)

For a third young @office worker, the office facilitated broader exposure to outside departments and leaders—a benefit quite likely to generate promotion opportunities:

So sitting at home, kind of isolated, your exposure to people that you don't work with every day is very minimal, especially to upper leadership and other departments that you just don't see. So I think opportunities to put myself out there have been limited because of that. It just doesn't happen because people are out of sight, out of mind. (Victoria, investment analyst)

But while it makes sense to think that young people prioritize career growth, what's interesting here is that young people believe career growth happens in person. And they are not wrong! Recent headlines have unequivocally reflected this reality. *Remote Workers Are Losing Out on Promotions*, The Wall Street Journal declared.[16] *Inc. Magazine* agreed.[17] *If Workers Want a Promotion, They Have to Go into the Office at Least 4 Days a Week*, they warned. It seems that single non-parenting @office workers have been one step ahead of these headlines! No need to order *them* back—they often are the first ones in.

However, we stumbled on an unexpected—and a little bit concerning—disconnect. You see, in our interviews with senior leaders, they often assumed that young employees want to work-from-home. "As our workforce is aging out and we're bringing younger folks in, that's what they're looking for" opined one senior leader, a home-preferring worker herself (Katie, associate vice president of sales). Another senior leader, also with an @home preference, was under the same impression: "As younger people enter the workforce, we've got to offer a lot more flexibility" (Travis, division director). But while "flexibility" meant work-from-home to these senior leaders, it simply meant flexible work hours to single non-parenting young workers. So be forewarned, company leaders. Your assumptions about the young generation of workers may be inaccurate. They may love their freedom and independence, but when it comes to work and career, they see value in being in the office. You must get on the same page with your young workers on what "flexibility" means, or else, your organization has a lot to lose.

To wit, we saw some concerning trends in our data. For example, one senior leader, again with an @home preference, shared this:

> It's been a couple years, probably actually before the pandemic, since I've mentored someone. But we do have pretty active [mentoring] programs. We actually rely very heavily on peer mentoring because, quite honestly, they're the ones doing the work. And we in leadership are, you know, our role is different as oversight and managers. (Paul, claims manager)

Hmm, delegating mentoring to peers? That may not be the best idea when what young employees really want is in-person exposure to senior leaders. Another poor idea is relying on online get-to-know sessions for relationship-building. Almost to a tee, our young @office workers decried this practice, especially when used as a replacement, rather than a substitute, of in-person relationship-building efforts. And yet, another senior leader with an @home preference thought that their summer intern "got all the relationships he needed" despite the whole team working fully from home. He then added: "He's now in the office two days a week at least, I think" (Jason, senior data analyst). We wonder why…

If you remain unconvinced that young workers want YOU, their boss, to be in the office, we'll let one of them put it apologetically, yet bluntly:

> My first manager at the time was never in the office. That's a whole other story, but she just wasn't a good boss. Sorry about saying this on live recording here, but she just really was not a great boss, and was really hands off, not a great leader, sorry about that. But I had the opportunity to start working with the CFO, and she was, she came in every day. And so she was a really great resource to connect with and kind of became a great mentor. (Charles, accounting intern)

So, senior leaders, especially you, @home preferring ones: please re-consider what your single, non-parenting employees—who are very often young and new to the world of work—want and need. Singlehood, via the young age and lower work experience that often comes with it, sharpens employees' career growth instinct. This instinct makes them hungry to learn and to grow professionally, which they perceive is best done in person. This pushes single, non-parenting employees to develop an @office (or @hybrid) preference, and strongly pulls them away from an @home preference.

But is there another instinct, outside of career growth, that singlehood sharpens?

Let's step back a bit. Remember how married employees—whether men or women, whether parents or not—mostly preferred @home? Marriage seemed to sharpen employees' homing instinct. Does singlehood sharpen employees' community instinct? Arguably, unattached people—regardless of age and work experience—would long for a community to help fulfill humans' fundamental need to belong.[18]

Without exception, our single non-parenting @office workers craved community. Community-at-work served a number of functions. For some, community-at-work provided energy:

> I would say, in the office, energy is a big word for me. You know, we had a big meeting here a couple weeks ago, and just to be able to see everybody, there's just a different energy in the office when people are in and you get to catch up with people. It's hard being at home and just talking through a computer all the time. Luckily, I have a roommate, but I think you feel more connected when everybody's around, you feel more energy. So energy is definitely a big one. (David, client services consultant)

For others, community-at-work was a source of happiness:

> The majority of my stuff is in person, but that's because I choose to make it in person. I feel happy that I get to see my colleagues. (Matthew, sales representative).

Community-at-work made work more fun:

> I love having people in person. (laughs) It's really fun. (laughs) I really like the in-person component of it. We've done things like a hot dog eating contest and stuff like that that's fun in person. So it's an opportunity to meet people in a fun setting. (Nicole, data analyst)

Community-at-work made work more enjoyable:

> To be able to be in the office with the team, it's more collaborative, and specifically for me—a single guy that lives at home by themselves—certainly more enjoyable. It's not as enjoyable to be home to no one but me. So for me, I enjoy the interaction that I could have with my coworkers. (Christopher, account manager)

And perhaps most importantly, community-at-work tied workers to the company:

> I definitely think that in-person is way better. My first two teams were all virtual. I honestly couldn't even remember any of the names of the people that I did work with. I couldn't tell you what schools they went to, I couldn't even tell you a basic fact about them personally. But with the last group that I had, there were like 13 of us that were located in Philadelphia, I can tell you pretty much all their names, and tell you some personal facts about them. Like, I actually got to know these people. And I definitely felt a stronger connection to the company itself, and have really seen myself potentially staying here. (Sophia, intern)

Conversely, working from home—all alone, lacking community—caused single non-parenting @office workers to look for more communal pastures elsewhere:

> If I wasn't, you know, at my house, doing my internship here, it probably would be the worst summer of my life because I didn't, I didn't meet anyone. When I'd go in, there'd be no one at the office. I mean, like I said, if I didn't have my girlfriend, if I didn't have my high school friends who all came back for the summer, if I didn't have the, you know, a few people who stayed here from college over the summer, if I didn't have them, it would have been the worst summer my life, hands down. I kind of gave up on the company then because there was no company culture. (Daniel, intern)

Our finding that community appeals so strongly to single non-parenting employees that it turns a good half of them into office-preferring people (and another third into @hybrid preferers), is particularly important in modern society. Why? Because—as the U.S. Census Bureau reported in 2023—46.4% of the U.S. adult population, or nearly every other adult aged 18 and over—is single![19] That's a whole lot of people who lack an easily accessible and socially acceptable place for community. And, that's a whole lot of workers who expect to find community-at-work. Long live the office?

Wrap-Up: Who Are the @Office Employees
So, who are the @office preferring workers, demographically speaking? When you close your eyes and picture an office-preferring employee, who should you see? In terms of gender, when picturing a woman, you should see an executive. In terms of marital status, you should see a single person. However, not any single person would do. You should specifically see a single non-parenting person. Let us re-state that picturing these characteristics doesn't guarantee that you'd be right. But, it significantly increases your chance of being right in how you imagine an @office preferring employee.

Are you one of these @office people? What is your reason to prefer office work? Are you a high-level female boss? Are you worried that your company is losing its culture, and wishing for people to return to the office again? Or perhaps you are a single, non-parenting individual. Do you find it easier to advance in your career, to receive mentoring and advice, to learn your job, when you're in the office? Or maybe you feel alone and isolated, and you are longing for a sense of connection and for an opportunity to have some fun with friends? If yes to any of the above, then being on team @office is your thing.

But you could again say to us, "Wait! My demographics are just a tiny reason why I prefer to work from the office. You're just scratching the surface here!" And again we'd say to you: Guilty as charged! We will get into much deeper reasons why some workers prefer "to office" in later chapters.

Who Are the @Hybrid Employees?

And finally, let's talk about employees with an @hybrid preference. We start with our by-now expected reminder that gender on its own is not a demographic characteristic that predicts work location preference. Just as men and women were about evenly split in the @home and @office preferences, so they are evenly split in the @hybrid preference. Here is that gender breakdown graph one last time (Fig. 2.11).

But what demographic characteristics predict the @hybrid preference? Who should you see when you close your eyes and try to imagine an @hybrid worker?

In some ways, employees with an @hybrid preference resemble those with an @home preference. For example, married @hybrid workers were more likely to pick one or two office days as their "ideal" number of days to be in the office, approximating @home workers' preferences. In other ways,

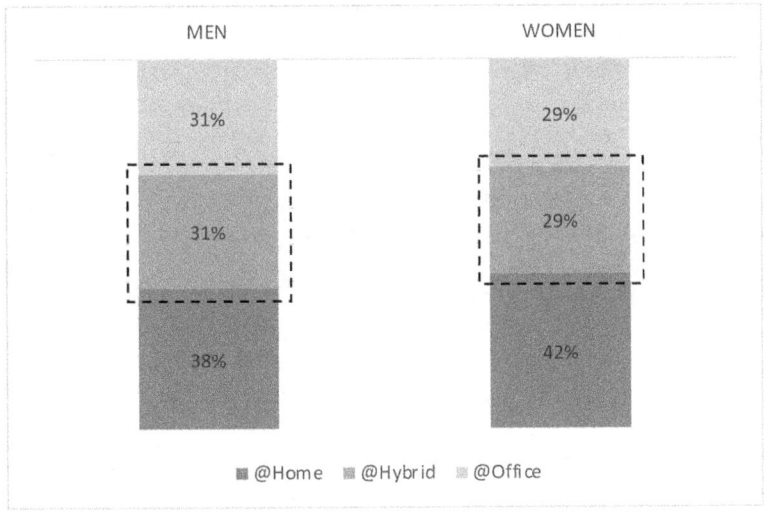

Fig. 2.11 Men and women are equally likely to prefer @home, @hybrid, or @office

employees with an @hybrid preference resemble those with an @office preference. For example, single @hybrid workers were more likely to pick three or four office days as their "ideal" number of days to be in the office, approximating @office workers' preferences. But these resemblances aside, we could identify no demographic characteristic to describe the prototypical @hybrid employee. Not a single one.

So, it seems that demographics funnel workers into an @home or an @office preference. But workers with an @hybrid preference? They appear much more idiosyncratic and difficult to be prototyped demographically. Perhaps preferring @hybrid is a mindset, not a demographic. A best-of-both-worlds mindset.[20] We can't wait to paint @hybrid employees for you in later chapters.

Reflection on Where We Prefer to Work In this chapter, you learned about the diversity of work location preferences employees have developed. You learned that some workers had come to realize they are perfectly happy working from home. Other workers had experienced the exact opposite realization—they understood they feel best when working in the office. And still others had found they like to mix-and-match, purposefully combining some work-from-home days with some work-from-office days. You also learned what demographic characteristics drive employees into these @home, @office, or @hybrid preferences.

But what happens when you consider employees' work location preferences and companies' workplace strategies all at once? What happens, for example, when an @office employee works for a remote-first company? Conversely, what happens when an @home employee works for an office-forward company? Or any other of the possible combinations of employee preference and company strategy?

In the chapters that follow, we will introduce you to the nine personas that emerge when employees' work location preferences combine (or in some cases—collide) with their company's chosen workplace strategy. We'll delve deeper, beyond demographic characteristics, to understand what makes these personas tick. And we'll introduce the notion of alignment. We'll explore how aligned versus half-aligned versus fully misaligned employees experience their work.

Notes

1. A. Mitchell, "Collaboration Technology Affordances from Virtual Collaboration in the Time of COVID-19 and Post-Pandemic Strategies," *Information Technology & People* 36, no. 5 (2023): 1982–2008, https://doi.org/10.1108/ITP-01-2021-0003; Zoom, "Navigating the Future of Work: Global Perspectives on Hybrid Models and Technology" (Zoom, 2024), https://click.zoom.com/navigating-the-future-of-work.
2. M. B. Perrigino, B. B. Dunford, and K. S. Wilson, "Work–Family Backlash: The 'Dark Side' of Work–Life Balance (WLB) Policies," *Academy of Management Annals* 12, no. 2 (2018): 600–630, https://doi.org/10.5465/annals.2016.0077.
3. O. R. Royle, "Wall Street Keeps Pushing to End WFH, but Their Own Senior Staff Would Rather Quit than Comply," *Forbes*, August 10, 2023, https://fortune.com/2023/08/10/wall-street-return-to-office-employee-mandates-wfh-hybrid-remote-work/.
4. A. Tangel and M. Maremont, "Private Jets and Pop-up Workspaces: Boeing Eases Return to Office for Top Brass," *The Wall Street Journal*, September 11, 2023, https://www.wsj.com/business/airlines/boeing-ceo-private-jets-return-to-office-9bee2035.
5. C. Cutter, "Starbucks's New Boss Gets an Unusual Perk: Remote Work," *The Wall Street Journal*, August 19, 2024, https://www.wsj.com/business/retail/starbucks-ceo-brian-niccol-remote-work-9429b303?st=nwroxmdeumgzjgz.
6. J. Barrett, "Could the Coronavirus Pandemic Shift Gender Roles Once and for All?," *Forbes*, May 11, 2020, https://www.forbes.com/sites/jenniferbarrett/2020/05/11/could-the-coronavirus-pandemic-shift-gender-roles-once-and-for-all/?sh=648e62344240.
7. B. Schulte and H. Swenson, "An Unexpected Upside to Lockdown: Men Have Discovered Housework," *The Guardian*, June 17, 2020, https://www.theguardian.com/us-news/2020/jun/17/gender-roles-parenting-housework-coronavirus-pandemic.
8. H. Hickok, "Are Men-Dominated Offices the Future of the Workplace?," *BBC*, May 6, 2021, https://www.bbc.com/worklife/article/20210503-are-men-dominated-offices-the-future-of-the-workplace.
9. M. Fox, "Is the 'Zoom Ceiling' the New Glass Ceiling? Experts Worry Remote Work Will Hold Women Back," *CNBC*, January 18, 2022, https://www.cnbc.com/2022/01/18/experts-worry-remote-work-may-hurt-womens-career-advancement.html.
10. A. Taub, "Pandemic Will 'Take Our Women 10 Years Back' in the Workplace," *The New York Times*, September 26, 2020, https://www.nytimes.com/2020/09/26/world/covid-women-childcare-equality.html.

11. S. Thatcher, C. B. Hymer, and R. P. Arwine, "Pushing Back against Power: Using a Multilevel Power Lens to Understand Intersectionality in the Workplace," *Academy of Management Annals* 17, no. 2 (2023): 710–50.
12. S. Subramanian, "A New Era of Workplace Inclusion: Moving from Retrofit to Redesign," *Future Forum* (blog), March 11, 2021, https://futureforum.com/2021/03/11/dismantling-the-office-moving-from-retrofit-to-redesign/.
13. L. Dhanani et al., "Inclusion near and Far: A Qualitative Investigation of Inclusive Organizational Behavior across Work Modalities and Social Identities," *Journal of Organizational Behavior* 45, no. 9 (2024): 1413–30, https://doi.org/10.1002/job.2779.
14. D. D. King et al., "When Thriving Requires Effortful Surviving: Delineating Manifestations and Resource Expenditure Outcomes of Microaggressions for Black Employees," *Journal of Applied Psychology* 108, no. 2 (2023): 183–207.
15. S. Murphy, P. A. Fisher, and C. Robie, "International Comparison of Gender Differences in the Five-Factor Model of Personality: An Investigation across 105 Countries," *Journal of Research in Personality* 90 (2021): 1–12.
16. T.-P. Chen, "Remote Workers Are Losing out on Promotions, New Data Shows," The Wall Street Journal, January 11.," *The Wall Street Journal*, January 11, 2024, https://www.wsj.com/lifestyle/careers/remote-workers-are-losing-out-on-promotions-8219ec63.
17. J. Stillman, "CEOs and Data Agree: If Workers Want a Promotion, They Have to Go into the Office at Least 4 Days a Week," *Inc.*, February 13, 2024, https://www.inc.com/jessica-stillman/ceos-data-agree-workers-promotion-office-4-days-week.html.
18. A. Colbert, J. Bono, and R. Purvanova, "Flourishing via Workplace Relationships: Moving beyond Instrumental Support," *Academy of Management Journal* 59, no. 4 (2016): 1199–1223.
19. United States Census Bureau, "Unmarried and Single Americans Week: September 17–23, 2023," *United States Census Bureau* (blog), September 17, 2023, https://www.census.gov/newsroom/stories/unmarried-single-americans-week.html.
20. A. Mitchell and P. Brewer, "Leading Hybrid Teams: Strategies for Realizing the Best of Both Worlds," *Organizational Dynamics* 51, no. 3 (2022): 1–9, https://doi.org/10.1016/j.orgdyn.2021.100866.

PART II

Personas in Remote-First Companies

What are remote-first companies? The defining characteristic of remote-first companies is that they do not require or expect office presence. Remote work is the *modus operandi*. This means two things. One, the office takes a backstage under remote-first; indeed, some remote-first organizations are officeless. Two, technology rules; it replaces "the office" as the predominant interactional arena.

Consider Airbnb as an example. Airbnb officially became a remote-first company in April 2022. In an all-staff email, CEO Brian Chesky outlined the five pillars of Airbnb's remote-first strategy, dubbed *"Live and Work Anywhere"*[1]:

1. You can work from home or the office
2. You can move anywhere in the country you work in and your compensation won't change
3. You have the flexibility to travel and work around the world for up to 90 days each year
4. We'll meet up regularly for gatherings
5. We'll continue to work in a highly coordinated way

Airbnb believes two ingredients are needed to make their remote-first strategy a success. The first is trust. Airbnb leadership has asked managers to trust the people on their team, pointing to the great results everyone accomplished during lockdown. The second is structure. Airbnb recognizes that being remote-first can create huge coordination and information sharing challenges. The company is leaning on planning. It is creating a single company calendar, standardizing product roll-out dates, and in general, creating rhythm and predictability around work activities in order to infuse structure into the dispersed work experience. Airbnb believes that going remote-first will unlock creativity and innovation, all while making working for Airbnb really fun.

Dropbox is another example. That company made a permanent shift to remote-first during lockdown. Back then, CEO Drew Houston told employees that once the office reopens, it will be off limits to individual work.[2] Those who insist on having an out-of-home desk are awarded a stipend for membership in a co-working space, like WeWork. To make it clear that the purpose of the office has changed, Dropbox re-branded its facilities as "Dropbox Studios"—or spaces for meeting and collaboration between teams. To stay connected, Dropbox employees can stop by "the studio" once a week or once a quarter…or never, really. But rather than simply cutting its real estate budget, Dropbox funneled a large portion of it into a travel budget. This enables the company to fly its employees to its offices (well, "studios") for meetings and social events. Dropbox believes that their version of a remote-first strategy promotes both flexibility, and human connection.

But don't assume that only tech companies gravitate toward remote-first. Research by FlexIndex.com, a platform tracking flexible work adoption, shows that in addition to technology, over 80% of organizations in insurance, telecommunications, professional services, media and entertainment, financial services, and non-profit offer flexibility, which includes remote-first.[3] To wit, consider Allstate. The insurer not only adopted remote-first post lockdown, but began to aggressively shed office space. By the end of 2020, Allstate had already sold its headquarters in Northbrook, Illinois, and donated items from the campus—office supplies, décor, sporting equipment, kitchen appliances—to more than 40 nonprofits. Real estate savings were funneled into funds to support employees' home offices.[4] In 2022, Allstate opened a smaller office space in Northbrook to facilitate employee interaction as needed. The company also maintains some office spaces in downtown Chicago. The smaller office footprint—coupled with heavy investments in work technology—meets the needs of Allstate's workforce which is 99% hybrid or fully remote.[5] Allstate CEO Tom Wilson says remote-first is working well for the company: "Our employees decided they wanted that and we're finding a way to make it work."[6]

As these examples show, under a remote-first strategy, working from a remote location is the default or primary method of working. Remote-first companies believe that employees can be productive from anywhere. They do not expect their employees to be in the office. They do not recruit based on office proximity. They do not promote based on who shows up to the office. They do not dodge pay based on geographic location. To substitute for the office—the place where culture, connection, and collaboration would traditionally happen—remote-first organizations rely on technology. With that, some are downsizing office facilities and rebranding the office into a place for fun, whereas others are eliminating the office all-together and settling into virtual space instead.

The remote-first company we studied fits this mold. Remember, we called it Promethean in a nod to the daring, non-traditional approach this company's taking. As we previously described, Promethean realized that its employees are just as productive at home. The company polled its vast workforce, 25,000+ strong, and heard a loud "we don't want to come back" answer. Honoring employees' wishes is a top reason for Promethean's remote-first strategy. A second reason is saving on real estate; this allows the company to increase their products' pricing competitiveness relative to rivals. A third reason for the strategy is Promethean's realization that remote-first opens up the talent pool; the company now hires based on expertise. As a result, most employees work on dispersed teams, interacting with teammates and team leaders—some whom they've never met in person—mostly through technology.

Though Promethean's employees told the company they wanted to keep working from home, the remote-first strategy the company adopted still created extreme persona diversity. You see, while the majority of employees called for a remote-first approach, not everyone at Promethean came out of the COVID-19 lockdown with the realization that they had an @home work preference. About 60% did. We call these @home preferring employees **Avatars** because they developed a comfort with technology that surprised even them. About 15% of Promethean employees realized they similarly loved work-from-home, but also missed the office. We call these @hybrid preferring employees **Centrists** because their philosophy on remote work was, arguably, more measured than their company's. Finally, about 25% of Promethean employees discovered they had an @office preference. We call these @office preferring employees **Community-seekers** because they kept on searching—often, in vain—for some type, any type, of social engagement and interaction with their colleagues.

So, Promethean had a majority of fully aligned personas (60% were Avatars) but also not insignificant minorities of half-aligned personas (15% were Centrists) and fully misaligned personas (25% were Community-seekers). This 60-15-25 persona breakdown should hold true in most remote-first organizations like Promethean—large, national companies with a previously strong in-office culture and imposing office spaces in midsize-to-large cities. Naturally, the persona breakdown might look different under other circumstances. But, as our research and consulting experience has taught us, we can guarantee you one thing: You will find Avatars, Centrists, and Community-seekers in all remote-first organizations, whether large or small. You can't run from persona diversity.

As an organization, it is not easy pushing a strategy when your team members are not on the same page. As an employee, it is not easy enjoying your work experience when sharp fault lines divide you from your colleagues. Clearly, company strategy and employee preferences should be much more aligned. Finding alignment begins with awareness. So, let's learn about Avatars, Centrists, and Community-seekers.

Notes

1. Airbnb, "Airbnb's Design for Employees to Live and Work Anywhere," *Airbnb News*, April 28, 2022, https://news.airbnb.com/airbnbs-design-to-live-and-work-anywhere/.
2. C. Cutter, "The Death of the Office Desk Is upon Us," *The Wall Street Journal*, January 31, 2021, https://www.wsj.com/articles/the-death-of-the-office-desk-is-upon-us-11610553529.
3. FlexIndex, "Flex Report: Tech Deep Dive," 2024, https://www.flexindex.com/reports/tech-industry-2024.
4. Allstate, "How Allstate Employees Are Redefining Their Workplace," *Allstate Corporation*, April 19, 2024, https://www.allstatecorporation.com/stories/flexible-workplace.aspx.
5. Allstate, "Allstate Took a Leap Forward on the Future of Work—and We're Not Looking Back," *Allstate Corporation*, April 16, 2024, https://www.allstatecorporation.com/stories/future-of-flexible-work.aspx.
6. K. Delaney, "A Surprising Case Study in Remote Work at Scale," *Charter*, July 23, 2023, https://www.charterworks.com/allstate-remote-work/.

CHAPTER 3

Meet the Avatar, the Centrist, and the Community-Seeker

INTRODUCTION

In remote-first companies, @home preferring employees evolve into Avatars, @hybrid preferring employees evolve into Centrists, and @office preferring employees evolve into Community-seekers. In Chapter 2, we shared a demographic analysis of employees with @office, @hybrid, and @home preferences. Here, we focus on deeper, more psychological factors that drive employees with these different work location preferences to become Avatars, Centrists, and Community-seekers when they work in remote-first organizations. See (Fig. 3.1).

NUDGED OR PUSHED TO REMOTE WORK

Hot-desking, desk sharing, hoteling... Do you remember these pre-pandemic office innovations? If you too had been subjected to this almost universally hated office re-design practice, we bet you can sympathize with the scores of Promethean employees who remember feeling "weird" about it:

> What made me feel kind of weird about all this is that the company decided to sell off a bunch of real estate [and] lease out part of the main building. And it's like, But, but, but, you're putting people in my little cubicle! That was my home! Now, it's a hotel space. And anytime I go in the office, I have to hook up to the hotel space, and it's like, 'Why, why am I here, I mean, seriously, why?' (Kate, instructional designer, avatar)

But post-pandemic, hoteling suddenly became ... shall we say, tolerable, to a large crowd of supporters: the Avatars. You see, hoteling gave these @home preferring employees another nudge, "another reason" to just stay home:

© The Author(s), under exclusive license to Springer Nature Switzerland AG 2025
R. Purvanova and A. Mitchell, *The New Workplace*,
https://doi.org/10.1007/978-3-031-86046-1_3

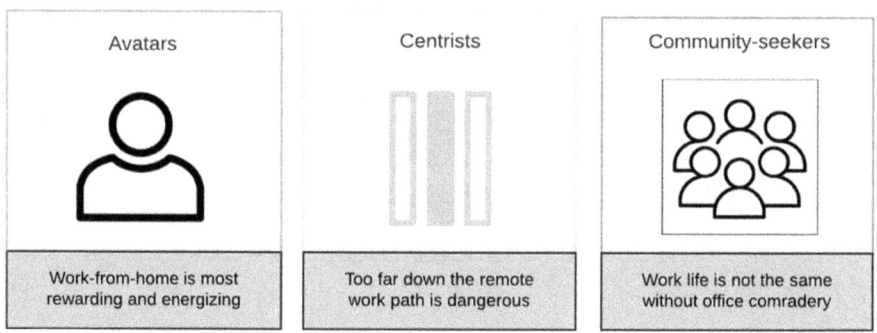

Fig. 3.1 Personas in remote-first companies include Avatars, Centrists, and Community-seekers

So that's another reason why I moved to work-from-home full-time: I was gonna lose my personal workspace. I had my own workstation. They were moving everybody to that hoteling idea, and the floor was also going to be different. So, I just decided then that I didn't want to do the hoteling piece because for many years, I had my own workspace. (Zara, risk director, avatar)

The company nudged employees even further; an employee explained: "You have a certain allowance for a desk and a chair. They provided all of the technical stuff, you know, monitors and keyboards and mouse and stuff like that" (Patty, risk manager, avatar). So, Avatars, who initially felt de-homed from the corporate office, rushed to re-home themselves at the home office.

Avatars loved designing their home offices. One "kicked my husband out of the office, and it is now mine" (Patty, risk manager, avatar); another "told my wife, we're making me an office, this is gonna be a thing" (Michael, senior product analyst, avatar). But all kidding aside, Avatars were serious about creating a space that "is work and feels like work" (Paul, claims manager, avatar); a space that's "very similar" to the office: "I've done stuff where, at this point, the feel of my working environment is very similar to when I was in the office. Everything seems and feels very similar" (Carl, data product consultant, avatar).

Unsurprisingly, in the process of creation, Avatars became truly attached to their home office: "I mean, all my stuff, all my work stuff is here. It's my dedicated space. I don't share it with anyone. So, I guess, it's kinda like, this is where I work. This is my stuff" (Taylor, innovation product manager, avatar). The more Avatars' attachment to their home office grew, the more detached they felt from the corporate office: "It's kind of like going to a strange place. It's just kinda like, you're just visiting" (Tim, senior product consultant, avatar). Its symbolism lost, the corporate office was no longer a source of employees' work identity: "When I go, it's almost like remembering that, Oh, yeah, I'm a Promethean employee and I work here" (Travis, division director, avatar).

In contrast, Avatars were fully at-home in the home office. They even found ways to put the home office to work. One used his home office décor as an icebreaker in client meetings:

> I have bike wheels up on the wall. And I liked that early on because it was an icebreaker. I work with a lot of external clients, and we don't always start the conversation there and then. You're making that personal connection. Whereas, like, I could not bring—I wouldn't want to bring—my bike wheels into the office. (Kyle, associate vice president of product, avatar)

Many used the home office to better connect with coworkers, seeing colleagues in their natural environment, not on the office stage, performing the work-from-office script:

> We have a toddler now so he can just walk in if he wants. Another person on the team has a daughter just a little bit older than my son. Another person, he used to be in our group, had a younger daughter, but school age. I always feel like it's well received, like, if he comes in and we're just having an informal meeting. And I've had other people's kids come in, or dogs… Like, my dog is right now sleeping here on the floor by me. Or we sometimes get to vent about whether the mailman comes, or if we're having work done at the house, or just random stuff.
>
> And you know, it kind of lets the guard down a little bit. It's like, you always just got to see what version everybody put forth at work, and you didn't get to see much in the home life. But like, you guys can see inside my house, and I can see inside yours. So, it kind of adds more of a human element to work, I think. It just kind of peels back the version you would put forth at work, so… (Michael, senior product analyst, avatar)

In the end, what started as a rude un-settling out of the office turned into a welcomed re-settling into an even better space: the home office: for Avatars.

Centrists were a different story. Unlike Avatars, Centrists bought into the company's reasoning for hoteling: "Yeah, they've understood that our physical brick and mortar real estate is a little too much. So they've reworked a lot of the floors" (Adam, senior software developer, centrist). Centrists also knew that because the workforce was so geographically dispersed, teams would mostly interact via technology anyways: "I lead a team of about 60 […] and only three are here in [name of city]" (Liam, director of sales, centrist). They were also not in a rush to build out their home office: "I have to get a really nice expensive chair for here at home. I still need to get one. I'm literally sitting on a metal folding chair" (Noah, risk manager, centrist). So, the company's move to hoteling was not what nudged these @hybrid preferring employees to the Centrist persona: "It's basically hotel. That plays no merit into what I feel" (Julian, innovation consultant, centrist).

But whereas hoteling was of little personal import to Centrists, what moved these employees over to the Centrist persona was their concerns with hoteling's long-term effects on others. Centrists questioned who would ever want to come back to the office given the "annoyance" of "trucking your stuff" every day:

> Yeah, if I had to truck all that stuff around—and we have some people who do, they bring, like, their whole keyboard and their headset, and their mouse, and all that, all this stuff. And yeah, no kidding, I wouldn't want to go to the office. That's super annoying, right? So, I think that's something that we need to, if we're actually going to, you know, say it's a desire that we want people to come into the office, we have to make it easy and convenient...unless you aren't going to do it. (Noah, risk manager, centrist)

They also decried the emptying of the office the switch to hoteling promoted:

> It's funny, you know, because—and I feel bad saying this—but I work for a Fortune 100 company, and I can go in and it's normal to go into the office and only see one or two people. It's very normal. As a matter of fact, it's very rare if you see more than 5 or 10 people in the office in a day unless it's something special going on. I'm not comfortable with that. (Julian, innovation consultant, centrist)

Centrists wondered about the "tipping point" where people "choose not to come in because—unless some critical mass of people decided to come in—the people that did come in don't necessarily get the full value" (Noah, risk manager, centrist). This concern echoes research on the contagious effects of the "lonely" office which has documented that employees often choose to work remotely not necessarily because they need to or want to, but because they assume others won't be in the office.

So don't be confused: Centrists may roll with the punches on office design. But, they are still going to call out unforeseen, unplanned, or unacknowledged long-term negatives ... *for others*.

Who was really distraught over the new office setup were the Community-seekers. The hoteling arrangement made these @office preferring employees feel *personally* displaced:

> I do like my own space. I do wish it wasn't hotel. That was the change I was not very happy with—as someone being work-from-office more than others. It is kind of sad to not be able to ever have the chance to personalize my desk, have pictures, or even just my notebooks and stuff at the office. We have a drawer, but it's not the same. So that's kind of a bummer. And it is kind of frustrating sometimes, coming in and having to, you know, set up your desk every single time you come in. So those little things make a huge difference to some people. (Hannah, senior analyst, community-seeker)

Community-seekers also felt displaced from a place of community:

My boss was pretty sad when she had to clear her desk off. I cleaned up some of the white boards and stuff, and it was kind of sad, you know, seeing old notes from team members who used to be on the team. You definitely lose that personal, that personality of the team when all the desks are emptying, everything looks the same. There is still random stuff sitting around that is people's stuff that hasn't been claimed. And it's very weird. (Hannah, senior analyst, community-seeker)

Not only were they de-homed from the corporate office, but—unlike Avatars and Centrists—most Community-seekers could not re-home themselves in their home office. "My office is in my bedroom," one Community-seeker said, unhappily (Victoria, investment analyst, community-seeker). Another elaborated:

I wish I had, you know, a second room, just for my desk, for a separate office. I would really enjoy that because for me, you know, work moved into my actual life a little bit too intimately. I absolutely hate it. I still hate it. I hate, you know, on a weekend, waking up and walking into my, you know, my common space, and you know, seeing my desk stare right at me. I'm like, Urgh! Cause you almost feel like I have to log in, it's right there. I can just log in for a couple of hours on a Sunday. Which I never, I never used to do that, I never. Any work I did was in an office, it was always out there. And now, my work is always here, so... (Emma, middle market sales manager, community-seeker)

In search of a home, in search of their lost community, in search of better work-life separation, Community-seekers kept on coming into the office. But—confirming Centrists' fears that the empty office would dissuade people from coming in—most Community-seekers eventually retreated:

At first, I probably went twice a week, and then every Friday, and then, honestly, I kind of stopped [going in] because, you know, for lack of better words, no one's in the office, like, it was just me, and... It's a ghost town. (Daniel, intern, community-seeker)

In all, hoteling pushed @office preferring employees toward the Community-seeker persona. And whereas some did find small pockets of community as we will see next, most kept on searching, in vain.

Virtual Reality Versus "Real" Reality

What superpower would you like to have? Invisibility? X-ray vision? Shapeshifting? Our personal favorites are super speed (Ina, she loves the Flash) and flying (Alanah, she's a fan of Supergirl).

Well, Avatars had acquired a superpower of their own. We call it projection: the ability to cast yourself into environments displaced in space and time. When you use projection, your body is comfortably sitting somewhere (say, your home office), but your mind, your psyche, has teleported to a different space—the virtual office. And in this new, virtual space, you can interact with others' projections of their selves, and you could feel feelings, and you could experience a sense of connection. All without having to leave your comfy physical reality. A handy power for the remote-first environment, right?

Avatars developed this superpower once they re-built the office at home and felt something's missing: the human touch. So, they realized they should try and "move out" the human connections that were happening in the corporate office over to the new, virtual office:

> The only thing is those human connections. Everything else, at first, we missed. Okay, maybe I missed the cafeteria. Well, then you brought the cafeteria inside the workspace in your house. So, you can build out everything because everything is material. The human connections are the only ones that you are not able to pick up. But we are finding out alternate ways of just moving those out too. (Helen, IT applications manager, avatar)

But how did Avatars "move out" those human connections? That's where projection came in. Avatars embraced the idea that they could cast themselves into virtual reality—you know, the reality created by Teams or Zoom, not even anything fancy. There, Avatars could re-engage with their colleagues.

At first, it was simple things, like starting the morning with an energizing team huddle (virtually), doing coffee or lunch or happy hour with teammates (virtually), attending a networking event to put yourself out there (virtually), shooting the breeze with a work friend to pass time (virtually), venting to the team leader about a client (virtually). In those virtual engagements, Avatars felt that they "are making a connection" with their colleagues, perhaps even more so than the connections they made in "real" reality:

> While I can't go walk and get coffee with somebody, it's really nice to be able to, like, see everybody and have these conversations. I feel like we're making a connection. Everybody's always willing and able to meet in virtual meetings, or I could just add some time on their calendar and make some time with them. Like, I have a daily meeting with one of the other operations leads, just so we can get to know each other and really, like, talk about all the work that we're doing, and just really get to know him on a personal level as well. And with other people, I would make time to connect and get to know them more on a personal level at least once a week. Every other Friday, we have a team get-together—there's no agenda, there's nothing we have to get to, it's just time that we can get together and just talk about what's going on with our projects, or if we have anything else to talk about, or we just get to know each other, just kind of make those personal connections, like a water cooler meeting. And also, the most helpful thing is that people have their cameras on. So it's nice

to make these virtual connections. I mean, I definitely feel more connected to my co-workers at this company than I did where I was before, and I was in an office environment. (Taylor, innovation product manager, avatar)

Soon, Avatars began to "move out" things more firmly moored in the physical, "real" reality of the corporate office. They were throwing surprise birthday or work anniversary or work recognition parties, working out with work friends, getting inspired by company-sponsored motivational speakers, raising money for charities, enjoying magic shows, interacting with lamas from a petting farm, lighting Diwali lamps to celebrate teammates' cultural heritage … all virtually. Here are some of these stories:

> You can schedule, you know, virtual workouts with your friends. You can still virtually get the same experience. (Zara, risk director, avatar)
>
> I hit a milestone work anniversary. I'm working from home, and you know, my team kind of did a surprise party, little surprise party, you know. My boss presented me with my certificate and all that good stuff. And that was, that was just really nice because it makes you feel like you're not just part of a work team, but just, part of a social group. (Kate, instructional designer, avatar)
>
> For some virtual team building event, you know, we had a lama that joined our Teams call. They [the petting farm] will actually Zoom a lama with you, and then, you know, you can see them. I mean, they just look funny. So, I mean, we have some silly moments like that. And yeah, we had a magician that joined once, and that was really nice. I mean, silly stuff like that. (Nabil, senior product manager, avatar)
>
> I am from India, and we celebrate Diwali—that's a festival of lights, once a year. My team, we used to have it on-site, and people came dressed up, and it was a big celebration, good food, and all that. And then, when we went remote, I could never believe that, but our team worked together and put together a video that showed all the previous memories. And also, they did a virtual video recording where they passed the lights to each other. And seeing that? [pauses] It was just thrilling. That is something that I have never through could be done virtually. So, those kinds of new moments, they're really thrilling. Is it the same? Probably not. But it still makes up to some level. That's one of my favorite memories. (Helen, IT applications manager, avatar)

The frequency, meaningfulness, and realism (enabled by camera usage) of the experiences Avatars had in the new virtual office reality further increased Avatars' connection to the virtual workspace. This is perfectly aligned with research on immersive virtual environments dating to well before the pandemic. This research had uncovered that people are more likely to enjoy and to return to virtual reality spaces—think immersive multiplayer videogames like *Second Life* or the like—if they have meaningful experiences there. Who knew the virtual office had so much in common with videogames!

You know what else pre-pandemic research had uncovered? That occasional in-person gatherings—which rekindle and solidify relationships— help sustain virtual interactions in the long term. Well, lo and behold! Avatars began augmenting their virtual reality with "real" reality. Sometimes, they inserted snippets of "real" reality into their virtual interactions. Teams timed gift delivery to teammates' homes at the exact moment the team celebrated virtually:

> We have daily team huddles. And in December, on our team huddle, my associates arranged to have my Christmas present delivered while we were on our huddle. So that was kinda cool! They surprised me with a delivery while [on the call] so they could see my reaction on camera. So that was fun. And it just, I don't know, it warms my heart, makes me feel good. (Patty, risk manager, avatar)

Or people ran around their houses collecting items for a virtual scavenger hunt:

> And we did a scavenger hunt within your own home. Only one person knew what was going to be on there. And we're a super competitive group, so like, we left our cameras on and audio too. And people were literally running all over their houses, and bringing stuff back, and having that excitement and that competitive juice flowing. It was a ton of fun. That's probably the most fun I've had at home. (Kyle, associate vice president of product, avatar)

Other times, Avatars fully stepped out of virtual reality and back into "real" reality for brief in-person get-togethers. Some of these were company-sponsored: "The company provides—once or twice a year—they provide for all associates to come together and meet. We do have a space, small space that is rented out" (Helen, IT applications manager, avatar). Some were spontaneous: "When I come out to Arizona, I actually meet up with them. I've had dinner with my co-worker there and his spouse. So, yeah, we've been able to do, you know, personal link-ups" (Tim, senior product consultant, avatar). And some were scheduled as part of teams' regular work rhythm:

> We usually have retro [an Agile meeting to wrap up a sprint] every two weeks. We meet up everyone on our team. We talk about what went right, wrong, you know, what we need to improve on. We usually take those days to go into the office so we can have those meetings at least some of us in person, and some of us through a call. But it's kind of a good opportunity because we can, you know, kind of go back to normal and have at least a little bit of, you know, one-on-one or talk to people instead of just all virtual. (Sophie, senior software engineer, avatar)

In all, Avatars turned their workplace from a physical location—the corporate office, to a feeling, an experience, a geographic fantasy—the virtual office. This feat required an occasional dose of in-person engagement in "real" reality, a very large and consistent serving of meaningful and varied virtual interactions, and a healthy degree of realism as enabled by the use of cameras. Oh, and, of course, a superpower: the ability to cast yourself into virtual reality for the long haul. The superpower of projection.

Like Avatars, Centrists had also acquired the superpower of projection. They enjoyed "finding ways to stay engaged in a unique way, you know, doing things that we would probably do in the office, but doing them in a virtual setting. I think that's really cool" (Adam, senior software developer, centrist). Like Avatars, Centrists described numerous instances of casting themselves into the new virtual office reality and enjoying experiences such as virtual Christmas parties, scavenger hunts, catch-ups with work friends, board games, knowledge sharing sessions, bingos…you name it. Here is an example:

> Something that's kind of funny, I guess, I don't know why this is different, but like, if it's someone's birthday, we have like our team meeting, everybody tries to sing happy birthday through the Zoom, you know. But then it's always, it's like even worse than it would be normally because you can't really quite match up, like cadence and beat, and everybody's at a slightly different place in the song. And for some reason, that's like, always just kind of funny and delightful. Whereas if you were just sitting there and everyone was singing to you in the office, you maybe would be more embarrassed. And this is more, it's more embarrassing for the other people, I think. So maybe that's part of it, is like shifting, shifting the embarrassment. I don't know…but these are fun things that come to mind. (Noah, risk manager, centrist)

But, unlike Avatars, Centrists' embrace of the new virtual workplace was not wholehearted. Centrists were vocal about the dangers of over-dwelling in virtual reality. They were concerned, for example, about being overbooked in constant virtual engagements, with no time left to eat:

> I already know when I wake up that I'm gonna work more hours when I'm at home because you get off of one call, and you gotta hop into the next call, and then you gotta hop into the next call. We've made it kinda acceptable to just every call, every call, just come on, next call, next call. There's times where I don't even get a lunch; there's times I'm eating lunch during a meeting, you know, so. (Julian, innovation consultant, centrist)

They were concerned about "networking, and making different connections, and seeing people that you haven't seen in a long time; that is kinda obsolete, now, out of sight" (Julian, innovation consultant, centrist). They were concerned about friendships falling by the wayside:

> I don't have quite as many informal relationships, like, I don't know that I've made a new close work friend since 2020. Like, I still have all of my ones I had before, but I'm not sure I have a new one. I'm trying to think. I don't, not really, not really. And just, that's kind of one thing I feel is what sometimes keeps

people at companies, keeps people wanting to be there and wanting to engage and, you know, stick around for them. And I think those kinds of relationships are very difficult to develop when you are not in the room. (Noah, risk manager, centrist)

To lessen the negative effects of these virtual reality downfalls, Centrists made sure to partake in "real" reality, splitting their time between the home office and the corporate office:

I work from home probably three or four days a week, and I go in the office one or two days a week. Being able to get in the office every once in a while, it's really nice to stay connected with people that you're not on Zoom calls with all day long, so it's beneficial in that space. I go in the office to see my peer group or others that I interact with in different business units. […] I do enjoy pulling people together in person, traveling, spending time together at a more intimate level. (Liam, director of sales, centrist)

And so, unlike Avatars who only dipped a toe in "real" reality from time to time but cast themselves into virtual reality the majority of the time, Centrists kept one foot firmly in "real" reality and the other—in virtual reality.

You might be surprised to hear that Community-seekers not only partook in the new virtual office reality their company and their colleagues were building, but that they, in fact, also helped build it:

Our company has made some moves in terms of, you know, offering our fitness classes at home because people can't go to the gym there, or they don't want to, or choose not to. And like, I'm on the Engagement Council, so we try and plan as much as we can with volunteer events in person and not in person. And we've tried to, you know, transition everything that once was in person to online as much as possible. Sometimes we do a lot of like coffee chats and things like that, and try not be so work focused because you do, you know, have your hallway chats when you're in the office, so we kind of transition those to virtual. (Hannah, senior analyst, community-seeker)

However, you won't be surprised to hear that Community-seekers did not prefer this new virtual reality. The reason? They never embraced the superpower of projection that their Avatar and Centrist colleagues willingly and comfortably wielded; they never bought into the notion that virtual reality is a good, or at least agreeable, substitute of "real" reality.

To wit, Community-seekers felt they couldn't really build meaningful, high-quality relationships with colleagues through technology. One thought interacting through Teams is "ways apart" than having a conversation: "It's not, it's not the same. Like, that green 'I'm available' button on Teams versus, you know, walking by someone and then having a conversation? They're just, they're ways apart for me" (Max, risk manager, community-seeker). Another agreed—to her, the "blank screen" was way different than passing by people:

When I come in person, there are people that I'll see every single day on my way up to my cubicle. And that pattern of seeing people, it's kind of, when I'm logging on, it's a blank screen. That feels a little bit disconnected from the camaraderie, the community environment, if that makes sense. (Nicole, data analyst, community-seeker)

Community-seekers also felt that because they couldn't truly get to know their coworkers virtually, they also couldn't enjoy the virtual interactions that their Avatar and Centrist colleagues enjoyed:

The fact that we keep coming up with new activities to do online is really funny to me. I didn't realize that there were that many options. I think it's good. But I also think that since I don't know all my co-workers well enough, they're fun but up to a point. Because it's a little too, I think, a little too sterile of an environment to really make decent connections. So, we're just playing a game where we're doing something that's an activity provided to us. (Victoria, investment analyst, community-seeker)

Community-seekers even felt it was difficult to maintain existing connections virtually: "I would say, moving to a work-from-home environment, it's a lot more difficult to, you know, keep those connections. Since I'm not physically seeing those people every day, you just don't really interact with [them] anymore" (Emma, middle market sales manager, community-seeker).

Additionally, Community-seekers had a hard time visualizing their job as "real" in the new virtual office reality: "To just work from home every single day, it doesn't feel like your job's real. But when I get to the office, I just feel like, you know, this is my real job, I'm a real adult in the real world" (Hannah, senior analyst, community-seeker).

So, Community-seekers doubled down on dwelling in "real" reality. Though offices were empty, some Community-seekers got lucky: either their office floors were "re-designed so that people who are in the office are by each other" (Nicole, data analyst, community-seeker), or they found a group of like-minded, office-going colleagues:

There's two other folks that I go to the gym with every day. So I'll have people talking about the gym later today, you know. [Looks away for a second.] Oh, I just got a message. One of the guys that I used to work for--my old boss, he's like, Hey, want to go for a walk during the day, you know? We go for a 10 or 15 min walk through the skywalk. We'll talk about--he just got back from vacation in Mexico--we'll talk about that. So that's, I don't do that, as intentional as I try to be at home, I don't just reach out and say, Hey, you know, how is your vacation, you know. Or like today, we have one of my associates, they just had a baby, first time seeing him since they had the baby. So you know, it's just definitely a sense of, like, friendship, you know, kind of belonging. That's stuff to get excited about. (Max, risk manager, community-seeker)

To a tee, these lucky Community-seekers chose to come in most days to "meet my coworkers, and kind of get more affiliated with my company culture, since it's in the building that you can kind of see that" (Victoria, investment analyst, community-seeker). And the unlucky ones? As we already learned, they retreated to the "real"—and lonely—reality of their bedroom-turned-workspace home office.

In all, to Community-seekers, the new virtual office reality was a relationally impoverished place. As we all know (and research confirms), people don't enjoy environments where they feel friendless. "Real" reality is where Community-seekers had real interactions with real people which produced "little sparks of happiness" (Daniel, intern, community-seeker). And so, "real" reality is where they dwelled.

What's a Cost and What's a Benefit?

You've heard of cost–benefit analysis, right? It's when you assign value to all possible costs and benefits of a choice. If the benefits outweigh the costs, then great, objectively, that's the right choice.

Well, not to burst anyone's objectivity bubble, but assigning value to costs and benefits—or even agreeing on what's a cost and what's a benefit in the first place—is far from an objective proposition. Case in point: The cost–benefit analyses of Avatars, Centrists, and Community-seekers.

In our interviews, Avatars would consistently list off a bunch of costs of work-from-home: loneliness and poorer social life, working more, blurry work-life lines, damage to company culture, limited career prospects. Missing the cafeteria omelets and hash browns also made this list. These costs, however, were not heavily valued; Avatars did not see these costs as costly. The list of benefits was also long, and sometimes cheeky: "No communal bathrooms!" (Paul, claims manager, avatar). But two items made an almost ubiquitous appearance: flexibility and convenience. These two items trumped everything else. Here's a thought on the trumping power of flexibility:

> Some of the benefits of working from home in terms of not traveling that long, saving time, and flexibility for the family and all of that, that overweighs the personal connection. So everybody, from everybody's angle, that has been accepted, even from my angle. Like, I would like to be in person there, but now, seeing these benefits, and having felt that, it feels like, Okay, we like this, why give up this? That's the question that comes to my mind, and I'm satisfied. (Helen, IT applications manager, avatar)

And here's a thought on the trumping power of convenience:

> I think there's quite a few things I did enjoy [during the pre-pandemic days of in-office work]. It was a good place out of college to work. It had a very fun culture. I always liked going and walking around the park, and doing lunches with people. There were a bunch of different groups I was in, like a Tableau

user group, and I was part of the emerging leaders program and some others. So there were a lot of those types of more social activities that I enjoyed doing. And because of that, you built relationships with lots of people. And so the natural, just running into people and talking to them over lunch, or having conversations and doing stuff, that just doesn't happen now. And I do think there's aspects of that I miss. But from a cost-benefit, it's like, I don't know… At this point, a lot of it is just convenience, from cost-benefit perspective. (Carl, data product consultant, avatar)

So, flexibility and convenience tipped Avatars' cost–benefit analysis in favor of work-from-home.

Centrists struggled with computing a definitive result of their cost–benefit analysis. Every time they'd add an item to their list of benefits, they'd also add that same item to their list of costs. Take flexibility, which, remember, Avatars always saw as a huge benefit. Centrists saw flexibility as both a good and a bad:

I would share that the work from home environment has definitely created a mindset where people are not as schedule-minded, so to speak. If you get your work done, you're done with meetings by 3; like, nobody's watching. Again, there's more flexibility now than there ever was when we were full-time in the office. But, I've gotten attuned to that well enough that I can look at my daily schedule and go: All right, I gotta build time into my schedule to get emails done, or I gotta just stop and come back to it later, in the evening, you know, something like that. So work-from-home has added flexibility in ways that has both added to the time I spend at work, and retracted from it. So it's probably a net neutral. (Liam, director of sales, centrist)

Or take convenience, another huge benefit to Avatars. To Centrists, convenience was a benefit, but a benefit outweighed: "I think maybe I'm a tiny bit more comfortable and relaxed here at home, but I'm a little bit more excited at the office. It kind of cancels out" (Noah, risk manager, centrist).

So, no cost and no benefit clearly stood out to Centrists, leaving their cost–benefit analysis kind of even.

In sharp contrast, Community-seekers' cost–benefit analysis generated a very clear result, which, predictably, was diametrically opposed to Avatars' computations. Community-seekers understood flexibility as a benefit, but as a benefit to others, not to themselves. So, they didn't assign a high value to it: "I don't have children, but I can imagine flexibility there would be very helpful. For someone young like me, I don't really need that flexibility as much" (Hannah, senior analyst, community-seeker). Convenience did not even make the benefits list; rather, <u>in</u>convenience was a high-cost item on the costs list:

There's less distractions [in the office]. I live in an apartment complex so there's dogs always around, and there's maintenance people coming in and out. And I'm at home, so I'm tempted to do laundry or cook, or something like call my mom. When I'm at the office, I know I have some concentrated deep work time to look forward to. The Internet's better. I know there won't be very many people here, so I know I'll be able to get work done with less distraction. (Victoria, investment analyst, community-seeker)

Another huge cost? Work-from-home's toll on mental health:

My wife said, "This work-from-home isn't good for you." And I agreed. Like, it was just mentally, for me, the isolation piece... I mean we have Zoom, we use Teams, we have that video technology which you still get this type of interaction. But just, the lack of social interaction was tough for me. I mean, I did not enjoy it. I'm a very social person. I enjoy, you know, going, getting coffee and stopping at people's desks. And not having that was difficult. So, I actually went in. As soon as we could, I was back in. But for me, just my mental health piece was, I was much, much more comfortable in the office. (Max, risk manager, community-seeker)

With flexibility not an important benefit, and inconvenience and poor mental health seen as heavy costs, the scales tipped toward disfavor of work-from-home for Community-seekers.

In all, our three remote-first personas valued the costs and benefits of remote work quite differently. And that's the final factor we discovered that differentiates the Avatar, Centrist, and Community-seeker personas.

Reflection on the Avatar, the Centrist, and the Community-seeker So, what makes Avatars, Centrists, and Community-seekers tick?

Avatars were nudged toward remote work. The initial nudge came from the company. When Promethean began to implement its remote-first strategy via tactics such as redesigning the office to a hoteling arrangement and supporting employees in furnishing their home offices, the Avatar persona began to emerge. A new superpower Avatars acquired—the superpower of projection—helped them feel welcome and at-home in the new virtual office reality the company was building. And when these budding Avatars, who previously weren't fans of remote work or hadn't even considered it, assigned high value to the flexibility and convenience remote work affords, the Avatar persona was fully born.

Centrists were neither nudged, nor pushed, into remote work. Centrists accept remote work as the new way of working, though they do have some qualms about hoteling, the virtual office, and the company's remote-first strategy broadly speaking. Interestingly, these qualms are mostly focused on potential negative effects on others, not on themselves. You could say that makes Centrists' qualms a tad theoretical.

Like their Avatar colleagues, Centrists are capable of projecting themselves into virtual reality, though unlike Avatars, they prefer a much heavier dose of "real" reality. They like to experience both worlds. And, completing their rather even-keeled persona, Centrists' cost–benefit analysis of remote work lands on neutral.

Community-seekers were pushed into this persona. They felt displaced by the company's remote-first strategy, removed from a community they liked—the community they had previously found at the office. Community-seekers never developed (or chose not to utilize) the superpower of projection, strongly preferring to interact with others in "real" reality rather than in virtual reality. They struggle to see tangible benefits of remote work for themselves, and though they do understand it is beneficial for others, that's not helpful. In contrast, Community-seekers see—and personally feel—a number of heavy costs of remote work to themselves, including, importantly, negative impacts on their mental health.

Notes

1. H. Mitchell, "Why Employees Hate Hot-Desking," *The Wall Street Journal*, May 13, 2023, https://www.wsj.com/articles/hot-desking-pros-cons-8ee52377.
2. K. Rockmann and M. Pratt, "Contagious Offsite Work and the Lonely Office: The Unintended Consequences of Distributed Work," *Academy of Management Discoveries* 1, no. 2 (2015): 150–64.
3. L. Goel et al., "From Space to Place: Predicting Users' Intentions to Return to Virtual Worlds," *MIS Quarterly* 35, no. 3 (2011): 749–71.
4. J. F. Nunamaker Jr., B. A. Reinig, and R. O. Briggs, "Principles for Effective Virtual Teamwork," *Communications of the ACM* 52, no. 4 (2009): 113–17.
5. G. D. Rowles, "Place and Personal Identity in Old Age: Observations from Appalachia," *Journal of Environmental Psychology* 3, no. 4 (1983): 299–313.
6. A. Colbert, R. Purvanova, and J. Bono, "Workplace Relationships of the Working Poor," in *Proceedings of the 77th Annual Meeting of the Academy of Management* (77th Annual Meeting of the Academy of Management, Atlanta, Georgia, 2017).
7. R. F. Baumeister and M. R. Leary, "The Need to Belong: Desire for Interpersonal Attachments as a Fundamental Human Motivation," *Interpersonal Development*, 2017, 57–89.

CHAPTER 4

Aligned and Misaligned Personas: Same Remote-First Company, Different Work Experiences

As we just learned, Avatars, Centrists, and Community-seekers are quite different. They differ in how they came to be (Avatars were nudged toward that persona, Community-seekers were pushed), they differ is which reality they prefer to spend their work time in (virtual or "real"), and they differ in what they consider to be costs and benefits of remote work. These differences between the personas have implication for how each persona experiences work. Why? Because as we show in the image above, some personas' work location preferences—Avatars', and to an extent, Centrists'--align with their company's remote-first strategy. That's entirely untrue for Community-seekers who're completely misaligned. As our book argues, alignment matters for employees' work experience. Let's see how. (See Fig. 4.1).

Aligned Personas: How Avatars Experience Work

Avatars fit perfectly in remote-first companies. You feel great when you find yourself in a context that fits you, right? That was true for the Avatars we studied at Promethean, too. When we asked them to describe their feelings for their organization, here's what they said:

> The one thing that I love the best is the flexibility that this place has offered. I have had the life that has changed! I'm very loyal, and my loyalty will always continue. (Helen, IT applications manager, avatar)

> I still feel just as connected [to the company]. If anything, you know, maybe a little bit more loyal, just because they've done whatever they can to make sure that it fits with what we wanted for our lifestyle. I've had a couple of employees who have been able to move closer to aging parents because of the flexibility.

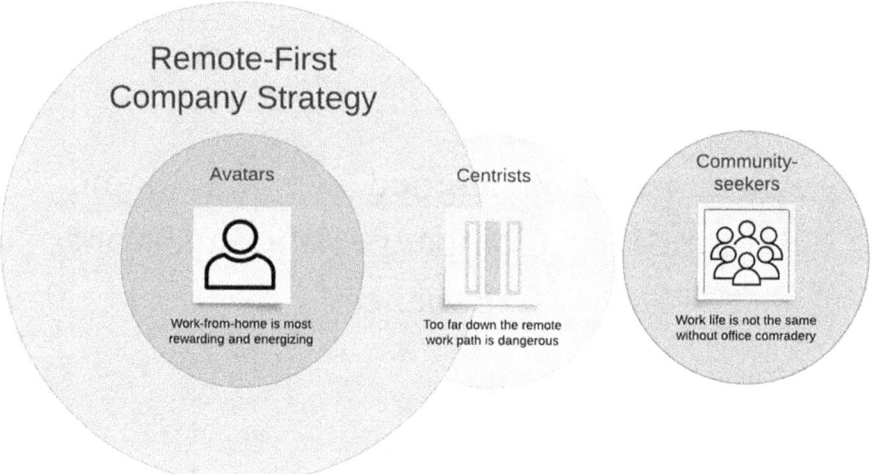

Fig. 4.1 Avatars are fully aligned in remote-first organizations while Centrists are half-aligned and Community-seekers are misaligned

> So for me, I think just seeing some of that, it just kind of adds more of, you know, they take care of you. (Patty, risk manager, avatar)
>
> I feel, well, I feel obligated, but I don't feel obligated in the bad way, I feel obligated in a good way, it's part of my responsibility and part of my pleasure to be able to give back to them for what they've been able to do for us. (Kate, instructional designer, avatar)

Wow! Employers, take notice. In an era where employee commitment and satisfaction are at an all-time low, in an era where there's constant talk about quiet quitting, grumpy staying, and bare minimum Mondays, to hear such passionate employee testimonials about their loyalty, connection to the company, and sense of responsibility to give back … that's gold right there!

So, what causes these strong positive emotions that Avatars feel? In our analyses, we kept on coming back to two reasons—a sense of calm and a sense of freedom.

You don't imagine the workplace as a place where you'd feel calm, right? Just the opposite—we usually imagine the workplace like this: "Our office was very *Wolf of Wall Street*—high intensity, busy, cow bells ringing" (Katie, associate vice president of sales, avatar). Oh, the stress!

And now? Now, the beginning of the day is "just calm":

> Usually, just calm. I don't have to rush when I'm at home. It's very calm. If I need to make breakfast, I can just step away, make breakfast, come back, you know. I don't have to worry about being somewhere right on time or anything, so it's pretty calm. I just log in, usually just check my emails. We have our daily meeting at 9:30, so in the mornings, it is a little slower. People are logging in,

you know. So yeah, it's pretty calm. I have time to, you know, take my dogs out, come back, I don't have to worry about rushing or anything. (Sophie, senior software engineer, avatar)

The actual workday? Calm again, like a "regular day":

I mean, I'm working, and I'm getting stuff done, but it doesn't feel like I have to go into work. Going to the office feels like much more of a production. But with working from home, it's just another day. I'm just kinda like, I'll have meetings, and I'll talk to some folks, and I'll get some stuff done, and it's just like a regular day. But, I don't know, because you're home, it's just more comfortable, and it doesn't seem like you're, I mean, you ARE working, but it still feels like it's more on your terms. (Travis, division director, avatar).

How about the end of the workday? You knew it! It's calm, a "smooth transition" to personal life:

When I end my workday, it used to be very tiring. Like a full, completed workday, and after that, there is no more energy to keep you going. But you still have to plan for whatever you have on your personal side, you still have to keep things going. And now it's an integrated environment. There is no transition. There is no need for transition. It transitions smoothly, naturally, by itself. So as your day ends, you start your other work smoothly. (Helen, IT applications manager, avatar)

We're pretty sure these experiences describe what Zen feels like. In Buddhist philosophy, you become "one with" when you enter Zen. This calmness that Avatars are describing suggests "oneness" with work. So, Avatars may have stumbled on a new concept—work-life oneness. Hear how this Avatar described this work-life oneness, this "togetherness":

You know what, my in-laws are farmers. And they don't see this as work, it's more of a lifestyle. I don't see that here--with this one being on a computer and all that kind of stuff--but I do feel like it's part of my life more. It's not necessarily a lifestyle, but my work is more of a... I don't know... It's more "together" as opposed to leaving and then coming back. So it just, I don't know, I wouldn't be, it can't be, I wouldn't be able to, I don't think I'd wanna go back into an office. I don't know... I just think it felt separated. It felt like I was going for a job, you know. Where now, it feels more like a... I don't know... It just feels more like...together. (Tim, senior product consultant, avatar)

So yup, Avatars have reached Zen.

And just in case that's not profound enough, there's another highly prized state Avatars have reached. Freedom.

In describing the company's remote-first policy to us, one thing became very, very clear: how, where, and when people work was 100% their choice.

Leaders proudly talked about giving freedom, and connected that to employees' "maximizing their contribution":

> I would even use the word--and I'm an officer of the company--but I would even use the word "proactive" about having people work from home. You can work from home 100%, you can do the hybrid thing, or you can go into the office. We're very much tailoring it to what every individual would like to do. And I think it works very well because, given the choice, everyone chooses what is right for them. So I feel like everyone is maximizing their contribution to the company because they are doing what is best for them-- either in the office or out of the office. (Kara, associate vice president of division, avatar)

We are not surprised to hear that. In academese, "freedom" goes by the term autonomy. Autonomy has powerful effects. When employees feel autonomous, when they feel they're working on their terms, they perform their jobs better (or "maximize their contributions" as the leader above testified). They are also more committed to their organization (or "connected" and "loyal" as we heard Avatars talk about above). And—like a gift that keeps on giving—autonomy improves another highly prized organizational metric: retention. Predictably, Avatars pointed to their freedom as a "reason why I'm staying":

> I mean, it is one of the reasons why I'm staying. Because, you know, you can contrast that with someone like Chase which is one of the major employers in our area. You know, their people are mandated to go into the office, company keeping your attendance record, and all of that stuff. And no, I'm not going for that. I mean to me, it's my choice, and I think Promethean respects that. I don't really want to work for a company that treats adults like kids. (Nabil, senior product designer, avatar)

And:

> I will say, it probably is keeping me at Promethean, you know. It's one more perk that our company provides that I would worry about going somewhere else. My wife calls this 'golden handcuffs' [laughs], but if I do choose to look for an opportunity, I'm going to be looking internally first rather than externally because I don't wanna lose this. I think that's probably my takeaway more than anything: it's become a benefit, a non-monetary benefit. (Paul, claims manager, avatar)

Though it's funny to think that the cost of freedom is being handcuffed, Avatars are passionately committed to their company and do not want to leave. Exactly as you'd expect from research on autonomy.

But let's go back to job performance for a moment. We feel compelled to dispel a pesky, persistent myth that Avatars are not working. We understand where this myth comes from. Hearing how someone is cleaning out their dishwasher in the middle of the workday easily gives the impression of "not working." But think about this state of "oneness" that Avatars have reached with work. Oneness means they switch back and forth between work and life. So Avatars ARE working; it just looks different. Here's how one company leader described this new, autonomous, integrated workstyle:

> I might go to the gym, go do something, come back, work a little bit more... Because I'm working from home, I kinda feel like whether it's on the weekend or at night or off hours, I can pop in my office anytime, do a little work, and then move on. When I was working in an office, at the end of the day, that'd be it. I'd usually just pack up my stuff, close up my laptop, head home, and I usually wouldn't work at home at night. And I'd say, with working from home, I do that a little bit more, but I don't think it feels like I'm working 24/7 either though. It feels like I'm more working on my terms. If I need to get something done, it's very easy, I'll just log on, you know, get something done, and then kind of move on. (Travis, division director, avatar)

In all, finding themselves in complete alignment with their company's remote-first strategy, Avatars are in a state of Zen. They're one with their employer, one with work, and one with life. Who wouldn't want that?

Half-Aligned Personas: How Centrists Experience Work

In remote-first companies, Centrists are halfway aligned to the company's strategy. This makes for a little bit of a mixed work experience.

Centrists often feel lonely working from home:

> I would be lying if I didn't say it's more business focused for the most part. [Question: OK. Is there anything that you maybe remember fondly from a work-from-home day?] Oh, man! Good question. Just me by myself. Yeah. Yeah. (Liam, director of sales, centrist)

They also miss the company-wide, in-office social activities of the past:

> We used to have big Christmas parties. Yeah, we don't get to do that anymore. But that's something that I remember, and I miss. (Julian, innovation consultant, centrist).

So, Centrists go to the office to spruce up their work experience with some social interaction:

> Just getting to do stuff with the people. So like, when we were in the office a couple of weeks ago, we were all sitting there working, and we were all like, Urgh, that meeting was kind of a drag. Let's go get cookie dough! So we all walked down, we all walked over to the cookie dough shop. And you know, the four of us, we walked there, grabbed cookie dough, walked back, and just

kinda had a fun personal connection type thing. And that's the kind of stuff that I want. That's why I go to work, is to do those kinds of things. (Noah, risk manager, centrist)

But then again, they don't really miss these social aspects of office life with a capital M:

It's cool to see, kind of, catch up with those people, old friends, every now and again. But yeah, I guess I don't necessarily have, like, a reaction of, Oh, wow, I'm just thrilled to be here. It's like, just, 'Yup, just another day', you know. (Adam, senior software developer, centrist)

Centrists applaud the company for giving people freedom. Like Avatars, they feel an increased sense of commitment to their organization for that reason:

The company has been pretty good to me. They've been very flexible, which has been a huge blessing. So, I feel more of a commitment to the company. From the standpoint of working from home, they, I feel, figured it out: 'This is what works best for most people, and we're just going to continue to do that.' One of our company values is like, you know, we value people. And right from the get-go, our CEO has been very upfront. He's like, you know, 'Work isn't everything.' (Adam, senior software developer, centrist)

They are also thankful for opportunities which—if it weren't for the remote-first stance of the company—they would not have had:

Three years ago, I actually applied for the job I have today, and I was told I'd have to move to Ohio to have it. Three years later, that ship has sailed, and I have a job that I wouldn't have had three years ago without having to move, right? And I can tell you more stories of letting people go cause we were moving away from work-from-home. And now, I keep them, you know. Now, we hire where you sit. In fact, one of my leaders that reports to me, he's moving from San Antonio to Virginia, right, so his daughter can go to a school there. So it's just enabled a lot more flexibility for our folks, our team, and a whole lot of more ability for us to run the business. (Liam, director of sales, centrist)

But then again, Centrists are not exactly all in on remote-first. They worry about the effects of remote-first on others. They are concerned about people whose jobs depend on the office:

Completely honest, I think this is the new normal. I can't see it as reverting back to saying, Hey, everybody, come back in the office and work. […] But you know what it does make me feel? It makes me feel bad for the people who actually have or had jobs, so let's say, cleaning people or people that worked in the cafeteria or people that, you know, worked in the coffee shop. Because their lives were actually affected more because there's no working from home for them. So you know, within my company, you've got to think about, we have security officers, we have, you know, the cleaning people, we have people who, you know, come and just set up, like, a pop-up shop on a random payday. We don't have that anymore, you know. I often think about mailroom workers, because if we're not in person, you have nobody to drop mail off to, so I could see the mail room being obsolete within the next, you know, 18–24 months. I can see these things be obsolete, which sucks. It really makes me feel bad for them. (Julian, innovation consultant, centrist)

They are also concerned about future workers joining remote-first companies without the benefit of having deeply meaningful and developmental in-person experiences—experiences which Centrists had enjoyed in their own early careers:

I kind of worry about, like, your students entering this workplace, going to work for a fully remote thing, and like how they're even gonna feel about work. Are they gonna feel at all connected to their company? Are they gonna feel like they're part of something? Or, are they just gonna feel like, I signed in the computer for seven hours a day, and yeah, it's kinda cool, I get paid and I don't have to go anywhere, but I don't like it, I don't enjoy it, I'm just kinda here, being a robot on my keyboard. I worry about that a little bit. I think, I hope that we get back to a place where, you know, you have some exposure to being in the office with people you work with, building human connections. But I think we'll have to keep some elements of the flexibility that we've already awarded. (Noah, risk manager, centrist)

We said above that Centrists' work experience is "mixed." Given the evidence above, that's a pretty accurate description, but to make this more vivid for you, we'll call Centrists' work experience "sunny with a chance of clouds." About what you'd expect from half-alignment.

Misaligned Personas: How Community-Seekers Experience Work

In remote-first companies, Community-seekers are fully misaligned with the company's strategy. This misalignment leads to two very damaging outcomes: disconnectedness and disengagement.

Community-seekers feel disconnected from the organization: "I feel disconnected to the organization as a whole because the only thing connecting me is a computer" (Hannah, senior analyst, community-seeker). Unpacking what "disconnected" means, it's the feeling of not really being plugged into the social fabric of the company. To wit, some Community-seekers describe having very few strong connections: "I have personal, strong connections to two or three or four people in my team, but as a part of the whole, I would say, it is lacking a little bit" (Victoria, investment analyst, community-seeker). Others have none:

I mean, everyone's nice sort of thing, but it's nothing more than, you're a face on the screen. There's no walking into a meeting room, sitting in the meeting room for 10 min, talking about what you did in the weekend. You pop up the Zoom and you get going, you know. There's none of that interpersonal or personal stuff. And you know, I like a lot of people, they're great human beings, it's just, you know, at the end of the day, you don't really know them because you never, you know, you've never been within five feet of them. (Daniel, intern, community-seeker)

Being poorly connected to the organization's social fabric makes it difficult to talk to colleagues. One Community-seeker vividly described how her solitary workdays made her feel: "I kind of don't expect to talk much during the day. I kind of, nobody's gonna really interact, I'm not going to interact with very many people today. My hermit days" (Victoria, investment analyst, community-seeker).

Even when Community-seekers try to find their voice and air their frustrations, no one listens:

Where I struggle with now is, I feel like nobody understands where I'm coming from. And so, it's really hard when I'm trying to express my frustrations. [...] I'm unhappy at home, working from home, and I want to see you people and feel a part of something. And you guys do not feel the same way at all. And I've ran into that roadblock many times where I'm trying to talk to people about it, and they just look at me [gestures disbelief], you know. That really has made a huge difference in the way I perceive my job and my willingness to work, too. I mean, it definitely makes me, honestly, not really wanna work as much because I just don't feel that strong of a connection anymore to a team. (Hannah, senior analyst, community-seeker)

Stop and think about this for a second. Can you imagine what it feels like to not hear the sound of your own voice (let alone the sound of other people's voices) for the entire day? And can you also imagine what it feels like to be dismissed, like your experiences and feelings of loneliness and isolation are not real or don't matter? Therapists would have a field day with this.

No wonder, then, that—as the employee quoted above suggested—the disconnectedness grew into disengagement from work. Here's another Community-seeker on that point:

The reason I liked what I was doing is I really enjoyed the people I was working with. But now, I wouldn't say I'm ever, like, excited to wake up and go to work, candidly. It really did change my outlook on work, like, Oh, what am I doing? Is this even meaningful? I just feel like I'm, you know, making money for a cash cow now, and I'm not really doing anything to fulfill me. Working in [this industry], to be completely frank, can be kind of bullshitty, pardon my language. Like, no one's calling cause they have anything nice to say to you. So you kind of need people to, like, bounce those kinds of experiences off of. Like, Oh, yeah, I can't believe this guy, you know, stuff like that. And now, in the work-from-home setting, you're kind of in your own little bubble, and you think, this is only happening to me. That is horrible. You kind of just get in your head. And it really does eat at you.

So I would say, I have lost a lot of motivation towards my job. I think I've started to care a little bit less because, you know, I still log in, I do my job, but I think it's like, Oh, if something gets messed up, I'm like, All right, it's not the end of the world, or you know, it'll get done. So for me, working from home has kind of turned me into that mentality of you just don't have that attachment to your job, you're just like, Oh, it's just a job. I hate to say it, but I think that's probably it. Oh, it's just a job. Like, what are they gonna do, fire me? I'll find another job. (Emma, middle market sales manager, community-seeker)

This is another "stop and think" moment. These Community-seekers are talking about something very profound. They are helping uncover how misalignment alters the very meaning of work. Instead of being an experience that infuses meaning in your life, work becomes an experience that detracts from meaning. Work turns into a "blah" and a "meh":

When you work from home, you kind of just stumble into, Okay, now I'm downstairs with a cup of coffee and sweatpants, working, you know. The overall sense for me is just kinda like "blah" [gestures "boring"]. (Max, risk manager, community-seeker)

I don't know, just kind of a "meh" for lack of better words. Just, I mean, nothing positive, nothing negative, just kind of a, you know, we're gonna punch in / punch out sort of thing. No real dread of the day, but again, you know, no real excitement about, Hey, I get to work. It's just a "meh." I check my email, see if anyone left me any work to do. Just kind of, Oh, boy, here we go again, we gotta re-reach out to 100 people to try and give me work or something to do. I mean, you know, besides the satisfaction of clicking "submit" on a big project that you got done that you spent, you know, a week on? Nothing real satisfying, to be completely honest. (Daniel, intern, community-seeker)

You can guess what comes next, right? Yup! Talk of quitting.

Here is a sample of the earful we got: "There are a handful of other reasons why I think I would look for another job. But I think that some kind of regular hybrid work schedule for everyone would definitely be a perk for me" (Victoria, investment analyst, community-seeker). And:

I think about it a lot more recently because I have friends who are work-from-home Monday and Friday but everybody is required to be in office Tuesday through Thursday. I would love to have that more than anything, and I very much have looked for that, and have ideas of places that I am thinking about possibly moving to. (Hannah, senior analyst, community-seeker)

And here's from an intern who declined a lucrative job offer: "I declined their $35 an hour job offer because I was looking for in-person, like, that was the number one thing on my list" (Daniel, intern, community-seeker).

So, whereas Avatars' satisfaction with remote-first raised their intent to stay with the organization, Community-seekers' dissatisfaction with remote-first raised their intent to leave. This is not to say that Community-seekers will quit *en masse* (just like not all Avatars will stay). But feeling disconnected, disengaged, demotivated, depressed, disenfranchised, and dissatisfied—all these d's… What a D+ work experience. The cost of misalignment.

> *Reflection on Aligned and Misaligned Personas in Remote-First Companies* So, how does alignment affect employees' work experience in remote-first companies?
>
> **Avatars**—the persona who is fully aligned to the remote-first strategy—have a positive work experience. They're fully enjoying work. In fact, it's beyond enjoyment; Avatars have reached Zen. They have learned to take full advantage of the flexibility and freedom afforded by remote-first, which had allowed them to become one with work and one with life. Avatars are so grateful to Promethean for enabling this positive work experience that their commitment and loyalty to the company is palpable. Even though they recognize this might be keeping them from pursuing other, potentially better, career opportunities elsewhere, Avatars are happily staying put—the "golden handcuffs" of remote work.
>
> **Centrists**—the persona who is half-aligned to the remote-first strategy—have a mixed, sunny-with-a-chance-of-clouds work experience. Centrists accept work-from-home as the new normal, and happily bask in its sunshine. And when the clouds of missing the comradery of human interactions blow in, Centrists go to the office to re-engage with others. But there are clouds Centrists can't disperse on their own: the concerns they have about office-dependent workers, dying downtowns, and disconnected, possibly disenfranchised, young employees. Because Centrists lack Avatars' "It's happening everywhere" attitude on this issue (Paul, claims manager, avatar), they can't blow these clouds away. Centrists wish companies would find middle ground, dialing back a little bit from remote-first.
>
> **Community-seekers**—the persona who is fully misaligned to the remote-first strategy—have a poor work experience. Denied the opportunity to interact with colleagues in person, Community-seekers feel completely disconnected from the organization's social fabric. This disconnectedness grows into disengagement from work. To Community-seekers, remote work is not meaningful because it is lonely. The logical outcome? Talk of quitting. Importantly, some Community-seekers have found a way to avoid this vicious spiral of disconnectedness and disengagement. They are the lucky ones who report to offices where @office preferring colleagues have been grouped together, or they have enough

office-going friends to create a social work experience. But outside of those rare exceptions, Community-seekers' work experience is a D+ . At best.

As we said: same remote-first company, different work experiences.

Notes

1. R. Maurer, "Employee Engagement Falls to Lowest Point in over a Decade," *Society for Human Resource Management (SHRM)*, May 5, 2024, https://www.shrm.org/topics-tools/news/employee-relations/employee-engagement-falls-gallup.
2. P. McGlauflin and E. Burleigh, "The Workers Are Not Alright: Most Employees Are Quiet Quitting and It's Costing the Global Economy Nearly $9 Trillion a Year," *Fortune*, June 12, 2024, https://fortune.com/2024/06/12/employees-quiet-quitting-low-engagement-9-trillion-global-loss/.
3. M. Llorente-Alonso, C. García-Ael, and G. Topa, "A Meta-Analysis of Psychological Empowerment: Antecedents, Organizational Outcomes, and Moderating Variables," *Current Psychology* 43, no. 2 (2024): 1759–84.
4. J. Guynn, "Are Remote Workers Really Working All Day? Here's What They're Doing Instead," *USA Today*, September 18, 2024, https://www.usatoday.com/story/money/2024/09/18/remote-work-from-home-survey/75266226007/.

PART III

Personas in Office-Forward Companies

Let's do a one-eighty and talk about office-forward companies and the personas they create.

What are office-forward companies? The defining characteristic of office-forward companies is that they see the office as the secret sauce that makes them successful. Work-from-office is the *modus operandi*. However, office-forward companies also understand that remote work is a staying feature of the post-pandemic workplace, and see it as a supplemental business practice.

That sounds fine and dandy, but let's be honest: thanks to Elon Musk and other Musk-eques leaders, we imagine office-forward companies as hellish places where employees' souls go to die. And why wouldn't we? In June 2022, Musk issued an ultimatum to Tesla employees to come into the office 40 hours a week (at least), calling remote work "phoning it in."[1] He told employees that if they wanted to keep working remotely, they should "pretend to work somewhere else" unless they are a "particularly exceptional contributor." Even earlier than that, in February 2022, Goldman Sachs CEO David Solomon told employees to return to the office five-days-a-week (or more), calling remote work an "aberration that we will have to correct as quickly as possible."[2]

But whereas office-forward gets a bad rap from such bombastic and divisive return-to-office rhetoric, in reality, most office-forward companies are (relatively) normal places that, importantly, respect flexibility. Consider Disney as an example. In February 2023, Disney officially adopted office-forward.[3] But, Disney expects a four-day office presence; employees have flexibility to work from elsewhere one day per week. Disney's rationale for adopting office-forward was creativity. As CEO Bob Iger explained, "In a creative business like ours, nothing can replace the ability to connect, observe and create with peers that comes from being physically together." Chipotle is another example. Chipotle got on the office-forward bandwagon in June 2023.[4] Like Disney,

Chipotle is sensitive to employees' need for greater flexibility, so the company expects four days a week in-office. Chipotle' rationale for office-forward was culture and business objectives. Leadership explained that "to preserve our unique, collaborative culture and achieve our aggressive growth plans," employees need to be together. Frankly, even Goldman Sachs' and Tesla's rationales for office-forward are not groundless (and might have been significantly better received if they had been explained in a sensical way). In the case of Goldman Sachs, the company hires a new class of about 3000 analysts every summer.[5] Mentoring these new hires—the future of the company—through the grueling 2-yr apprenticeship program proved difficult to do in the work-from-home setting. And in the case of Tesla (and likely other manufacturers), office-forward is a sign of solidarity with factory workers.[6]

As these examples show, under an office-forward strategy, working from the office is the default or primary method of working. Office-forward companies believe that the office facilitates employee productivity, learning and development, creativity and teamwork, and culture. Office-forward is also a way to show solidarity with workers who must report to the workplace. Office-forward organizations believe that technology is a handy tool, but a tool with limitations. And so, flexibility and remote work are (generally) respected, but the office is seen as the most appropriate arena for culture, connection, and collaboration. This means that office-forward employers often favor local recruitment and may request employees move in proximity to the office. They may promote or tie compensation based on office attendance. Given the primacy of the office, office-forward companies invest in their office facilities, rather than divest of real estate as remote-first companies often do.

The office-forward company we studied fits this mold. Remember, we called it Apollonian in a nod to the traditional approach this company's taking. Most employees at Apollonian interact in the office with most colleagues most of the time. Some employees work remotely (mostly due to talent availability or personal accommodations), and all employees have flexibility to connect remotely into work if life came calling. Still, Apollonian visualizes its office spaces as physical manifestations of its relationship-based culture. Post-pandemic, Apollonian further updated its offices across the U.S. to add more office perks and to ensure every employee has a personal workstation.

Similar to Promethean, the remote-first company that we introduced you to in Chapter 1, Apollonian dealt with extreme persona diversity. About 50% of Apollonian employees came out of the COVID-19 lockdown (or "forced work-from-home" as they called it) with the realization that they had an @office work preference. These @office preferring employees morphed into … wait for it … **Officers!** (We know, original.) About 30% of Apollonian employees realized that work-from-home had a lot to offer, but so did being in the office. We call these @hybrid preferring employees **Progressives** because their philosophy on remote work was, arguably, more farsighted than their company's. Finally, about 20% of Apollonian employees discovered they had an @home preference. We call these @home preferring employees **Producers** because they prized the get-my-job-done approach to work that the home office afforded.

So Apollonian had a majority of fully aligned personas (50% were Officers) but also quite large minorities of half-aligned personas (30% were Progressives) and fully misaligned personas (20% were Producers). This 50-30-20 persona breakdown should hold true in most office-forward organizations like Apollonian—midsize companies with strong, relationship-based cultures located in midsize cities. The persona breakdown might look different under other circumstances. But, as research from FlexIndex.com has reported, employers across a wide range of industries and sizes have adopted office-forward.[7] So, one thing is certain—you will find Officers, Progressives, and Producers in all office-forward companies. As we've said before, you can't run from persona diversity.

Like in remote-first companies, leaders in office-forward organizations need to align their strategy to their employees' preferences. And, employees in office-forward companies need to figure out how to exist within this structure and how to coexist with the personas their colleagues had adopted. Finding alignment begins with awareness. So, let's learn about Officers, Progressives, and Producers.

Notes

1. G. Kay, "Elon Musk Reportedly Issued an Ultimatum to Tesla Staff: Return to the Office or Quit," *Business Insider*, June 1, 2022, https://www.businessinsider.com/elon-musk-tesla-remote-work-return-office-or-quit-report-2022-6.
2. G. Colvin, "Goldman Sachs Is Ordering Employees Back to the Office 5 Days (or More) a Week. Inside CEO David Solomon's Mission to End Hybrid Work," *Fortune*, March 10, 2022, https://fortune.com/2022/03/10/goldman-sachs-office-hybrid-remote-work-david-solomon/.
3. J. Hart, "Thousands of Disney Employees Push Back on Mandate to Work in Person Four Days a Week," *Business Insider*, February 17, 2023, https://www.businessinsider.com/disney-employees-petition-against-working-four-days-in-office-2023-2.
4. D. Sirtori and M. Boyle, "Chipotle Calls Corporate Staff into Office Four Days a Week," *Bloomberg*, June 6, 2023, https://www.bloomberg.com/news/articles/2023-06-06/chipotle-cmg-tells-corporate-staff-to-be-in-office-four-days-a-week.
5. Colvin, "Goldman Sachs Is Ordering Employees Back to the Office 5 Days (or More) a Week. Inside CEO David Solomon's Mission to End Hybrid Work."
6. Kay, "Elon Musk Reportedly Issued an Ultimatum to Tesla Staff: Return to the Office or Quit."
7. FlexIndex, "Flex Report: Tech Deep Dive."

CHAPTER 5

Meet the Officer, the Progressive, and the Producer

INTRODUCTION

In office-forward companies, @office preferring employees evolve into Officers, @hybrid preferring employees evolve into Progressives, and @home preferring employees evolve into Producers. In Chapter 2, we shared a demographic analysis of employees with @office, @hybrid, and @home preferences. Here, we focus on deeper, more psychological factors that drive employees with these different work location preferences to become Officers, Progressives, and Producers in office-forward companies. (See Fig. 5.1).

DISPARATE ACCESS TO FLEXIBLE WORK

Think back to your pre-pandemic work experience. Did your job allow you flexibility, or were you chained to your office desk? If the latter, we bet you loved the taste of freedom lockdown gave you. And, if your company decided to go back to the office post-pandemic, we bet you reacted with frustration, even anger…and promptly fell into a Producer persona (or maybe a Progressive persona, but that's only if you missed the social aspect of office life).

This is exactly what happened at Apollonian. Pre-pandemic, Officers had all the flexibility they wanted: "I had a fairly flexible schedule, so you're in charge of your own schedule. I probably was in the office three days, three to four days a week, not full days, but, you know" (Elena, division vice president, officer). In sharp contrast, Progressives and Producers were office-bound: "For my entire career before COVID hit, I reported to a traditional office setting and worked their traditional business hours, eight to five, Monday through

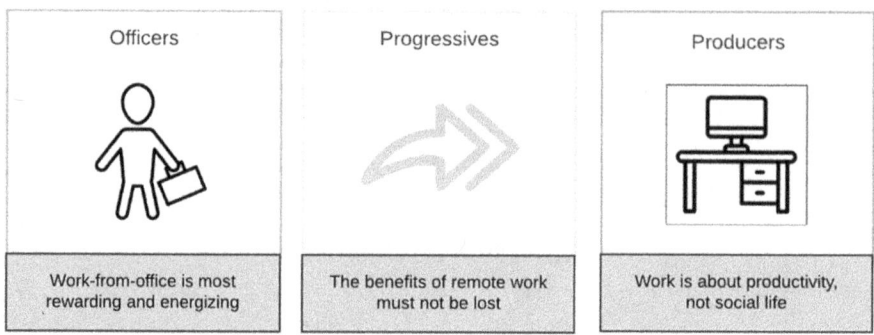

Fig. 5.1 Personas in Office-Forward Companies include Officers, Progressives, and Producers

Friday" (Abby, senior program manager, producer) and "I mean, we never worked remote prior to this" (William, client services consultant, progressive).

Only one Officer (repeat: one!) felt he didn't have flexibility pre-pandemic. In contrast, not a single Producer or Progressive felt they had flexibility pre-pandemic. Think about this disparity. It doesn't sound fair, right? Research on fairness at the workplace has long established that perceived unfairness pushes employees to act differently. But do you know what's worse? Removing access to remedial practices. Just listen to these employees: "Like, I mean, you do trust us, right? We've been doing this, you know, for however many months." (William, client services consultant, progressive), and.

> It feels a little two-sided. We were getting communicated when we were at home: You guys are doing a great job, customers haven't noticed a drop at all, you know, you're at work, productive, we are performing well, we're being profitable, rah-rah, everyone's crushing it. But then, as soon as they want you back in the office, that message kind of goes away. Remember when you were telling us we were doing great at home? (Amanda, client services consultant, progressive)

So, to some employees, office-forward represents an affront to what was a fairness-restoring practice: work-from-home. This provides our first clue why some employees—those who lacked flexibility pre-pandemic—developed into Producers (resenting office-forward in principle) and Progressives (resenting office-forward for its perceived disingenuousness).

But, perceptions of unfairness and the resultant lost trust are just one reason why some employees developed into Producers and Progressives. And also, this doesn't quite explain why some employees developed into Officers.

Just a Work Space or My Place

Do you know what an implicit association test is? It asks you about the first word that comes to mind when you hear a clue. Want to try this? Here is your clue:

O F F I C E

When we ask Officers what their company's office means to them, here is what they say: "amazing space," "beautiful office," "light, bright, and colorful," "inviting space," "makes me proud," "I love this building," "really cool building that matches our really cool culture," "our company's culture in a building." Here is what Progressives say: "just…the people," "good emotions," "I love the people," "I'm happy to be here," "welcoming and friendly people," "people's energy." And here is how Producers describe the office: "it does have a fun feel," "it does feel good to go back there," "it was awesome," "it will be good again," "faster internet," "free refreshments and things."

Translating these descriptions into one-word associations might produce something like this:

- Officers: I hear "office," I think "company culture"
- Progressives: I hear "office," I think "work friends"
- Producers: I hear "office," I think "a workspace"

Isn't it amazing how this simple exercise reveals so much about the psychology of the personas in office-forward companies?

Officers are not just people who prefer to work from the office. They are defenders of their company's beloved culture. And because they associate the company's culture with the physical office space where that culture resides, the destruction of the office means the destruction of the culture. So, Officers are on a mission to restore this culture by calling people back in. Said one Officer:

> We're to a point where it's not written, but it's kind of unwritten that you should be in the office. We're hoping that it would be even more strongly recommended that people are in the office because that's just part of our culture, that's what makes our company a good place to work—it's the people, and the interaction, and the collaboration, and all of that, and, you know, being in our building. (Sara, division vice president, officer)

Progressives are not just people who prefer keeping one foot in the office. They are relationship-oriented individuals who don't want to lose their work friends. Because the office is where those friends are, it draws them in:

> It's knowing that you're not alone in your endeavors, and being able to have them there as, you know, as friends. I think first and foremost is they, they are my friends, and resources. I think that's welcoming. I think that's probably the biggest thing that makes me come in every day, is just knowing that I get to

work with good people like that. You know, I talked about the physicality of our office. And while it is a lovely space, that's not what's going to get me in the door. It's about what, or who, who is there. Who's filling the space and what energy they're bringing. So I think that's probably the biggest touchy-feely thing—I just, I really value their partnership and their friendship. And it makes doing what we do so much better. I love what we do and I love who we do it with, yes. (William, client services consultant, progressive)

Producers are not just people who prefer to stay away from the office. They are employees who have one care: getting their work done effectively and efficiently (you know, producing). No need for touchy-feely. The office is just a workspace. And perhaps more importantly, it does not offer greater functionality than the home office. To Producers, this makes it even more illogical to have to go in. Said one Producer: "Here at home, I have the same number of monitors that I have there" (Theo, senior project manager, producer). Another elaborated:

> I wouldn't really say there's been much of a change functionally between home and going into the office. We still do a lot of Zoom calls. I'll be in the office, and I'm still just messaging my coworkers over Teams instead of getting up and going to find them in the office. Still a lot of emailing. Even for the meetings that we do as a team in the office, given that we have a couple fully remote employees, there's always a Zoom link so those employees are doing it over Zoom and doing all their work virtually. So I think, the same functionally. (Katherine, assistant project manager, producer)

To best appreciate the stark difference in how Officers and Progressives on the one hand versus Producers on the other think about the office, consider the terms *home* versus *house*. A *home* is where you live; it belongs to you and you belong to it; it holds all your cherished memories; it's a part of your identity; you miss it when you are away. A *house* is a structure; it's where other people live; you may admire its features, but that's just a fleeting emotion that you quickly forget about; it's just another space. In brief, you get attached to a *home*, not to a *house*.

Officers and Progressives are emotionally attached to the office, albeit for different reasons. For Officers, the office is a part of their identity; for Progressives, the office is a place where friendships are forged. Regardless of the different reasons, the point is, Officers and Progressives are attached to the office. Producers show no signs of such emotional attachment (in fact, we suspect they may find it bewildering that anyone *could* be attached to an office). Unsurprisingly, Producers are "all for hoteling where they share office desks or what-not" (Graham, account manager, producer), "especially if it meant that I was able to work from home, you know, just as I choose" (Katherine, assistant project manager, producer). In contrast, this idea is unacceptable to Officers:

I feel welcome because I have my own space. I know a lot of companies are starting to go to, you know, where you bounce around. Sounds terrible to me. I wouldn't feel as welcomed if I walked in and they just said, Sit wherever. But here, I have a designated spot and that's my little cubicle and I love that. I feel welcome. (Clara, sales representative, officer)

De-personalizing the office space is unacceptable to the company, too. "We don't need more reasons for people to not come in" shared an executive when chatting with us about the company's decision to keep a workstation for every employee.

In all, attachment to the office as a work*place*, a home-away-from-home versus thinking of the office as simply a work*space*, a location among many others where work gets done, is our second clue to what drives employees in office-forward companies into different personas.

THE MITCHELLS VERSUS THE MACHINES

In the 2021 movie *The Mitchells versus The Machines*, a family of technophobic parents and tech-savvy kids must overcome differences and learn how to use technology together to free humanity from rogue robots. Trust us: there's method to the madness here. We are bringing up *The Mitchells versus The Machines* because there are spot-on parallels between the movie protagonists (the Mitchell parents, the Mitchell kids, the machines) and the three personas in office-forward companies.

Officers are like the Mitchell parents. Their views on technology started out skeptical at best. "It's not natural" was perhaps the most consistent thing we heard Officers say, period. But, like the Mitchell parents, Officers learned to appreciate technology when they were forced to up their tech game. Some realized technology can help overcome distance:

I do work with a few other people in our different geographies like over in Kansas City. When we were working in the office every day pre-pandemic, we just weren't used to hopping on a Skype call. Now, we use all these different tools, and it's definitely made us all more connected across geographies. (David, client services consultant, officer)

Others realized technology can help generate savings:

Then I think about the sales piece, that was interesting because our main intro is really educational from a sales perspective. So that used to be a day trip, flight maybe and overnight, to do that meeting in-person. That's all Zoom now, and probably will stay Zoom, and that's doable, and I think that's good. It's efficient. (Evan, sales representative, officer)

Still others realized technology can help drive creativity and stimulate the development of new products and services, or new internal practices and procedures. Said one Officer: "A ton of creativity. I mean, from what we've done and how we created and what we added to our portfolio that we have never had before" (Elena, division vice president, officer). Another added: "We created an entire best practices set on how we can hold virtual trainings to show that there are ways we can interact and engage with our audience. So it was good. It was a good learning, forced learning" (Jessica, area director, officer).

But though Officers' views on technology improved, along with their willingness and ability to use it, Officers still hold a strong "not natural" sentiment about technology:

> I think that the hard part is, you know, you can connect with someone via Zoom but it's not the same. It's not the same as going and sitting in a meeting and for the first five minutes just having a conversation about what's going on in someone's life, or how is their weekend, or whatever it was. You get on Zoom and you just immediately start whatever your agenda is, and that's kind of it. You just, it loses a personal touch. And as much as you can try and force that, it's just--to me--it's not the same, just a different level of communicating with someone. (Sara, division vice president, officer)

Moreover, Officers are somewhat tired of technology: "I think people just got the Zoom fatigue, that's absolutely a real thing, and people just got tired of it" (Evan, sales representative, officer). It's safe to say, then, that Officers' views on technology evolved from an evil to a necessary evil. Just like the Michell parents.

Progressives are like the Mitchell kids. They embrace technology for its social connectivity, which is not surprising given that—as we already learned—Progressives are relationship-oriented. Progressives enthusiastically describe how they use technology to stay connected:

> We started doing happy hours where it would be like four o'clock or 4:30, and we'll hop on this Teams call. We would just touch base quickly on items for work, like this is what I'm hearing, this is what's expected of us, and then we would hop on to a happy hour. And what we would do is we would either play connected games on our phone, or there were a couple of times where we have one of our team members pick a drink (if you want to drink--you didn't have to), but it would be like a margarita, and then we would all make a margarita at home and then just kind of chit-chat and talk about life. (Megan, account manager, progressive)

But, just like the Mitchell kids came to understand their parents old-fashioned views on technology, Progressives eventually came to realize that Officers may have a point—technology is really "not the same." It may give you a great feeling when you are all "together," but once you leave the virtual meeting space, you realize you are all alone:

> When we did our first member meeting on Zoom (which was a 4-hr Zoom event that replaced our 2-day in person conference), afterwards, it was this big feeling of accomplishment. Our team was just like, Great! And then, it was like, you're just by yourself. Like, you just had such a good feeling, and then, you just log off the Zoom… (Zoe, project manager, progressive)

However, though Progressives agree that technology is challenging, they also believe that one could make it work, with purpose and intention:

> I think when the leadership team is putting in the effort to do things like that consistently—even if it's a coffee, virtual coffee, with a leader that you might not interact with typically—I think that that is helpful. Because it's just about trying to replicate the things that are good about the office. And so those interactions, like that coffee with somebody in a different department, might be a good substitute. I think it's kind of harder and it doesn't happen as effortlessly, but you can do it if you do put in that effort to schedule things like that. (Lily, project manager, progressive)

It's safe to say, then, that Progressives' views on technology evolved from an enthusiastic (some might say, uncritical) embrace of technology's social connectivity to a more measured, balanced view: technology is "not the same," but it has its pluses and one can smartly make it work to serve a purpose. Just like the Mitchell kids.

Producers are like the machines. They embrace technology for its cold-hearted efficiency. This totally fits what we've already learned about Producers: they question the value of the touchy-feely; they simply value productivity. Technology is the perfect tool to increase productivity. Because it enables work-from-home, it effectively puts some distance between Producers and the office. This allows Producers to avoid time-wasting, borderline unpleasant, office interactions, and be productive:

> From a productivity perspective, I think I get more done at home because I'm not interrupted with, you know, conversations and interactions that don't really apply to my work. Interruptions, I think, is probably the biggest one. Office drama, for lack of a better term. Just the things that don't really matter to working or to our jobs that often can take up a lot of time. [You've got] more control over interruptions, you know. Right now, the only thing that takes my focus away from a project is if the phone rings from a client or if there's an email from a client. It's all work related, you know, it's not a coworker coming up for something irrelevant. (Abby, senior program manager, producer)

Even when Producers must go in—an unfortunate consequence of their company's office-forward strategy that they must endure—they use technology to cut down on unwanted in-person interruptions right in the office:

> I would message someone on Teams rather than go up to their desk. It is a culture thing, you know. I'm thinking of one of my teammates, he sits a couple

desks away from me, but sometimes, he'll just send me a message. I think it's nice. Would they care if I came up and interrupted them? Probably not. But I just, I guess, I see it as, you know, if it can be avoided, then why not just message them on Teams? (Katherine, assistant project manager, producer)

This, of course, creates a closed loop: Producers communicate through technology even when in-office, then question "the value of going in" because they can communicate through technology just as well from home (Theo, senior project manager, producer).

But Producers don't just think of technology as a way to avoid in-person interactions (or as they see it, in-person interruptions). Technology offers an added benefit: it allows Producers to control who they interact with, and when: "I have set up bi-weekly Zoom meetings with some people, or weekly Zoom meetings with others that I work daily with" (Graham, account manager, producer). So technology introduces relational order: it tames otherwise disordered, spontaneous and unstructured workplace interactions, making them predictable and putting them on a schedule.

It's safe to say, then, that technology appeals to Producers. As soon as it became an omnipresent feature of the workplace, as soon as Producers were able to avail themselves of technology's unsuspected benefits, they felt right in place: "I would say I feel welcomed in this virtual space" (Graham, account manager, producer). Feeling welcomed in virtual space? Just like the machines.

Who knew that a silly family movie might be so revealing of differences among personas in the workplace! We told you—there's method to the madness.

But here's a caveat. *The Mitchells versus The Machines* banks on an easy (read: lazy) cliché: there are generational differences in comfort with technology. Sure, some research does support that. But, generational differences are effectively about age, whereas our Officers, Progressives, and Producers ranged in both age and work experience. So don't fall for lazy clichés. Dig deeper. Why do Officers embrace technology slowly and hesitantly? Because they'd use technology as a substitute for in-person interaction if they must, but they'd rather interact in person. Why do Progressives embrace technology passionately yet with a grain of salt? Because they'd take any opportunity they got—whether in-person or technology-mediated—to connect with others, but they need these connections to be purposeful. Why do Producers embrace technology as a second nature? Because they'd rather build a world they can control so they can do what they are paid to do—their job, effectively and efficiently.

And there you have it, clue number three: the value of human interaction at work. Is the workplace an arena for social relationships, or is it a place to get work done? And is human interaction changed for the worse or for the better when it happens on a real or a virtual arena? These are quite philosophical issues, don't you think? Whether they realize it or not, employees' stance of these issues drives them into different personas in office-forward companies.

Reflection on the Officer, the Progressive, and the Producer So, what makes Officers, Progressives, and Producers tick?

Officers need "to office"—a curious neologism many Officers kept using. They idolize their company's culture, and associate the culture with the physical workspace. Officers are emotionally attached to and identify with the workspace; they often describe it as a home-away-from-home. Officers typically hold jobs with built-in flexibility, which they take for granted. But they often come to the office even when they don't necessarily have to "because this is where I feel good" (Ethan, sales representative, officer). Officers enjoy interacting with colleagues, and believe the best interactions happen in person. This explains why they often express disapproval of home-preferring coworkers who "empty their dishwashers while I'm here, building community with my colleagues" (Clara, sales representative, officer).

Progressives genuinely love their company's culture. Like Officers, they are attached to their company's "beautiful" office space, and do appreciate being in the office. However, they sometimes "feel torn" about coming into work and would rather "roll from my bed onto my coach." They liken the experience of going to the office to going to the gym: hard to go, but happy to have gone because "the energy here is so much higher" (Lily, project manager, progressive). Progressives are "excited to see all my peers' smiling faces" in the office, though they also think that "you can get there" if you used technology with the intent to replicate what's best about the office—the human connection (Amanda, client services consultant, progressive). However, the office-forward strategy—which robbed Progressives of newfound flexibility—sharpened their fairness and equity instinct. Like their Producer colleagues, Progressives deeply believe that a more flexible (read: hybrid) workplace strategy would better address the needs of all workers, not just of some.

Producers don't miss the office. Once they tasted flexibility, they were sold. Producers don't crave the social interactions taking place in busy, loud, events-filled offices. Partly, that's because they believe that work is about productivity. The office is simply a location where you get work done; no emotional attachment here. Partly, it's because they see the office as a place filled with "office drama" (Abby, senior program manager, producer). But the home office? That's a place filled with serenity, and this makes it significantly more conducive to task accomplishment. Plus, Producers' home offices now boast the same setup, double monitors and all, and Zoom creates a space where Producers feel welcomed and most importantly—in control. Quietly, Producers are eager to regain some of the flexibility they lost when their company adopted office-forward. They come to the office because they must, but their souls long for home.

Notes

1. J. M. Robbins, M. T. Ford, and L. E. Tetrick, "Perceived Unfairness and Employee Health: A Meta-Analytic Integration," *Journal of Applied Psychology* 97, no. 2 (2012): 235–72.
2. S. A. Friedler, C. Scheidegger, and S. Venkatasubramanian, "The (Im)Possibility of Fairness: Different Value Systems Require Different Mechanisms for Fair Decision Making," *Communications of the ACM* 64, no. 4 (2021): 136–43.
3. R. Purvanova and A. Mitchell, "The Corporate Office as a Workplace: A Pandemic-Spanning Exploration of Organizational Place in Context," *Group & Organization Management*, 2024, https://doi.org/10.1177/10596011241284325.
4. C. Calvo-Porral and R. Pesqueira-Sanchez, "Generational Differences in Technology Behaviour: Comparing Millennials and Generation X," *Kybernetes* 49, no. 11 (2020): 2755–72.

CHAPTER 6

Aligned and Misaligned Personas: Same Office-Forward Company, Different Work Experiences

As we just learned, Officers, Progressives, and Producers are quite different. They differ in how they see the office, in how they view workplace relationships, in how they use technology. This makes sense—different personas have different characteristics. Importantly, these differences extend to how Officers, Progressives, and Producers experience work despite the fact they all work for the same company. This touches on the big *Ah-ha* of our book: alignment matters. Let's learn how personas who are more or less aligned to their company's office-forward strategy experience the office-forward workplace (See Fig. 6.1).

ALIGNED PERSONAS: HOW OFFICERS EXPERIENCE WORK

In office-forward companies, Officers are perfectly aligned to the company's strategy. As a result, Officers enjoy a positive work experience in the office. But this simple statement really means two things. One: Officers enjoy work when in the office. This makes sense, right? But now consider two: Officers cannot enjoy work outside of the office. It might help to see this as a formula:

$$Positive\ Work\ Experience = f(Office)$$

Let's unpack.

Officers' stories of life-at-the-office are like a testament to the fun-at-work doctrine. You hear about fun at the in-office bar: "We have a bar here, so there's good happy hours here. I mean, we just like to have a good time at the office" (Evan, sales representative, officer). You hear about fun on Fridays:

© The Author(s), under exclusive license to Springer Nature Switzerland AG 2025
R. Purvanova and A. Mitchell, *The New Workplace*,
https://doi.org/10.1007/978-3-031-86046-1_6

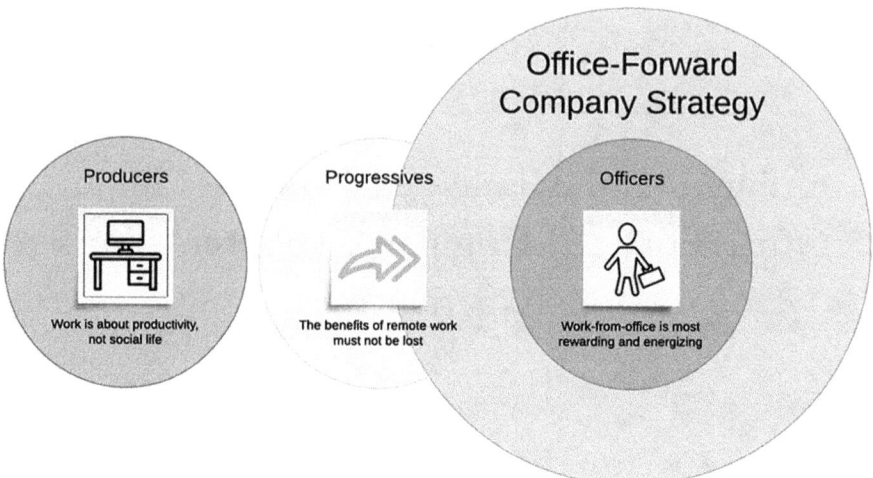

Fig. 6.1 Officers are fully aligned in office-forward organizations while Progressives are half-aligned and Producers are misaligned

"On Fridays, everyone comes down, and they have snacks, and there's candy. It just is a good environment. People enjoy seeing other people. It's just a good culture here" (Sara, division vice president, officer). You hear about all sorts of fun in the cavernous office atrium which "we turn into an event space, it can accommodate 800 people, and it's incredible" (Cole, client relationship manager, officer). Sometimes, it's like fun at a dance club: "One time, we hosted a silent rave and obviously we had great food catered in and drinks at the office and it just turned into a really fun environment for our people" (Cole, client relationship manager, officer). Sometimes, it's like fun at a concert venue: "They had a band come in and like disco ball things and it was a cool, fun thing" (Christopher, account manager, officer). You even hear about fun in the parking lot, ice cream vans and food trucks and all. If there's one complaint Officers have about fun at their workplace, it's that there isn't enough of it! "They're slowly starting to bring those things back," said one Officer (Sara, division vice president, officer); "Slowly," agreed another (Christoper, account manager, officer). *Rev Up The Fun!* might be Officers' new rallying cry.

But if you're not exactly moved by Officers' stories of fun-at-work (we mean, *The Office* kind of ruined the concept years ago), how about Officers' stories of feelings of pride and joy and sense of accomplishment, or of finding meaning and purpose in their work, only when they are in the office? Here is how one Officer hit on these notes when explaining why it is important to him to go to the office:

For me, going into the office is a much better experience. I am in 5 days. Unless you're in the office to talk about what you're going through, you're really just doing your own thing at your own time. Like, I have my own clients, other people have their own clients, so it's not really a collaborative space. So, for me, that was the main issue I was having [with work-from-home in lockdown]—finding a sense of purpose within the organization because I felt like I was just working on my clients, nobody was really seeing what I was doing, no one was providing any feedback on what I was doing. Leadership was genuinely startled when I told them I've lost my sense of connection and purpose within the organization.

And so I think it helps to be in the office. From my perspective, working from home makes it more difficult to call someone and say, Hey, are you available to talk, rather than walking over to someone's desk and basically demanding that they're available and say, I have this question, let's talk about it and then I'll go back to my desk. And so when I'm in the office, I don't know, it just seems like much more of a collaborative environment to be able to be in the office with the team. And I think productivity—I'm just so much more productive in the office, more connected.

There also are people under me that are still training. I enjoy being there for those individuals, providing them that, you know, easy, easy access to be able to ask questions and not feel like they are asking a dumb question or anything like that.

And—and this is probably super weird of an answer—but we have a badge to get into work. It feels good to have the exclusivity of, Oh, I have somewhere to go, someone needs me to be there, or someone needs me. You know, that badge, it's not like it's super significant, but at the same time, it's like I have a place to go, I have a purpose, I have things I need to do within this building, within this job, that need to get done.

So for me, and it could be opposite for other people, but for me, and the way that I work, I enjoy any interaction that I could possibly have with my coworkers. And just the idea that I have a place to go to, a place of purpose! Yeah…I think purpose is a good word. (Christopher, account manager, officer)

Another Officer hit on some of these same notes as she explained how being in the office energizes and motivates her:

I am much more creative when I am here, I get much more done when I'm here. When I am at home, I don't think I've had a single day where I had been in the zone at home. Like, a day where I would feel like the day flew by because I could get so much done. And those are days I thrive off of! At work, I am super productive. It's just a different feeling here. I can see the whole building in one look. I can see the sales people upstairs, I can see who's walking around, getting coffee… I mean, it's just, you can just see the action which I think is one of those things that make me feel motivated. It's just seeing the energy, or feeling the energy that's here. And like, tomorrow morning, I have to work from home because we have a situation with some vehicles, and I am dreading it just because I don't, I'm not as productive at home as I am here. (Jessica, area director, officer)

A third Officer offered this almost poetic explanation of why the office makes him happy:

> There are a couple people in our office that have great laughs. You would almost think that they were fake—they're so loud. And they're not obnoxious but just loud and kind of alarming, and they're very frequent, and they're distinct. If you hear the person laughing, you'll know who it is, and you just know they're in the office. I think those are some of my favorite sounds. I don't know why I went to sounds, but yeah, those make me happy. (Ethan, sales representative, officer)

To translate Officers' reasons why work is most enjoyable in the office into academese, we'll throw in the term "intrinsic motivation." Intrinsic motivation is motivation from within (contrast that with extrinsic motivation which is motivation from external sources, such as money or the watchful eye of a supervisor). When you do something because you want to, you're intrinsically motivated; when you do something because you have to, you're extrinsically motivated. Research in the psychology of work has shown how powerful intrinsic motivation is. We are pushed (or motivated) to do something from within when we find something interesting, or meaningful, or personally rewarding, when we experience pride, or find purpose, or feel energized, when we have the opportunity to help others, to give back, to do good, when we sense a connection to others or to something bigger, some cause, some social entity, when something makes us happy, and yes—when something is fun.[1]

Do you notice a correspondence between these intrinsic drivers and Officers' reasons why they enjoy work only in the office? The office is where Officers experience these intrinsic drivers, and therefore, the office is where Officers experience work positively.

But work psychology research has not only uncovered the beneficial effects of intrinsic motivation. It has also shown the detrimental, de-motivational effects of the *absence* of intrinsic motivation.[2] When we are denied the opportunity to experience intrinsic motivation, it feels like we are just going through motions or that we are mere executors of others' wishes. Without intrinsic motivation, it's almost like life loses its meaning. That, in turn, affects mental health and well-being.

So what happens when Officers are prevented from experiencing the intrinsic drivers they find in the office? Hear this story:

> I do not like working from home. It's not a great time. It's very boring, frustrating ... I don't really know other words to describe it.
>
> I remember during the pandemic, when we got that dreaded email that said, Okay, we're doing this indefinitely, until we know more or know what's going on. I remember getting that email, and personally, I got tears in my eyes. I

had already been home for a month or two at that point. When I worked from home, I would not put makeup on, I wouldn't really get ready for the day. I remember one time looking at myself in a Zoom and thinking, Oh my gosh, I cannot believe I got to this point. Like, my hair was a mess! I enjoy getting ready for the day, I enjoy putting make-up and doing my hair.

So I remember, I really was reaching out to my leader and saying, I can't do this. Like, when I'm home, I will be the first to admit, I was not working my full 40 hours. I felt like, you know, when they say mental health, I took a toll on. I was one of those people you could have put into that category. I had no motivation. I am one that would wake up every morning and go to the gym. I was sleeping until I really wanted to, and then I would watch Netflix, and I just wasn't at my computer, I would do the bare minimum. And that's not like me at all.

So I reached out to my manager and I was like, I need to be in the office, you know, even if it's just for one day a week, just so that I can experience that. I was even trying to fake a bit and say, Oh, I have to print something, or I need my dual monitors for even a couple hours. And they'd be like, Okay, you can go in for only a couple hours.

So when we came back, I remember feeling relieved. I remember feeling excited. I remember feeling like…just getting back to myself and feeling very productive. That's actually another very, very important part is, you don't realize how comfortable an expensive chair is. I didn't have that at home, so my back would hurt from sitting at my make-shift desk. I don't live in a big house where I could just create an office all of a sudden, so it felt good to come back and sit here and feel like I had my space. And I just knocked stuff out and I mean, hours flew by. I remember drinking coffee or drinking tea, and just being so zoned in, and just…I loved it!

And now, I've really been in here 30–40 hours a week and not looking back, not wanting to work from home. I feel excited, I love coming to work every day. (Clara, sales representative, officer)

As this story illustrates, what happens when intrinsic motivation is removed is that the work experience becomes poor. In fact, the life experience becomes poor!

So, Officers are unable to positively experience work outside of the office. Unsurprisingly, then, Officers describe work-from-home as boring and frustrating, as disruptive to mental health, as lonely…pretty much the opposite of the intrinsically motivating work-from-office. Even when pushed to specifically think of any beneficial element to work-from-home, Officers can't come up with anything positive to say:

> "I can't think of anything that would draw me to it… I have a hard time saying what I enjoy about work-from-home" (Jessica, area director, officer);
>
> "Ooh, boy. I don't have a ton. I do not enjoy it. I just really don't" (Cole, client relationship manager, officer);

"I'm [hesitates]… Nothing I can think of. So, I'm probably 'no'" (Sara, division vice president, officer).

Officers are also unanimous that they would never take a remote job: "I personally would never take a job that was a 100% remote. If they call me tomorrow, and they're like, You no longer have a desk and you're not allowed back in the office, I think I would probably look for another job, another job that has an office" (Emily, assistant division vice president, officer), and "Like I said, I wouldn't. If they're like, Hey, do you want to work remote, I'd probably pass on that" (Evan, sales representative, officer).

So, like we said, for Officers, having a positive work experience is a function of being in the office. Remember, this means two things. One, Officers can only enjoy work in the office. Two, Officers cannot enjoy work outside of the office. Officers depend on the office for a positive work experience because the office is where they find intrinsic motivation. Let's clarify this in our formula:

$Positive\ Work\ Experience = f(Office = fun + purpose + mental\ health + other\ intrinsic\ drivers)$

Officers are a powerful example of how alignment matters. When employees' work location preference (in this case, an office preference) and company strategy (in this case, office-forward) fully align, it's like a match made in heaven. So yay for Officers—they are in workplace heaven!

HALF-ALIGNED PERSONAS: HOW PROGRESSIVES EXPERIENCE WORK

In office-forward companies, Progressives are halfway aligned to the company's strategy. Progressives enjoy a mostly positive work experience in their office-forward company. Did you catch the key word here? Yup—"mostly." So what tips the balance toward a "mostly" positive—and away from a negative—work experience?

On the positive side of the ledger, Progressives really enjoy the social aspect of in-office work. On first blush, this makes Progressives seem like Officers. But unlike Officers who talked about all sorts of over-the-top social events at the office: dunk tanks, and disco balls, and ice cream vans, Progressives—true to their relationship-oriented nature—talked about the more intimate stuff, the close, interpersonal bonds they have with their colleagues.

> Those informal, organic interactions that come up when you're in the office--whether it be just going down to get coffee in the morning and you see somebody that you wouldn't have interacted with otherwise, or what-not. I've noticed that I feel a lot closer to my team when I'm in the office more consistently. So yeah, now I come in at least Tuesday through Thursday. Sometimes I'll come in on like a Monday or a Friday in addition to that. My team is really, really close, so I think that is kind of motivating to go into the office. My specific team is in almost every day. Almost everyone on my team is married,

and only a handful don't have kids, most people are pretty young, I would say in their 30s, and people have anywhere from newborn babies to kids in elementary school. But I don't know, my team is really unique, I would say. We're just a really, really engaged group of people. And people are really close outside of work too. I haven't, I've never worked with a group of people that are this close. And it really, when I don't go into the office, I miss my team. (Lily, project manager, progressive)

Progressives enjoy experiencing these genuine connections with colleagues in the office. But they go one step further. Progressives enjoy capitalizing on these connections for collaboration purposes...

I sit next to Julie, she's right next to me, and Emily's a cube over. And we're not waiting for these meetings or sending Teams links or Zoom links to say, Hey, can we have a huddle to discuss this. It's just like the whack-a-mole—we all pop up from our cubes and we all talk about it right there. So that works for our team. Sometimes it's just easier to say, "Hey, stupid question" instead of sending a Microsoft Teams messages or something like that. (William, client services consultant, progressive)

...and even for productivity purposes:

To me, it's not just that social aspect, but also, I'm in sales. I do know that sometimes, call it kind of "accidental" work gets done. You run into somebody in a different department, and they talk about a client, or this opportunity, or ask questions. So I do like that aspect. Now, while I'm maybe not as productive in emails and day-to-day and getting some of that done [in the office], I do think there is a positive, you know, by being around people. It can bring on sales, bring sales to me, be beneficial for our customers. (John, senior vice president, progressive)

So the key to Progressives' (mostly) positive work experience in office-forward companies are the deep and meaningful connections they have formed with work colleagues. Deep and meaningful connections are one kind of intrinsic motivation. But notably absent from Progressives' positive side of the ledger are all the other intrinsic motivators that Officers experience in the office. In our conversations with Progressives, we heard a mere smattering of stories about how being in the office instills a sense of purpose, is best for mental health, or energizes and supercharges the drive to accomplish. Those stories were there, but they were few and far between.

But what wasn't that rare in our conversations with Progressives were stories of extrinsic motivation—you know, the type of motivation that comes from outside forces. Those stories—which were notably absent from Officers' accounts—fell on the negative side of Progressives' ledger.

Progressives resented the connection they perceived between being in the office and career growth.

> I think it's part of just being present, being seen. You could be doing all the work from home, but if you are not taking that one next step of seeing people and having them see you... Coming into the office may make you look like an overachiever but it's gonna get more notice. Even if others are working harder at home, unfortunately, I think, unfortunately, it's harder for people to see if you're working from home and only directly reporting to your team or your manager. Whereas at least being here, you are helping yourself from just external exposure. So it's just this perception sometimes of, Oh, well, they're working from home today. And it's a little passive. And I don't want to be that person that's talked about in that way, so it's like, Well, I'll just come in, you know? And then, it's not an issue. I can still choose to be at home. But it's more of our leadership's expectation that you are just going to be here. So if we can just ditch the perception that people at home don't work, or that people in the office are going to always get the promotions or always work harder. I just think it's unnecessary and not fair and I know that there's people that are going to look elsewhere if they are seeing that kind of culture of toxicity in an organization. (Amanda, client services consultant, progressive)

Progressives also resented the mandate, as they perceived it, to come in: "Our continuity teams in HR were pretty intense. And certain elements of the plan, we're kind of pushing back a little bit from mandatory anchor days in the office" (William, client services consultant, progressive). They resented the perceived policing of office attendance: "We scan our little badges all the time, and you can kind of tell, it feels like they are tracking it" (Amanda, client services consultant, progressive). In all, being extrinsically motivated—being rewarded for complying with mandates, being told what to do, being monitored and micromanaged—did not sit right with Progressives.

So, Progressives' work experience is a function of some intrinsic and some extrinsic motivators that they experience in the office. Thankfully, the intrinsic motivators Progressives experience—those positive work relationships with their work friends—are way more powerful than the extrinsic stuff, so Progressives' overall work experience leans positive. This echoes much research in work psychology on the power of workplace friendships to make the workplace a better place.[3] Still, seeing the pros and cons of both work-from-office and work-from-home leaves Progressives feeling torn. On the one hand, they love being in the office:

> I love my work. I love being around people. I love, I love the coffee machine, I love, you know... I don't know, it does bring a sense of comfort that when I need to work, all these things that I'm used to, this gets me in the habit. I like the brightness, I like the comfort, so I have a lot of good emotions. I'm happy to be there. (John, senior vice president, progressive)

On the other hand, they miss being at home:

> My wife, she's working upstairs, she's in a job that she now works fully from home. And it's always great to just text my wife--or she would text me: you

want to grab lunch in 10 minutes? Yep! We'll go up. Honestly, we would not talk all morning, but we'd make sure and take 15–30 minutes, come up, eat lunch together, then we go back down. So that, I love that, you know, just to have that, you know, that social aspect, but also just to kind of feel the closeness with her. That is great. (John, senior vice president, progressive)

So, Progressives enjoy their work experience. But, they also feel torn about it. This is a powerful example of the contradictory effects of half-alignment. When employees' work location preference (in this case, a hybrid preference) and company strategy (in this case, office-forward) do not fully align, employees' work experience is a mixed bag of good and bad.

Misaligned Personas: How Producers Experience Work

In office-forward companies, Producers are fully misaligned with the company's strategy. Producers' work experience in their office-forward company is, frankly, poor. They spend their time in the office dreaming of home:

Some days I genuinely feel like I go into the office just to go into the office. I don't talk to anyone--maybe it's a little bit of small talk--but I don't talk to anyone at work. I'm just there to be there, that's how I feel about it most days. Or like maybe I'm in the office and I'm talking to someone, or I'm in a meeting with other people, but I'm still kind of thinking, 'You know, I could be at home doing this.' A lot of the things we do in the office, in the back of my mind, I'm kind of thinking, 'Oh, we could do this at home.' (Katherine, assistant project manager, producer)

True to their newfound appreciation for technology, Producers miss some of the socializing and information-sharing that happened through the less personal, more anonymous technology-mediated channels the company utilized in lockdown:

Now since we're back, we are just not utilizing [virtual happy hours and such] as much, but it was fun to see people's faces, you know, just kind of to remember who you work with. And we do still get video updates from our CEO, but he was sending them more often--I don't know how often they were at one time--but more often. Now we still get them but maybe once a month. (Chloe, program manager, producer)

Producers also feel a little left out: "There are things I miss by not being in the office and being in the moment and hearing all those side conversations. Occasionally, I kind of need to remind them: Somehow, you have to get that word to me" (Abby, senior program manager, producer). But not all Producers "remind" their office-loving colleagues to include them; again, most Producers prefer to avoid in-person interactions: "I think I've kind of stuck to myself, you know. I don't branch out a whole lot. Not to say that I'm not social, but I more go to my desk, get my work done, get home, you know?" (Chloe, program manager, producer), and:

> I'm not necessarily longing for a deep personal connection with any of my coworkers right now, you know. And so without feeling the need to relate to them, I just don't think I know them personally, or care to know them really personally, and I don't mean that in a mean way, I just... (Katherine, assistant project manager, producer)

So Producers feel forgotten and lonely in the office, even though the office is full of people. Noting the contradiction, one Officer quipped: "You are only as disconnected as you make yourself be. Every day, the two people that don't feel like part of the team are the two empty chairs" (Ethan, sales representative, officer).

Be that as it may, forcing Producers back to the office is also not a good idea. We heard a slew of negative emotions in Producers' stories of having to be back. One emotion was fear—the fear that whatever flexibility to work-from-home remains at their office-forward company may soon go away: "It makes me nervous, that's for sure. I enjoy working from home and I hope that option continues" (Chloe, program manager, producer). Another emotion was powerlessness—being denied the opportunity to make personal choices: "How do I feel about the office? Required? That's not really an emotion, but that's just kind of how I see it—required" (Katherine, assistant project manager, producer), said one. Another agreed: "I think the biggest caveat is being able to have more freedom with my work schedule" (Graham, account manager, producer). A third emotion was defiance...albeit of the quiet sort: "If I were asked to come in every single day, it'd be kind of like, I don't know if I really like that" (Theo, senior project manager, producer). Those are precisely the emotions workers experience when they are solely extrinsically motivated. It does not feel good when big brother's watching...and yet, that's exactly how Producers feel in the office.

Another way to understand why Producers' in-office work experience is so poor is to understand what's so good about their at-home work experience. Why are Producers dreaming of home when at the office? Simple. Convenience and ease:

> Oh, my gosh! I just, I like to work at home! I don't have to commute, I don't have to wake up as early and do my makeup, my hair, the whole nine yards. I get to wear comfortable clothing when I'm at home. I really don't have an issue separating the work from home. Once I'm done working, I'm done working, and I'm already at home. So I like working from home. (Katherine, assistant project manager, producer)

Oh, and also—more me-time:

For me, I love it. I get to wake up whenever I really want. I'm a morning person so I'm always up before six, but I get to wake up, I get to enjoy my time instead of spending, you know, 30-45 minutes in traffic just to get to the office. I can spend 30-40 minutes reading a book or spending more time on myself, which I think a lot of people weren't doing before. (Graham, account manager, producer)

But what about the social connections that their Officer and especially their Progressive colleagues so prize at the office? You know, the work friendships that even research shows are so essential? How are Producers not going crazy, being isolated at home and all?

I go to a coffee shop sometimes. I do make it a point to get out and about when I'm not working to interact with people. I do belong to a book club with some other professionals in my community. So that's an opportunity for socializing. Plus, I'm in a lot of other activities that give me an opportunity to just not be totally reclusive. (Abby, senior program manager, producer)

And:

We have those co-working spaces out here in Colorado, We Work is one of them. I've been in those a couple times, and I really liked the atmosphere. I will say, it's very Millennial, Gen Z -focused inside, and I think that's probably why I like it so much. (Graham, account manager, producer)

So Producers would rather stay home alone, work at a loud coffee shop, or even pay good money to go work in a co-working space rather than go to the office. We take that as proof of how allergic Producers must be to the in-office work experience. But more seriously, this is a powerful example of the negative effects of misalignment. When employees' work location preference (in this case, home preference) and company strategy (in this case, office-forward) completely misalign, employees' work experience is poor.

Reflection on Aligned and Misaligned Personas in Office-Forward Companies So, how does alignment affect employees' work experience in office-forward companies?
Officers—the persona who is fully aligned to the company's office-forward strategy—enjoy their work experience. Their enjoyment comes from the intrinsic motivation Officers experience in the office and in the office only. The office is where Officers find purpose and meaning, have fun, are able to mentor others and give back, feel pride, and so much more. All of this has important downstream effects on Officers' engagement and productivity. So, aligned employees are engaged and productive employees, and that engagement comes from the heart.

It's interesting that Officers' stories are rarely told. Officers' very existence is infrequently—if ever—acknowledged in the media. Their story shows that even though office-forward companies may not be media darlings (and might even be media villains), the modern, post-pandemic workplace needs office-forward companies as part of the mix. Otherwise, a sizeable contingent of employees—office-preferring folks—will be denied the opportunity to find alignment and enjoy a positive work experience.

Progressives—the persona who is half-aligned to the company's office-forward strategy—have a mostly positive work experience. They experience strong intrinsic motivation (Progressives absolutely love the positive work relationships they've built with colleagues), but they also experience extrinsic motivation (Progressive feel pressured to go in). How do Progressives square this paradox? Well, for starters, it helps that Progressives agree with some of their company's reasoning for office-forward. They do believe that culture happens in the office, and they do love their company's culture. They happily go to the office to help sustain that culture. Now, Progressives disagree that work-from-home is bad, or that remote workers should not get promoted. But one interesting thing we noticed about Progressives is how pragmatic they are. They may disagree with parts of their company's philosophy, and they may resent the pressure to go in, but they go in nonetheless—not just because they miss their work friends, but also, to be seen, to keep themselves in the game. So, half-aligned employees (aka, Progressives) are engaged and productive employees…though part of that engagement may be a bit self-serving.

Producers—the persona who is fully misaligned to the company's office-forward strategy—have a poor work experience. They are in the office solely due to the extrinsic pressure the company applies on them to be there. With their wishes to work-from-home not respected, Producers resent the office-forward approach. An important caveat here is that a tiny number of Producers had worked out deals to be remote workers based on personal circumstances. These Producers are lucky—their individual arrangements shield them from the negative effects of misalignment. Outside of those rare exceptions, Producers feel miserable in the office. So, misaligned employees' engagement has taken a hit. What would come next is Producers looking for greener pastures elsewhere … or at least keeping their options open.

As we said: same office-forward company, different work experiences.

NOTES

1. A. Fishbach and K. Woolley, "The Structure of Intrinsic Motivation," *Annual Review of Organizational Psychology and Organizational Behavior* 9 (2022): 339–63.
2. A. Furnham and L. Treglown, *Disenchantment: Managing Motivation and Demotivation at Work* (United Kingdom: Bloomsbury Publishing, 2017).
3. Colbert, Bono, and Purvanova, "Flourishing via Workplace Relationships: Moving beyond Instrumental Support."

PART IV

Personas in Hybrid Companies

Unlike office-forward and even remote-first, the hybrid approach is a post-pandemic innovation. It took organizations some time to even settle on a term for this workplace strategy. Words like "blended" and "flexible" were strong contenders. "Hybrid," of course, won out the naming games. The strategy has become so popular that—according to McKinsey—nine of ten organizations have adopted hybrid.[1] We take this number with a grain of salt as "hybrid" has become a somewhat overused term. Still, undoubtedly, hybrid's in the air.

But, what exactly are hybrid companies? The defining characteristic of hybrid organizations is that they see an important role for the office, but they also recognize that work can effectively happen anywhere. A combination of in-person and remote work is the *modus operandi*. However, with hybrid, the devil's in the detail.[2] Some companies practice structured hybrid—they prioritize the office by requiring in-office work on specific days or specifying a certain number of days each week employees must be in the office, while still recognizing the value of remote work. Other companies practice fluid hybrid—they prioritize remote work while still recognizing the value of the office by asking employees to commit to some in-office work days.

Google's strategy is an example of structured hybrid. In April 2022, Google officially announced its three-days-in-office policy. The company's message to its workforce was that this will "maximize flexibility while still facilitating innovation, collaboration and camaraderie of in-office experiences." CEO Sundar Pichai also tied the hybrid strategy to doing good for the local communities that host Google's offices.[3] To prep for hybrid's roll-out, Google began to update its physical offices, which it sees as "vital anchors" to employees. However, because the company is struggling with filling up its offices with people, it is now tracking office attendance and tying it to performance.[4] It's also implementing desk sharing to cut on office costs, but employees have complained there are insufficient workspaces at the office. So, while Google is trying to thread the needle between office culture and employee flexibility via its structured hybrid strategy, employees don't see structured hybrid as flexible enough.

HubSpot, a collaboration software company, offers an example of the fluid approach to hybrid. Implemented in January 2021, HubSpot's fluid hybrid strategy neither proscribes in-office days, nor coordinates office attendance.[5] Rather, employees choose the home-to-office work ratio that works for them, on a schedule that works for them. There are three levels of choice. Some employees may choose to be in the office three or more days a week; these employees have a dedicated desk at the office. Other employees may choose to be in the office two or fewer days a week; these employees use a hotel desk (organized by team when possible) and receive support with their work-from-home set-up. Still other employees can choose to be remote; these employees receive support with their work-from-home setup. HubSpot asks new employees to choose their option before their start date; all employees have the chance to change their option once per year. According to CTO Dharmesh Shah, HubSpot's hybrid strategy values remote and in-office work. As Shah explained, leaning into both promotes equity and inclusion, and allows employees to build work around life rather than the other way around.

As these examples show, under a hybrid strategy, combining in-person and remote work is the default or primary method of working. However, hybrid organizations do not balance office and remote perfectly; they lean toward office (structured approach to hybrid) or toward remote (fluid approach to hybrid). Under structured hybrid, a ratio of office-to-home work is established (typical ratios are 2:3 or 3:2 office-to-home days). In some cases, specific office days (aka, anchor days) are identified. Structured hybrid companies often invest heavily in their office facilities, and may tie compensation or promotion to office attendance. As such, structured hybrid tactics are reminiscent of the tactics employed by office-forward companies. Under fluid hybrid, units (teams, departments, divisions) and even individual employees have discretion to set their own office-to-home work ratio. In some cases, the ratio could even be 0:5 (i.e., fully remote). Often, there are no anchor days, and employees are not required or expected to coordinate attendance schedules with others. Fluid hybrid companies recruit based on talent, promote based on performance, and do not dodge pay or threaten termination based on showing up to the office. They may downsize office facilities, and may assist employees with setting up work-from-home spaces. As such, fluid hybrid tactics are reminiscent of those employed by remote-first companies.

The hybrid company we studied fits the fluid hybrid variety. Remember, we called the company Harmonium in a nod to its efforts to "harmonize" office and remote work. As we previously described, Harmonium valued employee flexibility even pre-pandemic, so adopting fluid hybrid was a natural outgrowth. Harmonium encourages two-to-three days in office, and has identified Tuesday as the "team" day. However, interpretations of this guidance vary widely across the company. Some teams coordinate office presence; most do not. Hiring often happens across geographic boundaries, so many team members, team leaders, and even company executives are away from office hubs. Harmonium is a global company, too, which adds to the geographic diversity and dispersion of the workforce.

Just like Promethean saw persona diversity with its remote-first strategy, and Apollonian saw persona diversity with its office-forward approach, the hybrid strategy Harmonium adopted created persona diversity as well. About 45% of Harmonium employees realized they had an @hybrid work preference. We call these @hybrid preferring employees **Integrators** because they liked blending work and life, office and home. About 20% of Harmonium employees discovered they had an @office preference. We call these @office preferring employees **Traditionalists** because they wished for a return to normal, which to them meant office-based work. Finally, about 35% of Harmonium employees realized they loved work-from-home. We call these @home preferring employees **Rebels** because they rarely went back to the office, wishing instead that the remote-only workdays of the COVID-19 lockdown had never gone away.

So, at Harmonium, most employees adopted a fully aligned persona (45% were Integrators), and there were two sizeable half-aligned personas (20% were Traditionalists and 35% were Rebels). This 45-20-35 persona breakdown is unique in two ways. First, under hybrid, there's no misaligned persona; instead, there are two half-aligned personas. Second, compared to a clear majority of aligned personas in office-forward companies (Officers) and a clear majority of aligned personas in remote-first companies (Avatars), aligned personas under hybrid (Integrators) are not necessarily a majority. This has important implications for organizations adopting hybrid. Not only will you find persona diversity in your hybrid company—Integrators, Traditionalists, and Rebels will be present—but, unlike your office-forward and remote-first competitors, you may not have a strong majority of aligned personas to lean on for support with implementing your strategy. It's interesting that the most popular workplace strategy in the post-pandemic workplace—hybrid—might be the hardest strategy to square. Hybrid organizations have their work cut out for them in aligning their split workforce to their hybrid strategy.

As we keep on saying, finding alignment begins with awareness. So, let's learn about Integrators, Traditionalists, and Rebels.

Notes

1. A. Alexander et al., "What Executives Are Saying about the Future of Hybrid Work," *McKinsey*, May 17, 2021, https://www.mckinsey.com/capabilities/people-and-organizational-performance/our-insights/what-executives-are-saying-about-the-future-of-hybrid-work.
2. Mitchell and Brewer, "Leading Hybrid Teams: Strategies for Realizing the Best of Both Worlds."
3. K. Schlosser, "Google Set to Bring Employees Back to Seattle-Area Offices at Least Three Days a Week in Hybrid Model," *Geek Wire*, March 2,

2022, https://www.geekwire.com/2022/google-set-to-bring-employees-back-to-seattle-area-offices-at-least-three-days-a-week-in-hybrid-model/.
4. M. Kruppa, "Google Gets Stricter about Employees' Time in Office," *The Wall Street Journal*, June 7, 2023, https://www.wsj.com/articles/google-gets-stricter-about-employees-time-in-office-9a20f2e.
5. K. Burke, "The Future of Work at HubSpot: How We're Building a Hybrid Company," *HubSpot Blog*, August 19, 2020, https://www.hubspot.com/careers-blog/future-of-work-hybrid.

CHAPTER 7

Meet the Integrator, the Traditionalist, and the Rebel

In hybrid companies, @hybrid-preferring employees evolve into Integrators, @home-preferring employees evolve into Rebels, and @office-preferring employees evolve into Traditionalists. In Chapter 2, we shared a demographic analysis of employees with @office, @hybrid, and @home preferences. Here, we focus on deeper, more psychological factors that drive employees with these different work location preferences to become Integrators, Rebels, and Traditionalists when they work in hybrid organizations (See Fig. 7.1).

THE MYSTERY OF WHO'S IN

Imagine walking into your office. What's your first thought? On a typical day for Ina, it's "How late am I?" Alanah, who actually has time to settle into her office, is thinking "I like my space and I am happy to be here." These are probably somewhat mundane first thoughts (though we promise, we are not boring people!). But in our interviews with Harmonium employees, a peculiar first thought kept on popping up: "Who's In?".

> As I'm walking into the office, I'm thinking: Who's going to be in the office today? (Ella, product manager, integrator).

> I wonder: Well, you know, who's even going to be in the office today? (Robbie, senior content strategist, rebel).

> The first thing I think about is, Who else is in the office today? It's always a mystery. (Laura, leadership development manager, traditionalist).

© The Author(s), under exclusive license to Springer Nature Switzerland AG 2025
R. Purvanova and A. Mitchell, *The New Workplace*,
https://doi.org/10.1007/978-3-031-86046-1_7

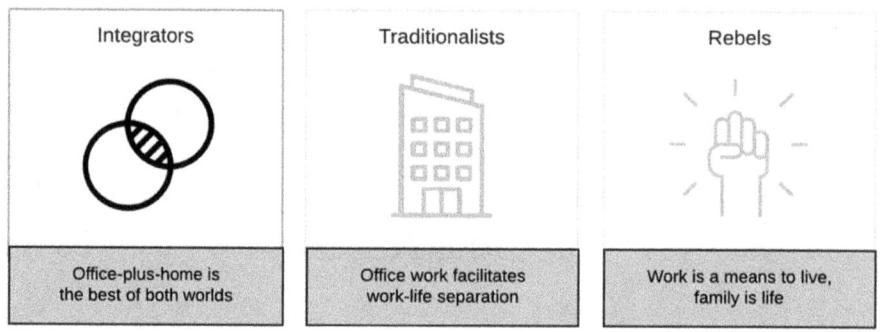

Fig. 7.1 Personas in hybrid companies include Integrators, Traditionalists, and Rebels

What caused this daily mystery? For one, Harmonium had jumped on the geography-blind hiring train. As one executive proudly explained: "As long as it's the right talent, the right fit for the team, it doesn't matter where they sit anymore" (Henry, director of consulting, integrator). Consequently, we barely spoke with people whose team members were all local. Instead, this was almost always what we heard:

> When I look at my team, there's probably four to six people in the metro, and then we have team members in Texas, Georgia, North Carolina, and Minnesota. And so, about 50% of our team is not within driving distance of the same office. (Ben, senior engineer, rebel)

With dispersed teams the new norm, there were fewer people to go to any local office. To boot, Harmonium's brand of hybrid strategy—fluid hybrid—decreased the probability that even co-located teammates would be in the office on any given day:

> Because you don't have to identify a specific day, people just rotate in and out. Some people come in more frequently, others are more likely to work from home. The last time I went, maybe one third of this space had actually been filled. (Raul, sales specialist, rebel)

As one employee explained, determining one's hybrid schedule had become the new "dress for your day":

> I can choose, it's extreme flexibility. My leader can't even tell you what days I'm in and out. And I don't know what days my team members are in and out. What I tell my team is: Look at your calendar if it makes sense to be in. It's similar to how we always said dress for your day. And now it's, you know, determine if you're in or out for your day. (Maggie, operations manager, integrator)

And so, for Harmonium employees, "Who's In?" was a daily mystery.

How employees reacted to this daily mystery was one tell-tale sign of their developing persona.

Integrators valued work-from-home, but they also purposefully went to the office to maintain their connection to colleagues. So, the community-threatening aspect of Who's-In bothered them:

> Not everyone's in [the office] on any given day, and some people have moved and are working remotely from, you know, Wisconsin, or Colorado, or somewhere. So, having a big semi-professional slash semi-social group that was just always in the office is something that I really miss. And I think it is unlikely that this kind of environment will really ever return, to the extent that you have any hybrid or remote work. (Kevin, junior analyst, integrator)

To offset the Who's-In effect of diminished in-office community, some Integrators switched teams:

> Over three months ago, I moved [to a different team]. Part of my move was that on my last team, no one came in. They had the option to come in, but no one came in and they didn't really partner together. But this team came into the office, and they collaborated. And so, I knew that this culture I was joining was more collaborative, and there was that expectation that people would be in, so when I did come in, I wouldn't be sitting here by myself. And that was a driver for it. (Lori, assistant director of customer experience, integrator)

Other Integrators made it a point to coordinate office attendance with teammates. Even coordinating with a few of them sufficed: "For me, if one of my teammates is going to be in on a day that works for my schedule, then I'll go really just to have lunch" (Tina, data governance specialist, integrator). Still others came into the office on their at home days to partake in team meetings in person:

> Even on those days where I typically will work from home, I'll still go into the office for meetings, even if it's for half the day. I just think it's very important to have facetime with people, you know, to really make those connections and to foster that atmosphere. Getting back to the office, rekindling those relationships is helpful and important to getting things done, and getting them done effectively. (Nikhil, chief operating officer, integrator)

Integrators also looked to their broader social network: "At 2 o'clock every day, there's a group of us that walks downtown to get coffee, and that's one thing I kind of look forward to in the day" (Patrick, treasury analyst, integrator). They were even willing to consider working in a co-working space "just to go see people" (Mindy, assistant director of client services, integrator). "Crazy how relational we are!" this Integrator exclaimed.

The daily Who's-In mystery caused Traditionalists consternation, too. But their reaction differed from that of their hybrid-preferring Integrator colleagues'. True to their office-preferring nature, Traditionalists took it upon themselves to role-model office presence, only to eventually realize that's not going to catch:

> There's a strange trend where some of the other teams in our department had just kind of started to fall off of coming in. And I've thought about that from the perspective of, What am I doing to contribute to the equation? And you're kind of met with this wall because there's only so much that you can do to inspire other people to be around by you being around. At some point, it just feels a little bit futile, like, Well, that person hasn't been in in five weeks, they're a lost cause who's never going to come back in again. And it's okay, it's what they need, but I've done what I can there. And I think about that a little bit because I'm one of the people who, when given the opportunity, leans a little more towards wanting to come in. It's an interesting experience to hear very consistently from a lot of people that 'Oh, yeah, if we didn't have this team day, I wouldn't be coming in ever.' It's interesting only because I come in, and like, three people I know come in, and we get lunch together. And I'm just like, Okay, I'll be here anyway, probably. (Grant, senior data analyst, traditionalist)

With their role-modeling efforts failing, others' absence grated on Traditionalists. Said one: "On some days, I'm coming in and it's like, Oh, yay, I'm gonna see so-and-so! And you know, you get there, and it's like, Oh, they're working from home today" (Luke, treasury relationship manager, traditionalist). Another was less forgiving:

> Listen. I always say Americans are way too fortunate. The problem is, we have it too good. I have very little tolerance for people complaining about coming to an office twice a week. Our parents did this hustle and bustle every day, and you're complaining about twice a week? So my patience and my tolerance for that is rather low. You tell me today that you have to pick up your kid at 3 o'clock, but you somehow managed to not pick up your kid at 3 o'clock pre-COVID? That, that's where I have an issue. (Matthew, sales representative, traditionalist)

However, most Traditionalists did understand colleagues had different preferences and needs: "My team is really young, you know, no kids, pets for the most part. But it makes sense for others because, you know, you want to be with your kids" (Ying, assistant analyst, traditionalist). Still, Traditionalists called for a more considerate and inclusive approach where each team member's needs are taken into consideration:

> It's a balancing act. You need to try and figure out what's your teams' responsibilities, what's the function of your team, and then, what's the personalities on your team. And from there, try to kind of fit and mesh what's going to work best for everybody. (Jake, client analyst, traditionalist)

Sounds like a reasonable request to us!

In contrast to Integrators and Traditionalists, Rebels—who preferred at-home work—were not concerned with the community-threatening aspect of the daily Who's-In mystery. Their reaction was to question the wisdom of going in at all given most interactions were going to be virtual anyways. Said one:

> I want to say, 95% of my daily workload has to do with California, so I don't have any reason to, you know, I don't do anything with anybody in the office. Most of my work is over the phone anyway, phone and emails and Zoom or Teams or whatever it is. (Raul, sales specialist, rebel)

Another concurred, pointing to the futility of going in if face-to-face communication would not occur:

> For me, what would draw me to the office is if everyone on my team was there at once, right? It's really just a draw to get everyone together to get some of that more face-to-face communication. That's the only pull or justification that I see to go in the office. (Ben, senior engineer, rebel)

And so, Rebels stayed home. Eventually, they began shying away from the office even when they knew social events were planned. Some found the timing of such events inconvenient: "They usually have events later, like, starting at 5 PM. Not having those during the day makes me not want to go as much cause that's my family time" (Vera, senior treasury manager, rebel). Others couldn't (or perhaps—wouldn't) break away from their work or meetings to attend social events:

> I thought about going [to the company-wide barbecue in June], but I guess it is a disadvantage of being at home. I had meetings surrounding the lunch hour, and so, I was going to go into the office, but timing… We pack our schedules a bit more when we are at home because you don't have the transit time of walking from a meeting room to your desk and back to the other one, you know. You just pop on and pop off, so the turn-around time is a little tighter. But that's, that's probably why. And it was, you know, I don't know, I just wasn't necessarily as eager to go down there, since as you know, again, nobody's down there. And so you're trying to reach out to, you know, 10 people, Hey, do you want to go down, and Hey, you know, I'm not really, I've got meetings. So, you know, it's not the same vibe down there when you don't quite know as many people. (Mark, onboarding coordinator, rebel)

Still others identified loss of social skills as a reason to not go: "I can pinpoint exactly what it is. For me, to interject myself into a social situation is always weird. But it's even more exhausting now because I haven't done it in so long. Especially if I don't know anybody, making the effort to be social is a lot more painful for me now" (Tracy, senior analyst, rebel).

In all, the daily Who's-In mystery that Harmonium's fluid hybrid strategy created proved troublesome for all personas. True to form, however, each persona had a different reaction. For Integrators, Who's-In upset the balance between getting work done and socializing with people. So, they found their own ways to re-create the work-social balance they seek. For Traditionalists, Who's-In was a daily reminder of the dark side of hybrid and remote work: the lonely office. So, they tried to influence others to see this perspective, often in vain. For Rebels, Who's-In was self-reinforcing: they rarely went it, then they cited the empty office as a reason to not go in. So, they grew more home-bound, and stopped attending even planned social events.

What You Say and What You Do

Managing people's perceptions is hard, right?

At Harmonium, the official message was "We value hybrid." But to Integrators and Rebels, it seemed that leadership was quietly role-modeling office-forward, whereas to Traditionalists, it seemed that leadership was downplaying the office. Each persona cited a different reason for this perceived disconnect between leadership's words and actions. Each had a different solution.

Integrators strongly felt that executives privately privileged office-forward. Said one: "I don't know how many traditional executives you'll find that really love the whole idea of the remote worker completely" (Kevin, junior analyst, integrator). Another agreed: "Because I work with the C-suite, I do see behind the curtain. I understand that while our policies say that we are flexible and hybrid, our executives would really very much like us all to be back in the office as most executives are" (Nina, senior communications strategist, integrator).

They pointed to two easy-to-spot trends as evidence. One was that executives were mostly in: "Our entire leadership structure is generally in the majority of the time. More often than not, the people who are consistently here are, you know, the leaders of the organization" (Patrick, treasury analyst, integrator). Integrators warned leadership that this would send mixed messages:

> I work closely with people that work with our Chief Human Resources Officer. And they're really trying to plug to him that, Hey, if you want people to stay, you can't say you can work from home but then promote being in person. So now I've noticed, on company-wide calls, one of our executives is conveniently always working from home that day [uses air quotes]. But I recognize their office, so I know they're just, well, faking a hybrid environment ... which is better than not, I guess. (Tina, data governance specialist, integrator)

Another trend that did not escape Integrators' attention? An uptick in in-office activities. Integrators were split on whether they personally appreciated these enticements. Some did: "They're trying to get people back in. I mean, they've done, like, employee barbecues, coffee with our executives, happy hour with our executives. I really like those efforts. They make me feel prioritized" (Mindy, assistant director of client services, integrator). Others—not as much:

> They tried lots of things, like free lunches and stuff. I don't know, I'm almost like a natural contrarian, I see through what they're trying to do. And I'm like, Yeah, forget it, I'm staying home. Like, I don't want to let you win by trying to trick me in sort of thing. (Alex, senior financial analyst, integrator)

But whereas Integrators disagreed on the effectiveness of in-office activities for themselves, they agreed on the poor judgment of de-prioritizing virtual connection options. Their main concern was their home-preferring colleagues:

> The point of inclusion of those who are remote should be a matter that everyone takes very seriously. Not just from a retention-of-talent, but from the human side. If these people are feeling excluded, that's going to play with their emotions. What can we do as an organization to try to be consciously inclusive so it's not band-aids like the happy hour. But what else can we do to really include them? (Eva, assistant director of communications, integrator)

The solution? Integrators felt that leaders should personally embrace hybrid work, lest they continue to create a disconnect between themselves and their hybrid and remote employees:

> There's a big disconnect between regular people and executives because they're all in every day working the same way they always have been. And so, they're not, maybe, having to make these same adjustments that people working hybrid have to. (Tina, data governance specialist, integrator)

Integrators also felt the company should actively invest in educating itself how to be a true "hybrid-first" employer:

> There are many, many things I love about Harmonium, but they are not a hybrid-first company. They are an office-first, hybrid-is-an-option company. And that means that we don't actively educate our teams on: How do you behave in a hybrid meeting? How do you have better etiquette? How do you think about the in-person conversations that you just had? Did you make sure to translate those to your team if they weren't and couldn't be there? My hope is that Harmonium invests in creating the collaboration and the employee experience that's necessary for this to work. (Nina, senior communications strategist, integrator)

Similar to Integrators, Rebels felt executives privately privileged the office: "Harmonium, I think their preference would be that we would go in" (Tom, product director, rebel), and "They're paying for the building, so they want people there" (Tracy, senior analyst, rebel). Notably, they didn't take issue with their direct leaders, but with the "disconnected higher-up's": "Our leaders are human, they understand. I think it's more the high-ups that are disconnected. They don't get that it's a little bit more complex than just getting everybody back in. There are other things at play" (Raul, sales specialist, rebel).

Also like Integrators, Rebels felt leadership was de-prioritizing virtual connection options, despite their professed embrace of hybrid. They blamed this on going back to the office: "We've backed off from the Zoom meetings now that we go to the office on Tuesdays" (Tracy, senior analyst, rebel). Rebels missed the remote social events:

> Our leader used to set up happy hours every other Friday. We would just get on Teams, and, you know, as everyone wrapped up their day, people were welcome to hop in and hop out as they saw fit and as it fit in their schedule obviously. It was just a time to hang out, tell stories, get to know your coworkers, right? So, I always thought those were fun, being able to do that from home and kind of just relax. I remember those warmly. (Mark, onboarding coordinator, rebel)

So, sadly, Rebels felt forgotten, as evidenced by the chorus of such sentiments we heard:

> They forget about us the remote people because they are hybrid now (Rachel, business analyst, rebel).

> I don't feel as connected because leadership hasn't figured out yet how to show their appreciation for us when we are hybrid slash virtual (Mark, onboarding coordinator, rebel).

> They'll schedule like maybe a happy hour or something after work. I can't go because I work in a different state than where my colleagues are (Karen, financial analyst intern, rebel).

Rebels proposed a simple solution—go back to remote-only meetings. As one Rebel said, "Virtual is the most inclusive, especially for a global workforce" (Ben, senior engineer, rebel). Another agreed, pointing out that virtual-only meetings level the playing field: "I feel that if you can create your meetings to just be virtual meetings, everybody's on that equal playing field. There's not that separation that occurs" (Sue, learning and development manager, rebel). Indeed, Rebels often felt excluded in hybrid meetings: "Sometimes they just forget you're remote or they forget that you're up on the screen on Teams, and they're talking with each other" (Karen, financial analyst intern, rebel). They felt anxious they had missed the important stuff, the stuff that happens after the meeting: "My boss is based in Philadelphia, and he would always ask, Hey, what did you guys talk about after the meeting was over" (Tom, product director, rebel).

Going back to remote-only meetings seems reasonable in a hybrid organization with a geographically dispersed workforce. Another reasonable solution? Be more human:

What I'd want to change moving forward maybe would be those connections. Maybe make more of an effort. Like I said, with my boss, everything is cut and dry with them, like, I hardly know much about them, and they don't know much about me. They still don't know my daughter's name. (Rachel, business analyst, rebel)

This was a commentary on a new development in the hybrid workplace—reserving chit-chat, spontaneous social stuff, fun—you know, reserving "being human"—for in-office interactions only. Rebels felt that infusing humanity (back) into virtual meetings would go a long way to making them feel included.

In sharp contrast to Integrators and Rebels, Traditionalists felt the office was de-prioritized, despite leadership's professed adoption of hybrid. So, Traditionalists saw a disconnect between leadership's words and actions, too, but their perception was diametrically opposed to Integrators' and Rebels'.

Traditionalists' biggest concern was that leaders dropped the ball on restoring a previously strong and fun in-office culture. One explained:

[Before the pandemic], there were a lot more events that were taking place at my employer's campus. There were a lot more social things that were going on that were publicized throughout different parts of the company. And then they just kind of stopped. And when we came back in, I think we were trying more at the beginning. But at a certain point, leadership was less focused on intentionally setting up, you know, different kind of ways to spend time together as a team outside of the context of getting the work done. There was almost nothing anymore. So, it just didn't come back. I don't think it ever quite recovered in any meaningful way. (Grant, senior data analyst, traditionalist)

So, Traditionalists reminisced about fun in-person moments from the olden days that were no longer. Here's one nostalgic example:

And I just remember, I don't know why, like, there wasn't anything crazy around it. But we just had this giraffe, this purple giraffe that we would hand out as an award to team members who are doing a good job once a quarter. It was a physical representation of, like, Hey, Joe did a good job. So, it's going to sit on Joe's desk, you know, until the next quarterly awards. We used to do fun stuff like that, you know, and play Olympic games in the office, we had soup challenges and stuff... (Laura, leadership development manager, traditionalist)

Traditionalists understood that the new hybrid work environment just couldn't support these activities given that "we're not back to full capacity and we will never be" (James, portfolio manager, traditionalist). But, they were puzzled—we'd say, with reason—as to why people would still log into meetings even when they came into the office:

One of the things that's kind of challenging and frustrating too is that there's this tendency now with using Teams as a crutch. So a lot of people schedule a meeting in a conference room on a Tuesday [the anchor day], thinking most people are gonna be in here. And you go in the room and there's one person there but three other people are sitting at their desk on Teams. And it's like, Well, if you're in the office, at least come to the room! I don't understand staying at your desk when you're in. For me, if there's a room, I wanna see people. (Luke, treasury relationship manager, traditionalist)

And so, to Traditionalists, leadership's dropping the ball on supporting in-office activities led to such cascading outcomes as by-gone fun office days and lack of in-person interactions even on office days. To Traditionalists, this defeated the purpose of hybrid, creating the perception of a words-versus-action disconnect.

It's troublesome that Integrators, Rebels, and Traditionalists disagreed on how "hybrid" Harmonium was. But even more troublesome is that the personas agreed that leadership says one thing but does another. Research on strategic leadership has well documented a commonsensical fact—that for a strategy to be successful, leadership must communicate clearly and role-model organizational priorities consistently.[1] Clarity and consistency. That's what helps get, and keep, everyone on the same page.[2] Seeing eye to eye.[3] Simple recipe, difficult execution.

TASK-LOCATION FIT

The old workplace was easy. It offered structure: You work 9-to-5 every day, rinse and repeat five days in a row, then you relax two days. It offered work-life separation: You work in the office, you relax at home.

The hybrid workplace is tricky. There's no structure: You work some combination of hours, mostly over five week days; you relax over the two weekend days but maybe do some work still. There's no work-life separation either: You work in the office some days, at home other days, you also relax at home.

How do you deal with this constant switching of work hours and work locations? And when you let work into your home on some days, how do you shoo it out of your home other days?

Well, here's a happy occurrence:

With joy and love, we introduce our new family member: Task-Location Fit.

Proud parents, The Integrators.

What great news! Integrators got themselves a new workplace skill: task-location fit. As one Integrator put it earlier, task-location fit is the new "dress for your day." Think about the tasks you have that day and where you'll be most successful in completing them. Are you going to be heads-down, working on spreadsheets all day? You might be more successful working remotely, without coworker interruptions. Are you planning on a feedback meeting with your supervisor or your team member? This conversation might be better handled in person at the office then. You get to decide!

This new skill—which researchers have actually already recommended for hybrid settings—was born out of necessity.[4] You see, Integrators initially struggled to adjust to the lack of rhythm in the hybrid workplace: "At first, it sucked, right? The hybrid situation was a little challenging because it's pretty volatile in the working styles day by day" (Connor, consultant manager, integrator), and "It probably took a couple of weeks of burnout. I was like, I can't, this is just not for me" (Lori, assistant director of customer experience, integrator). So how did Integrators adapt to this roller coaster work experience that hybrid creates? Well, they tricked their minds a little. One "unconsciously changed his brain to adapt":

> I found ways to build a routine. So, there are days I'm going in for sure: Mondays and Wednesdays. And then I also know, Ok, for sure, Tuesdays and Fridays I'll be home. I can kind of just like train my brain. I feel like I unconsciously have changed my brain to adapt to that schedule, so it doesn't feel volatile anymore. (Connor, consultant manager, integrator)

Another "flipped her mind" by focusing on the positive side of identifying and then prioritizing her daily objectives:

> And then, I flipped my mind: I just have to figure out what my priority is each and every day! I can do it all! I think about the positive--that there's more flexibility to say, Today, my priority is my family and I have to be there for my family but I might have to make up the work some evening this week. So, it's changed the way of thinking. It's not a 9-to-5 arrangement anymore. It's an arrangement that I'm going to provide an output or a thought leadership for the company, but we just have to be more flexible on when that's going to happen throughout the day or throughout the week. So it took some trial and error, but once you start thinking of daily priorities, it's doable. (Lori, assistant director of customer experience, integrator)

And so, Integrators learned to prioritize. The task-location workflow that emerged as most popular was this: "I prefer the work part at home but the social aspect in person" (Tina, data governance specialist, integrator). Another elaborated, explaining how he "bifurcates" his week:

> I'll just kind of arrange my week so that the days I'm at home, I'm saving that work that I need to really focus on. Or I'll just stack a number of calls in a given day when I'm at home. But when I'm in the office, it is great for collaboration. The days I'm in, I'm typically pretty stacked with meetings and a lot more of my time is spent interacting with folks on different things, whether both business and personal. I almost always have, like, a lunch scheduled with someone on the days I come in. So, it's much more relationship-focused. I really like, you know, the hybrid approach. Like I said, I can really plan my schedule, or you know,

bifurcate my time where it's best used throughout the week now. (Nikhil, chief operating officer, integrator)

However, the new task-location workflow had an important flaw: Integrators struggled with disconnecting from work on at home days.

"I have issues," said one (Eva, assistant director of communications, integrator). She went on to explain how life interfered too much with work on at home days, pushing back the end of her workday:

> In the office, it's almost a ceremonial close of my laptop. When 4:30 or 5 approaches, I mentally close my work chapter. But at home, I'm not able to create a separation. I feel like I break my day much more at home. I have dogs at home so I'm like, Ok, when do I need to take the dogs out? And is the concrete guy coming, and is the guy who mows coming, or There, I see the Amazon guy, oh my gosh, my thing that I ordered finally arrived! I have a lot of interruptions. So I pause my day, and then I come back. Like, after I put my daughter down in bed, I'm like, Oh, I have these three emails. So, I need to finish, but that "finish" doesn't come at 5. It comes after I complete my day's work. And because my personal life gets in the middle, the day's close is pushed back. (Eva, assistant director of communications, integrator)

Another Integrator also missed a symbolic, "conservative disconnect" from work on at-home days. For him, the issue was simply not knowing how to stop working in the absence of a clear stop sign:

> I don't feel like I can log off. You know, that 20-to-25 min ride home, that's a conservative disconnect. At home, I find it hard to log off because, I mean, let's face it--in most roles, there's always something else you can do, right? There's always something else you can work towards. It's much tougher to say, Okay, I'm just completely cutting it off at this point, we'll address that tomorrow. Like, later at night, I might come back to the computer and say, All right, I got to hammer out a little bit more. It's harder to say you have defined hours. All those hours start to bleed together. (Henry, director of consulting, integrator)

Regardless, Integrators unanimously loved switching scenery between the office and the home: "I love both. I really do love both" (Connor, consultant manager, integrator). And so, they kept on using their new task-location fit skill to navigate the ever-changing work experience in the hybrid workplace.

In contrast to Integrators, Rebels did not develop or adopt the new task-location fit skill. Frankly, they didn't need to because they rarely went in. Instead, they did develop another skill—personal flexibility:

> I've become a lot more flexible. Before, I was like, you know, Gotta get in at 8 o'clock, and then work till 5, and then boom, boom, boom. You know, I was very, like, boom, boom, boom. And now, I would say, No, it's okay to work a little bit in the morning, and then go take your kids to school or to a doctor's appointment, and then come back and work, and then you maybe work a little

bit at night. So, the flexibility piece of it has been good for me because I was pretty rigid before, and it's been good to kind of bring me down a level. What one week looks like doesn't look like what the next week looks like, and that's ok. (Tracy, senior analyst, integrator)

So, work bleeding into their personal lives didn't bother Rebels. In fact, they embraced that, they enjoyed the personal growth it stimulated. Unlike Integrators, Rebels did not feel the need to look for or create a daily or weekly structure. Rather, they felt "empowered" (Robbie, senior content strategist), "not micromanaged" (Raul, sales specialist, rebel), and "like a free person" (Svetlana, senior sales specialist, rebel).

Traditionalists, however, very much needed structure. But the new task-location fit skill that helped Integrators create structure for themselves was no use to Traditionalists. It wasn't structuring enough. For Traditionalists, intentionally going into the office at least four days a week was the only way to create structure. One said: "I struggled with the separation of, I'll say, church-and-state, or home life and work life. My [at-home] workdays drag to 8, 10, 12 hours a day sometimes. And so, for me, it's nice to go somewhere, then go home and leave work at the office" (James, portfolio manager, traditionalist). Another agreed: "The days where I'm not in the office just kind of bleed together, it's almost like I've never logged off" (Grant, senior data analyst, traditionalist). A third Traditionalist shared this powerful story of how she realized she needed the structure that going to the office provides:

> I don't mind sharing because this was really important for me, it changed how I look at everything!
>
> I had a miscarriage on a weekend. I actively was going through that process physically on Monday still. And instead of taking the next day off, I was in a presentation the very next morning, 8am.
>
> And I'm sure if I had told people at work, they would have said, no, don't come. But I felt like that meeting was so important, more important than my feelings of processing, of going through that experience. That really messed me up. I had never thought that I would have done that to myself because if that was a team member of mine, I would have said, take time off, we got this presentation, it's totally fine. But I wasn't generous with myself. That's when I realized that I was prioritizing the wrong things.
>
> I think that had Harmonium been a place that said you need to come back to the office and you're only working from the office, I probably would have taken the day off, to be honest. I probably would have said, I'm taking a sick day, we need to rearrange this. But because my computer was right there, I felt like, what excuse do I have to not just open my laptop and get this presentation over with versus, you know, the process of getting ready, going to work, and stuff. That's almost more of a don't-come-in versus your computer just being right there and logging in.
>
> So, I made an intentional decision: I'm going to start coming back into the office. I'm here, I'm concentrated, I'm going to get some stuff done, and then,

just shut it down. Because really, at this point, where I work from doesn't really matter to my team or my leader or the people I work with. But for me, it matters. I'm trying to create some structure for myself. I worked more hours at home than I ever did before. And so, I look forward to it because that means I can kind of turn this part of my brain off and focus on life stuff until the next morning. So now, I think I have a healthy balance where I have an attitude, you know, I'll get what I can get done in the time that I've designated for work, and outside of that, I need to be myself, for my family, for my home, and, you know, for my mental health. (Laura, leadership development manager, traditionalist)

It's interesting to consider these unrecognized effects of the hybrid workplace: the lack of structure, the lack of work-life separation, the constant switching between home and office. This rocky hybrid terrain discombobulated all. Integrators dealt with it by inventing a new skill: task-location fit. Rebels and Traditionalists? They took the rockiness of hybrid as further evidence that their instinct to (mostly) work-from-home (Rebels) or from the office (Traditionalists) was the appropriate path to stability and predictability.

Reflection on the Integrator, the Traditionalist, and the Rebel So, what makes Integrators, Rebels, and Traditionalists tick?

Integrators shine at finding balance; that's their thing. When faced with the Who's-In daily mystery created by the unpredictable attendance patterns of their colleagues, Integrators simply switched to teams with greater attendance predictability or found communities at the office they could join on days they went in. When faced with the challenge of constantly switching work locations between the home and the office, Integrators invented a new skill: task-location fit. They found rhythm—and therefore, sanity—by scheduling heads-down work on home days and setting office days for relationship-building. Now, this didn't fix their work separation "issues" on at home days, but their newfound structure still made them happy. Always advocates for balance, Integrators protested leadership's perceived over-emphasis of the office, arguing that true hybrid requires an equal measure of in-person and remote engagement activities, as well as equal concern for office-based and home-based employees.

Rebels look at hybrid and see a thousand reasons to just work-from-home. Why go in when no one is going to be there? I'm still going to be on Zoom, so... Why go in for social events when those could (and were!) done from home, just as effectively? Plus, my social skills are kind of rusty anymore. And why deal with the tiresome office-home switching when I can do my job at home? I don't have issues disconnecting from work; I don't need any artificial, ceremonial day-closures. And, oh by the way, I love my freedom. With hybrid confirming Rebels' lingering suspicion of the role of the office in the post-pandemic workplace, they did not understand why leadership would want to push the office, even on a hybrid schedule.

Traditionalists look at hybrid and see a thousand reasons to just go back to the office. They get that some colleagues had developed vastly different preferences, but they still can't help but feel a mild annoyance at people's stubborn absence from the office. Traditionalists also did not appreciate the stress caused by the constant office-home switching. To boot, they never figured out how to disconnect from work on at home days. They realized they needed structure, so they recommitted themselves to the 9-to-5, five-days-a-week rhythm of the olden, simpler days. To them, structure is a matter of mental health. Traditionalists were upset with leadership's loose hybrid policies, wishing for a greater emphasis on office. They do understand that the post-pandemic workplace has changed…but one can dream, can't they?

Notes

1. L. Nishii and R. Paluch, "Leaders as HR Sensegivers: Four HR Implementation Behaviors That Create Strong HR Systems," *Human Resource Management Review* 28, no. 3 (2018): 319–23, https://doi.org/10.1016/j.hrmr.2018.02.007.
2. T. Murase et al., "Mind the Gap: The Role of Leadership in Multi-team System Collective Cognition," *The Leadership Quarterly* 25, no. 5 (2014): 972–86, https://doi.org/10.1016/j.leaqua.2014.06.003.
3. S. Desmidt and B. George, "Do We See Eye to Eye? The Relationship between Internal Communication and between-Group Strategic Consensus: A Case Analysis," *Management Communication Quarterly* 30, no. 1 (2016): 84–102, https://doi.org/10.1177/0893318915609406.
4. Mitchell and Brewer, "Leading Hybrid Teams: Strategies for Realizing the Best of Both Worlds.".

CHAPTER 8

Aligned and Misaligned Personas: Same Hybrid Company, Different Work Experiences

As we just learned, Integrators, Rebels, and Traditionalists are quite different. They differ in their prescriptions for how (and even—if) leadership should implement hybrid. They also differ in how they react to the downsides of hybrid, such as the unpredictable office presence of colleagues or the constant switching between home and office. These differences between the personas that occupy the hybrid workplace have implications for how each persona experiences work. Why? Because as we show in the image below, the work location preference of one of the personas—the Integrators—is fully aligned with their company's hybrid strategy. But other personas' work location preferences—Rebels' and Traditionalists'—are only half-aligned. As our book argues, alignment matters for employees' work experience. Let's see how (See Fig. 8.1).

Aligned Personas: How Integrators Experience Work

In hybrid companies, Integrators are fully aligned to their company's strategy. A hybrid strategy by definition promotes a balance between employee flexibility and company culture. And, Integrators by nature enjoy balancing—aka, integrating—opposites: task accomplishment and relationship-building, home and office, work and life.

As we already learned, Integrators happily used their newly developed skill: task-location fit, to craft an enjoyable work experience. They liked figuring out where to execute what task (onboard my new team member in the office? prepare and practice my nerve-racking presentation from home?) and when to tackle different tasks (work on my Excel file with fresh eyes in the morning? catch up on my emails before bedtime?).

© The Author(s), under exclusive license to Springer Nature Switzerland AG 2025
R. Purvanova and A. Mitchell, *The New Workplace*,
https://doi.org/10.1007/978-3-031-86046-1_8

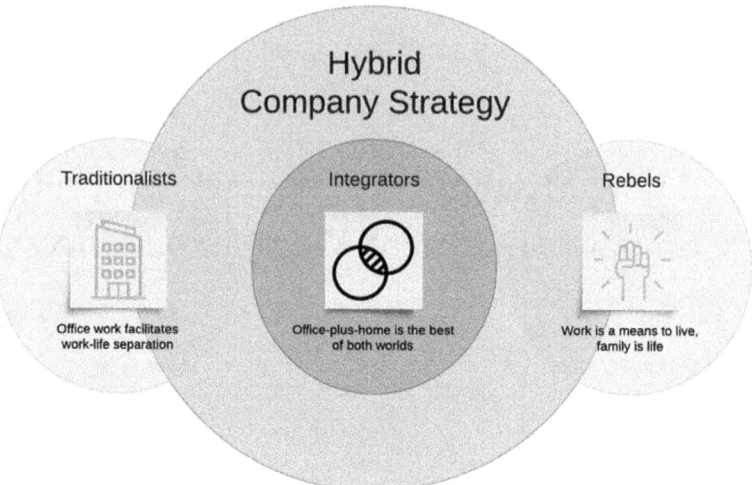

Fig. 8.1 Integrators are fully aligned in hybrid organizations while Traditionalists and Rebels are only partially aligned

But more than crafting their work experience, Integrators enjoyed crafting their work-life experience. One enjoyed getting his "stuff done and being productive and getting the best use out of my work hours" while still being able to "get to my young one's appointments or other errand-type things like going to the chiropractor during the week" (Nikhil, chief operating officer, integrator). Another was in the office the majority of the time because he thought it's "incredibly valuable" but enjoyed the ability to just "take a remote day and drive up to Minneapolis to visit friends or to South Dakota to visit family, work remote from their place, and then enjoy the weekend right away" (Patrick, treasury analyst, integrator). A third took pleasure in the ability to "be more engaged and active in his kids' activities" because he could "start and stop when I feel I need to, like if I need to coach my son's little league team at 4 o'clock" (Henry, director of consulting, integrator). And so, crafting one's work-life experience by mixing and matching work and life during the course of the day or the week was a key source of enjoyment for Integrators.

But, something unexpected happened as Integrators flexed work to accommodate life. They realized, they work to live, not the other way around. We'll let them tell you:

> Work is a means to live my life. It's important to me that I enjoy the work I do and those I work with, but it mostly goes to how the work helps me to live my life with those I love. (Maggie, operations manager, integrator)

> Why do I work, right? Do I work to live, or is it the opposite—do I live to work? Is it worth, you know, spending day and night working nonstop? What's important? How do I design the life that meets all the boxes? I don't think that

you can ever have complete balance. I definitely think that I've probably raised, you know, increased the importance of family and health over work compared to where I was before. (Nikhil, chief operating officer, integrator)

I do think I have focused more on quality of life than on climbing the corporate ladder. I make sure I'm on top of my to-do list, you know, I make sure I get my stuff done. But I have shifted to working for the people I lead and our customers versus working for my boss and our executives. I think that has shifted because my purpose for working has changed. Like, I think it's actually probably become greater than what it was before when I was really just trying to impress and please my boss, and please our executives, and meet demands. And I do think that life has slowed down a little, that I've been more intentional with boundaries, with setting time. And it's like, I haven't, like, de-prioritized work, but I've definitely allowed life to ... [pauses]. Well, I mean, I have "de-prioritized" work [uses air quotes] if that means that my life comes before work, you know what I mean? But it's not that I don't work hard anymore or anything like that. It's just, I think, I've had time to assess what really matters. (Mindy, assistant director of client services, integrator)

I really love my job. I don't know if I love work—it's pretty high up but I think it's gotten a little bit demoted. I take a lot of pride in my work, so I hope it doesn't completely shift to the bottom of my totem pole. But I do hope that I continue to have a life-first mindset. (Tina, data governance specialist, integrator)

A life-first mindset. On their quest to craft the perfect work-life balance, Integrators developed a life-first mindset instead. How paradoxical!

Importantly, however, Integrators' life-first mindset did not sour Integrators on work. Life-first did not diminish their drive or passion for work. To the contrary, Integrators' new life-first mindset improved their work experience. Why? Because Integrators felt gratitude. They were grateful that the hybrid workplace pushed them to see the importance of life: "Flexibility made a lot of people realize that there are other things in life, and you can enjoy them better, you can see them better, when you're not tethered to the desk" (Alex, senior financial analyst, integrator). They were thankful that hybrid removed the stigma of people needing to take care of their personal life: "Everyone now understands that we also have life to get done, and no one will be against you if that's what you need to prioritize" (Nina, senior communications strategist, integrator). They loved that colleagues are much more likely now to "grant grace to each other" rather than assume that people are "lazy when they're yellow on Teams" (Connor, consultant manager, integrator). They celebrated not needing to worry that their job is in trouble if they can't be there physically because "if I'm not there, I can do this virtually, it's not a big deal anymore" (Lori, assistant director of customer experience, integrator). They enjoyed being able to let down their guard, to be "more vulnerable, letting others see that I need help if I'm not having a good day, or if I need to unplug and actually be present at my daughter's silly school concert" (Eva, assistant director of communications, integrator). And so, gratitude that the hybrid workplace allows for a life-first mindset was another key source of enjoyment for Integrators.

But at the same time as they felt this gratitude, Integrators also entertained a constant, nagging thought: Is this for real? Could it be? Are people really not judging me?

Integrators worried whether their coworkers and bosses knew that they are working on at home days:

> I guess this is something I worry about. I get that I'm valued enough, that they know the products I've put out. But in the back of my head, it's this nervous thing, right? Like, do they know what I'm doing? Especially, you know, how the 360-performance review is once a year, right? And I've worked with these people, I know how they think of me. But it's this little latent fear at all times, right? (Alex, senior financial analyst, integrator)

Similarly, they also worried about whether they are present enough to be noticed for opportunities:

> In my mind, I still think that if I came in, I'd be top of mind, right? I truly do think in my mind that if I'm seeing people, whether it's passing them going in and out of the bathroom, or at the lunch hour, or something like that, like, that just keeps me top of mind for opportunities. (Connor, consultant manager, integrator)

But though Integrators' new life-first mindset stirred doubts and insecurities in their minds, they remained big fans of hybrid. Integrators saw their values reflected in the hybrid workplace. They appreciated that—like them—hybrid privileges both sides of the coin: flexibility (read: personal life) and culture (read: work in a fun social context). Said one: "I like the flexibility it provides, while not cutting off any of the culture or people aspect" (Tina, data governance strategist, integrator). Another put it more passionately: "Harmonium's flexibility and culture are things I can't really put a price tag on. I wouldn't even take a 50% raise in exchange for the flexibility our company offers. And, I like seeing people" (Maggie, operations manager, integrator). A third concluded:

> Yeah, there's definitely some trade-offs, but I look at it holistically. I like the ability to have 2–3 days in the office and a couple of days at home. And I'd say based on polls of my team members, it's a very consistent story around that. Hybrid resonates with people. (Henry, director of consulting, integrator)

This Integrator got to the essence of why hybrid resonates: "I can achieve self-actualization and a sense of self-worth through supporting both my ongoing personhood and my productivity" (Kevin, junior analyst, integrator).

And there you have it. In the end, despite the paradoxical twists and turns, hybrid resonates … with Integrators at least. On balance (pun intended), Integrators have an enjoyable work experience in the hybrid workplace which—like them—prioritizes both employee flexibility and company culture. Of course, that's what you'd expect from full alignment.

Half-Aligned Personas: How Traditionalists Experience Work

In hybrid companies, Traditionalists—an office-preferring persona—are halfway aligned to the company's strategy. At half-alignment, Traditionalists' work experience teetered, swaying into positive territory when they go to the office, and into negative territory when they work from home.

Traditionalists enjoyed their work experience on in-office days. A key reason Traditionalists cited for their better in-office work experience was greater productivity in the office. They explained how when they go "to work"—meaning, to the office, they feel "productive," they feel they are "doing work," and work itself feels "tangible":

> When you go to the office, you're sort of plugged in, and even working a couple of hours on a project without finishing it feels productive. At home, I'm just floating out here in my own space, sort of out there, in this no man's land. When I go to work, the sense is I'm doing work. This is the first time I've thought about this as I say it out loud, but I feel like at home, work doesn't become tangible. (James, portfolio manager, traditionalist)

Traditionalists credited their higher in-office productivity to the greater ability to focus in the office: "I have a lot of focus when I come in here" (Laura, leadership development manager, traditionalist), and "At work, I think I'm probably more focused" (Luke, treasury relationship manager, traditionalist). They also pointed to the in-person collaboration opportunities the office affords as another driver of their higher in-office productivity: "I'm more productive because I can have a quick chat with the person next to me. It's easier for us to communicate about a project when I can just stop by and talk to them" (Ying, assistant analyst, traditionalist).

The office setting also led to greater enjoyment of the in-office workdays. But it wasn't the physical features of the office, like office amenities or office technology that gave Traditionalists joy. In fact, the office itself was either a non-driver: "It's just nice to be there but, no, there's nothing really in particular about the office itself" (Matthew, sales representative, traditionalist), or even a slight disincentive as it was eerily quiet and lonely: "It's a huge space and it's very noticeable that nobody else is around" (Laura, leadership development manager, traditionalist). The lack of personal workstations was annoying, too:

> I had to wait until one of my former bosses got a promotion, and so as soon as that was done, I just kind of scooted on over with my stuff and said, Okay, this is mine now. And if someone came in in the morning before me and really wanted to sit there, yeah, they could technically. But I'd ask them what time they come in, and then come in earlier the next day. (Grant, senior data analyst, traditionalist)

Despite this, the office exerted important psychological effects on Traditionalists. They felt a sense of professionalism in the office, a sense of pride in the building:

> It feels more professional. I'm sitting at home in basketball shorts, but when I go to the office, I put on dress pants. It's not a super business-formal environment, but it is a professional environment. And if I really think about it, there is some level of, I guess, prestige. We are the biggest skyscraper in [name of city]. There is a professionalism that goes with going to that type of building, and it puts an importance on the work we do, it adds a sense of grandeur, somewhat, to the role. (James, portfolio manager, traditionalist)

As well, Traditionalists could only experience their work as meaningful in the office:

> I would say that there is a difference. It's not extreme but it's more in the idea that there are people—leadership and business partner teams—relying on you to be able to do their things. You feel that more presently when you're in the office. For me, the work itself is very abstracted away from impact on an actual person's life. I deal with investment data primarily. And so, when I'm not in the office, not only do I not really have any tie to what's the point of this job, what's the point of this data, but I also don't get that feeling that, you know, here's the other team that's relying on you, here's the manager who needs the report back. So that's where the difference lies for me. (Grant, senior data analyst, traditionalist)

In sharp contrast, Traditionalists did not quite enjoy their work experience on at-home days. The overwhelming reason? Lack of motivation. Traditionalists found it harder to pull themselves away from non-work-related activities, such as checking what's happening in the cybersphere in-between meetings:

> I feel less motivated at home. Not that I'm not getting work done but I have to push myself a little harder when I'm at home to stay focused, to stay concentrated, you know, to not pull up my phone and check and see what's happening online in-between meetings. So, I would say that there's maybe a degree of less, yeah, less motivation, less excitement when I'm at home compared to here in this environment. (Laura, leadership development manager, traditionalist)

Because they found it harder to self-motivate at home, Traditionalists felt "lazy":

So for me, it's a discipline thing. Last week, when I woke up, I wanted to work from home because I was being lazy. But I knew if I worked from home, I wasn't going to be as efficient as I was going to be in the downtown office. So I'm more self-aware about my self-discipline on those days. (Matthew, sales representative, traditionalist)

In the absence of the stimulating hustle and bustle of the office environment, Traditionalists were also just bored at home, which made them "drag their feet" and gave them "this nebulous feeling" that only further depressed their motivation:

Those days I feel like I'm more likely to put off even getting signed on. I'll still pick up my phone to look at the emails and the messages and make sure I'm understanding what's going on. But I think I drag my feet a little bit more because I know that the very first meeting of the day is when I actually have to be online and functional and present. So, I'm a little slower to get involved. I think it's more of a temptation to, you know, feed into being tired and not wanting to really get going. And I actually think that these days are a little less enjoyable because I don't get going. I don't have a reason, really, to get going. You know, I am not showing up in the office where there's a desk and there's people around. It's this nebulous feeling of, like, well, I have to be online. And it's less motivating. Those days, they're just the same. Bland. Beige walls all around me. Nothing to say bad about them, nothing to say great about them. Just non-descript. (Grant, senior data analyst, traditionalist)

So, what does half-alignment do to Traditionalists' work experience? Clearly, Traditionalists do not enjoy the at-home part of hybrid work. Traditionalists need the office, they need to "go to work" to enjoy their work experience, they need the Monday-Friday, nine-to-five structure the office promotes. Fortunately, under the hybrid strategy, full-time office work is possible. True, there are some nuisances, such as empty offices and desk sharing, but the overall in-office experience is still preferable. This makes Traditionalists an interesting case in which half-alignment does not mean a half-good work experience. In Traditionalists' case, half-alignment pushes Traditionalists over to (mostly) positive territory. As one Traditionalist aptly put it: "I'm definitely more of an office body than a home body. It's fulfilling for myself to go to the office" (Jake, client analyst, traditionalist).

HALF-ALIGNED PERSONAS: HOW REBELS EXPERIENCE WORK

Rebels—a home-preferring persona—are also halfway aligned in hybrid companies. Like Traditionalists, the other half-aligned persona in the hybrid workplace, Rebels' work experience teetered on the fine line between good and bad. But opposite to Traditionalists, Rebels' work experience threatened to go over the edge at any time.

As you might predict, Rebels' work experience swayed into negative territory when they went to the office. It started with a stressful, "draining" morning.

> I'm drained only because I have to wake up a lot earlier than I would when I work from home. So, it's just, I feel tired and it's like, Ugh! The morning just drags on. I literally just get ready in silence. No music. Just ready to get the long day over with. (Karen, financial analyst intern, rebel)

Some Rebels speculated that perhaps stressful mornings were more typical for women: "Guys are probably much different, but as a female, there's a lot more steps to getting ready" (Tracy, senior analyst, rebel). But, men also described stressful mornings on in-office days:

> It's going to sound silly, but I need to set my alarm earlier to make myself humanly presentable, right? My hair here is a little bit of a mop. And then, thinking about traffic, making sure my coffee is ready, worrying about parking. I would say these things are small stressors in our lives, but, you know, they are things we have to consider. (Ben, senior engineer, rebel)

What about the in-office day itself? That was "exhausting," perhaps borderline "depressing":

> In the office, it's everything. It's the stimulus, it's seeing people, it's having to be this person, this professional person in this office setting. I'm not going to say it's depressing, that's not the right word, but it's a more serious feeling. You get in, and you're at your desk, and it feels very formal, like, Okay, here we go, I'm in this serious mindset, I have to get as much done as possible, and it's serious. It's not just I'm mom at home, and we're relaxed, and, you know, there's no agenda for the day. It's you have to be on, seeing people, smiling, shaking hands... It is exhausting. (Vera, senior treasury manager, rebel)

Rebels not only found the social stimuli in the office too much: "I get very anxious very quickly; I feel more relaxed in my own home" (Rachel, business analyst, rebel), but they disliked feeling "watched," almost "micromanaged":

> We have these drop-in rooms, it's just like a little room where you can be by yourself. I like that a lot more than being in my cubicle and having 20 other people just sitting in the little cubes. And it's not so much the noise. It's just, I feel watched, I feel uncomfortable. The thought of being micromanaged—and I'm not saying they do—but it's just something that always, like, crosses your head. (Karen, financial analyst intern, rebel)

They also dreaded having to deal with "challenging" coworkers:

> Some of the business partners that I have...they're very challenging, to put it lightly. I would have to see them every single day in the office, and it got

to the point where I had a lot of anxiety just seeing them. And now, I can really separate it. That's more conducive to like my health. (Molly, marketing manager, rebel)

Unsurprisingly, then, Rebels couldn't wait for the end of the in-office day to come: "At the end of the office day, it's like, Finally! It's time I can go home! It's very rewarding" (Vera, senior treasury analyst, rebel).

Feeling exhausted, drained, depressed, anxious, surveilled, almost bullied ... these are not good feelings to have about your in-office work experience. These feelings stood in sharp contrast to how Rebels felt about at-home days. At-home days were relaxed, slower, wonderful, enjoyable, stressless, chill, smooth, comfortable, warm and cozy (you can snuggle with the cat, you can wear your fuzzy socks), lighthearted, playful, and fun (you can play catch with the dog, you can chase your toddler-turned-dinosaur around the house). And so, Rebels' work experience swayed into positive territory at home.

The sharp contrast between in-office days: gloomy and depressing, and at-home days: filled with joy and well-being, got Rebels to reflect on work and life. It is these reflections that turned Rebels, well, rebellious. These reflections opened Rebels' eyes to an uncomfortable realization: they had been prioritizing the wrong thing. They had been putting work over family and life. And so, in a "one-eighty," Rebels decided that life must come first:

> It's done a one-eighty on me. I hate to say it, but work was my top priority. I didn't take time off or do vacations. I put work above myself and my family. Work was right up there, it was one of the most important things. And now, I have that complete mind shift, you know. I know I need to take time for my own mental health and well-being. And family comes first. If there's something going on, I need to be able to put work aside. So, it has completely changed my mindset and what I value. And it has really enhanced my quality of life and my relationship with my family. (Vera, senior treasury analyst, rebel)

You might say, Didn't Integrators also develop a life-first mindset? The answer is, "Yes, but."

You see, Integrators did raise the importance of life. But for Rebels, that raise was stratospheric; life now towered over work. Integrators wanted to balance work and life, they wanted to integrate life into work and work into life. But for Rebels, the very concept of work-life integration became questionable; they were looking to prioritize life. Integrators felt the hybrid workplace is most conducive to their goal of work-life integration. But for Rebels, only work-from-home was most conducive to their goal of life prioritization.

So, Rebels concluded that work-from-home is the only work arrangement that lets you prioritize life. Work-from-home allows you to focus on yourself and your mental health:

> I was very, very work focused. Work was consuming my life. I think about where I was with my own stress that I was putting on myself, right? Like, it was

my own, I gotta do this, I have to be in these meetings, I have to, you know, be a part of this. And that meant being in person. But now I've realized, with the work that we are doing, we don't have to be in person. I could enjoy my life, and I could have a little bit more focus on myself, my own mental well-being, my, you know, my family, my husband, my niece and nephew. So yeah, I really had a mind switch, my perspective definitely shifted. (Sue, learning and development manager, rebel)

Work-from-home allows you to have quality time with your spouse:

My wife and I have always been pretty good about, you know, spending dinners together and eating with each other when we can. But it's become easier to, you know, maybe cook together or do the dishes together and all this stuff, where before, one was doing laundry while the other was cleaning up. And now, we get to do a lot of things together now, I think, because of the work-from-home aspect. (Mark, onboarding coordinator, rebel)

Work-from-home allows you to focus on your kids:

Before, I'd get home at maybe 7, what, 7:30. Well, my kids, they got to shower, get ready for bed, and go to bed at 9 o'clock. So, I would have an hour to be a parent. Now, working remotely, I can actually be a parent. I can see my kids a lot more because I am home. I can cook breakfast for them. When they come home from school, I can help them with homework. I can help them if they're stuck on something. We can take a quick walk outside or go play soccer or whatnot. We can cook dinner together. They can help me set up the table. We can have a conversation if I need to reroute them if they're going in the wrong direction, you know.

My company says, 'Bring your best self to work.' That's one of our big focuses. Well, I have kids. So, if my kid is not feeling well, that's in the back of my head. Is that my best self that's coming to work? I would rather be at home when my kid is on the couch with a fever. I can still do my work, but I can cater to them as well.

So, for me, work from home is the best of both worlds. Nobody ever wants to choose between work and your kids. You really can't do it. (Raul, sales specialist, rebel)

Rebels' realization that life could only be prioritized at home, not in the workplace, mimics research findings predating the pandemic that exposed flexible work strategies, like today's hybrid work, as bandages.[1] For example, work-life policies, such as flextime and telecommuting, were celebrated as great, progressive supports to women. In reality, they came with significant financial and career penalties to mothers who quickly found themselves on the dreaded mommy track for using them.[2] Similarly, work-life policies designed to support men, such as paternity leave, proved non-viable. Fathers shied away from them for fear of violating the ideal-worker norm: a provider, a breadwinner who grinds non-stop to pursue career success (and, by extension, life success).[3]

Rebels seem to have reached the same conclusion, whether intuitively or through experience—hybrid is a bandage. It's designed to appease employees by offering the illusion of flexibility. In reality, it charges employees with figuring out how to fit life into a slightly augmented work schedule (typically, three in-office days versus five). By creating the illusion of flexibility, it allows work organizations to avoid the much-needed change in how, when, and how much employees work.

And so, a note of cynicism entered Rebels' narrative. Some talked about how "no one will die" if work doesn't get done:

> Work dictated how my life ran. All of my other, like, extracurriculars happened around work. It was just that central being, and it took up a lot of my time, energy, and thought. And now, it's put everything in perspective. Yes, work's important, but no one's going to die if I get something done a couple of hours later than it had initially been planned. And so, I feel like yes, I still value the work that I do, but it's not the central focus of my life. (Molly, marketing manager, rebel)

Others agreed "we are not saving lives," but went even further. They questioned the very concept of work. Is work subjugating? Perhaps "job" is by far a more liberating concept:

> Yeah, we're not saving lives, right? My approach to work in general has become a lot looser because I value my time, I value my relationship with my family and my friends, and I don't want to put work in front of that anymore. That to me just seems silly anymore, it seems out of balance, especially, you know—and this is a whole other radical, but Harmonium isn't giving 15% raises every year, you know, they're not. It's… What we do is a job. Let's work our 40 hours, let's get paid, and then, yes, let's go and enjoy the rest of our life and not let work consume it. (Sue, learning and development manager, rebel)

What Rebels are really questioning is society's oversized devotion-to-work.[4] This term, coined by the renowned sociologist Mary Blair-Loy in the early 2000s, describes the expectation that employees must be devoted to their employers and careers, and that they must demonstrate this devotion by working long hours and putting a priority on career over personal obligations. Rebels are ready to break this expectation. It's a different devotion they are interested in: devotion to family, and friends, and health, and well-being, devotion to life. It was Rebels' half-alignment to their company's hybrid strategy that pushed Rebels to see this. To live their values, and to have a good work experience, Rebels need to work-from-home not just some of the time, but all the time. The impossibility of full-time work-from-home under the hybrid strategy ultimately pushed Rebels to rebel. This makes Rebels an interesting case in which half-alignment doesn't create a half-good work experience. In Rebels' case, half-alignment pushes Rebels over the edge.

> *Reflection on Aligned and Misaligned Personas in Hybrid Companies* So, how does alignment affect employees' work experience in hybrid companies?
>
> **Integrators**—the persona who is fully aligned to the company's hybrid strategy—have a positive work experience. Integrators enjoy solving the puzzle of finding work-life balance that hybrid promotes. On their quest for balance, Integrators realized they had been over-privileging work and under-privileging life. And so, they developed a life-first mindset, proclaiming they now work to live. Importantly, this does not mean Integrators shun work. To the contrary, they are grateful that hybrid normalizes the search for work-life balance, that it privileges both work and life. And while Integrators have a fear deep down inside that this flexibility might be too good to be true, they are taking each day as it comes, enjoying the hybrid work experience.
>
> **Traditionalists**—one of the two half-aligned personas under the hybrid strategy—have a work experience that teeters between good and bad, and ultimately tips toward good. Traditionalists experience a slew of positive emotions in the office. Even the occasional negative emotions, such as being upset that the office is half-empty or that someone took their preferred workstation, are not enough to overshadow the positive feeling on being "at work." In contrast, Traditionalists experience a slew of negative emotions on their at home workdays. What's interesting here is that what Traditionalists cite as reasons for a diminished at-home work experience, Rebels—the other half-aligned persona—cite as reasons for a great at-home work experience. Traditionalists see checking personal messages during work hours as unproductive, Rebels see it as taking a mental break from work; Traditionalists see sleeping-in as lazy, Rebels see it as relaxing; Traditionalists see the quiet home office as under-stimulating and boring, Rebels see it as a distraction-free space for focused work. In the end, because the hybrid workplace sanctions full-time in-office work, Traditionalists are able to create a work experience for themselves that is largely positive by going to the office.
>
> **Rebels**—the other persona who is half-aligned to the company's hybrid strategy—have a work experience that also teeters on the verge. However, in contrast to Traditionalists, Rebels' work experience ultimately tips toward bad. Rebels experience a slew of positive emotions on their at-home workdays, but a slew of negative emotions on in-office workdays. Rather than producing an overall neutral work experience, this emotional juxtaposition led Rebels to realize how much more they enjoy

life, and how "silly" it is to be so devoted to work. Rebels became interested in pursuing a different devotion: a devotion to life. Realizing that a devotion to life cannot be pursued within the confines of a hybrid workplace where office attendance is part of the mix, Rebels' work experience soured. And so, Rebels represent an interesting case where half-alignment produces not a half-good, but rather, a (mostly) negative work experience.

As we said: same hybrid company, different work experiences.

Notes

1. I. Padavic, R. J. Ely, and E. M. Reid, "Explaining the Persistence of Gender Inequality: The Work–Family Narrative as a Social Defense against the 24/7 Work Culture," *Administrative Science Quarterly* 65, no. 1 (2020): 61–111, https://doi.org/10.1177/0001839219832310.
2. Perrigino, Dunford, and Wilson, "Work–Family Backlash: The 'Dark Side' of Work–Life Balance (WLB) Policies."
3. E. L. Kelly et al., "Gendered Challenge, Gendered Response: Confronting the Ideal Worker Norm in a White-Collar Organization," *Gender & Society* 24, no. 3 (2010): 281–303.
4. M. Blair-Loy, "Work Devotion and Work Time," in *Fighting for Time: Shifting Boundaries of Work and Social Life*, ed. C. F. Epstein and A. L. Kalleberg (Russell Sage Foundation, 2004), 282–316.

PART V

Finding Alignment

This section of the book speaks to organizational decision makers, team leaders, and professional employees. We provide space for organizational decision makers to consider organization-wide alignment tactics so that they can achieve alignment between their company's workplace strategy and their employees' work location preferences (Chapter 9). We then suggest alignment strategies for team leaders to consider as they manage the persona diversity within their teams or departments (Chapter 10). We finally ask individuals to pause and think about what persona they had grown into and what that means for their work experience (Chapter 11). In this chapter, we also introduce our Workplace Persona Assessment. We discuss various ways in which readers can use our assessment, such as identifying the persona they had developed or using the assessment for team-building purposes, among others. Finally, we show how the various alignment tactics we recommend for organizational decision makers, team leaders, and professional employees, respectively, come together into a holistic "new workplace" strategy.

CHAPTER 9

How Do Organizations Align Their Workplace Strategy to Employee Work Location Preferences

What is your organization's workplace strategy? Office-forward, remote-first, hybrid? Perhaps you are just now settling into a strategy? Or maybe you want to change your strategy?

Here's the thing about strategy. You have to know WHY you want to pursue it. Why do you want to be an office-forward, or a remote-first, or a hybrid organization? To answer this essential why question, you must know what long-term objectives you may reasonably expect to achieve with your chosen strategy. What would you achieve with office-forward? How about remote-first? And hybrid? Equally important is knowing why not. What will you not achieve with your chosen strategy? To help you find your why (and why not), we'll start with a quick detour into researchland. We'll share what research has uncovered about the effectiveness—and lack thereof—of each workplace strategy.

Next, we'll help you think about the how. How will you implement your strategy? This is about tactics. Here, we'll return to the main idea of this book: alignment matters. The tactics we'll outline will help you align your workforce to your chosen strategy. What's best about our recommended tactics is that the personas you have in your workplace told us loud and clear what they want and need. We've put their words into actionable tactics for you.

Building Your New Workplace with a Remote-First Strategy

Why Do Remote-First: The Good and The Bad

Prior to the COVID-19 pandemic, remote-first was a boutique workplace strategy. In 2019—right before the pandemic struck—only about 400 companies were fully remote.[1] In lockdown, the pendulum swung to remote-first as a vast number of work organizations instituted work-from-home mandates. Today, the pendulum is swinging back, but many employers are sticking with remote-first. The reason? There are two reasons, actually: cost savings and a humanistic concern for employees. These are the why's of remote-first.

But do these why's work? Does remote-first help you save costs? Does it create a humanistic employee experience?

In terms of cost savings, remote-first allows you to ditch the office. Office spaces are pricey. In fact, they are often the most expensive line item on the budget sheet, following HR expenses. Downsizing or eliminating office spaces certainly helps save on real estate costs. And speaking of HR expenses, there are savings there too. Remote-first companies spend less on recruitment as these job opportunities are attractive propositions in the employment marketplace. They even spend less on compensation! Whereas office-forward competitors are raising pay to attract employees,[2] remote-first companies offer the ultra-flexibility that their remote-first strategy affords as a nonfiduciary benefit, cutting personnel costs. Research from Wharton reported, for example, that IT applicants are willing to take a 7% pay cut in exchange for fully remote work.[3] So, remote-first is a definite win for companies from a cost perspective: you don't pay for an office, and your labor costs may be lower.

In terms of humanistic employee experience, the ultra-flexibility afforded by remote-first is seen as a sign of ultra-caring for employees. This buys lots of good will. Remote employees are also happy. In a meta-analysis of post-pandemic research, the more workers worked from home, the higher their job satisfaction got, and the more they liked their leader.[4] These metrics—work happiness and a positive relationship with one's immediate supervisor—have always been key determinants of employee motivation, as well as of something we call employer stickiness. Once you like your job and your manager, you don't leave. You become a committed and loyal employee.

But, remote-first does have drawbacks. One study explored "Zoom fatigue." It showed that digital connectivity was good for employee engagement, but up to a point.[5] Too much digital connectivity was detrimental to employee job performance. Zoom fatigue struck back! Other research has showed that the more workers work-from-home, the more burned-out they get.[6] This is because work-from-home is associated with longer work hours. And, though remote-first strategies are touted for their positive effects on employees' well-being, occupational health science has started to document that we move less when we work from home.[7] Working alone at home not only promotes more sitting but also decreases our willingness to reduce sitting. Finally—the big one: workplace relationships. Research has already uncovered that employees have become more siloed. They report forming connections with fewer coworkers outside of their immediate work group,[8] as well as experiencing poorer relationship quality with existing work friends and acquaintances.[9]

So, from a humanistic perspective, the research on remote-first work is a mixed bag. Employees are happy with their job and happy with their leader; they are committed and loyal. But fatigue, burnout, poorer occupational health, fewer and lower quality relationships ... these negatives do detract from the humanism of the employee experience.

If your "why" for remote-first is cost savings, go for it. If your "why" is a humanistic employee experience, your footing is not as solid.

Realize, though, that the research above uncovers general trends. It does not account for the effects of persona diversity. What we shared with you in Chapter 3 and Chapter 4 does account for how the different personas in the remote-first workplace—the Avatars, the Centrists, and the Community-seekers—experience remote-first work. Remember, Avatars—the fully aligned persona—embrace the positives of remote-first, and importantly, discount its negatives. So, if you moved the other two personas closer to alignment, you might be able to implement a remote-first strategy successfully.

Let's focus, then, on how to implement remote-first in a way that aligns more of your workforce.

How To Do Remote-First: Aligning Your People to Your Strategy

When implementing remote-first, choose tactics that will:

- Keep Avatars aligned

Avatars—an @home-preferring persona who represent about 60% of your workforce—have a great work experience. Yes, they acknowledge the costs to relationships and office culture, but they love the freedom and convenience remote-first affords. They've reached a state of Zen where work and life are one. Because freedom and convenience trump the disadvantages of remote-first for Avatars, they must remain a strong aspect of your remote-first strategy.

- Align the half-aligned Centrists

Centrists—an @hybrid-preferring persona who represent about 15% of your workforce—have a sunny-with-a-chance-of-clouds work experience. They appreciate the freedom and convenience of remote-first, but miss the in-office banter and relationship-building. Because the relational poverty of remote-first is a top concern for Centrists, solving that must become a top priority of your remote-first strategy.

- Re-evaluate Community-seekers

Community-seekers—an @office-preferring persona who represent about 25% of your workforce—have a poor, D+ ork experience. They feel disconnected and disengaged. Because Community-seekers are fully misaligned in the remote-first workplace, they present a challenge you must address strategically.

The tactics we suggest below speak to these three priorities.

Office Space Tactics: The Home Office, The Company Office, The Virtual Office
- Under remote-first, most employees work from their home. Provide monetary and non-monetary support for setting up the home office.
  - Monetary Support: Provide a stipend for office furnishing along with specific requirements for type of chairs, keyboard/mouse, and other office items that would be best for your employees. A specialist could help remote workers set up their home office to the highest ergonomic standards to maximize occupational health.
  - Non-Monetary Support: Educate remote workers on how to use their office space at home for connectivity purposes. Their home office is their stage. Could office décor be a conversation starter? Could allowing the dog or the cat or even the baby to make a periodic appearance on camera humanize the work experience? Traditional professionalism expectations may make the remote-first experience even colder. At the same time, professionalism cannot go out the window. Help your remote workers navigate this paradox.
  - The Upshot: When people become attached to their home office, they are more likely to want to work from home. This is a way for you to align your people to the Avatar persona.
- Remote-first still needs to include a physical office. But "office" can mean different things.
  - Headquarters: A downsized version of your headquarters could accommodate both company-wide social events, and your office-preferring employees. However, an empty office is a huge morale-killer, worse than a desk sharing office. Know how many of your employees prefer to work from the office, and downsize accordingly.
  - Office Hubs: If eliminating your traditional headquarters space, consider opening up local office hubs. This may not be viable if your workforce is very geographically spread-out.

- Coworking Spaces: Consider providing a stipend to employees who prefer to work in an office. This may be in lieu of a home-office stipend.
- Temporary Spaces: Consider renting large spaces once per quarter (or biannually, or annually) to host company-wide events. Everyone loves a retreat!
- The Upshot: In-person social connectivity is important in remote-first. All personas want some degree of in-person connectivity. This increases or maintains employees' connection to the company. Additionally, office-preferring employees (your Community-seekers), and even hybrid preferers (your Centrists), will appreciate having some work space to report to.

- Remote-first unfolds in virtual space as employees interact in Teams, Zoom, or the like.
  - The Virtual Office: When employees work from home, they are physically located in their home office. They gradually forget where they work. You become less real. To keep the company top-of-mind for employees, establish a presence in virtual space. Does Microsoft Teams (or Zoom, or SharePoint) feature your company's branding? Are employees greeted by a virtual receptionist? Do you provide and require using company-branded virtual backgrounds during virtual meetings? Send them some company-branded décor items for their home office, too. These will serve of a physical reminder of you.
  - The Metaverse: Consider building a metaverse, a virtual version of your company.
  - The Upshot: In remote-first, technology is your workspace, not the physical office. When employees boot up their laptops in the morning, they enter your virtual office. Infusing your virtual workspace with your branding will serve as a constant reminder to all personas that they work for you. A metaverse will create even more—and more realistic—interaction opportunities, not just within teams, but across teams. This will begin to restore company-wide social networks, breaking down the silos—an especially big concern of Community-seekers.

HR Tactics: Recruitment, Selection, and Retention
- Remote-first must be properly communicated during recruitment.
  - Realistic Job Previews: The freedom and convenience remote-first affords is a huge selling point. Use it! However, in your job ads and during the recruitment process, communicate the full reality of remote-first work. What are the home-office requirements and recommendations? How much time is spent in virtual meetings versus solo work? What are the meeting protocol expectations

(camera use; break time between meetings)? What skills are needed to build relationships in a remote-first context? What virtual engagement opportunities are available? How about in-person engagement opportunities? What, if any, opportunities for in-person work are there?
  - The Upshot: Painting a realistic picture allows applicants to self-select out of the recruitment process, leaving those with greater potential to be aligned in.
- Remote-first must be an element of your applicant selection processes.
  - Selection Criteria: Soft skills for remote work must be included in your selection criteria. You should assess applicants' ability to connect and collaborate through technology. Would an applicant reach out over Teams to ask a question? Are they skilled in virtual networking? Are they able to get their voice heard in virtual meetings? Can they lead a meeting virtually? You should also assess applicants' organization and focus skills. Can they structure their workday? Can they stay focused on the job without immediate supervision? Can they disengage from work at the end of the workday?
  - The Upshot: Including remote-first skills in your selection systems will ensure you are hiring people who are more likely to be aligned.
- Remote-first is "golden handcuffs" for some but retention is not guaranteed for others.
  - Mentoring: Mentoring newcomers in a crucial retention tactic. Provide training to your leaders on mentoring in a virtual context. Virtual coffee with a leader is a start but it's not enough. Design mentoring programs for the remote-first environment. Be sure they include some in-person element.
  - Demographics: Beware the demographic profile of the aligned remote-first worker: the Avatar. Avatars are typically married people. They are not necessarily older with children, but they won't be your new college grads or your single individuals. As married individuals prioritize family connections versus connections with coworkers, consider how you will retain single individuals who are likely to inhabit the Centrist and Community-seeker personas. Employee resource groups might be one solution.
  - The Upshot: Proper mentoring and employee resource groups will help with embedding half-aligned (Centrists) and misaligned (Community-seekers) personas better in the social fabric of your organization.

Relationship-Building Tactics: Virtual and In-Person Relational Tactics
- All personas value workplace relationships. But the relational needs of the different personas differ.
  - Virtual Relational Tactics: Be creative as you design virtual social activities. Virtual coffee is cool but what else? Virtual book clubs? Skills development classes? Virtual gym? Start a virtual tradition, like #photofriday. Charge experts, such as your HR or marketing specialists, to help dream up options. Train team leaders to conduct daily or weekly huddles. Make Agile meetings a company-wide thing, not only an IT thing. Make sure the top brass is highly visible and engaged in virtual social activities.
  - In-Person Relational Tactics: Host periodic in-person gatherings, whether company-wide or department-specific. Provide teams with a social budget for things like a monthly dinner, an annual fly-out to a retreat location. If you do maintain some office footprint, make sure there are social activities happening there. Food truck, anyone? People who go to the office crave social interactions. And also, free food.
  - Reality Bridging Relational Tactics: Dream up ways to connect with remote employees physically. Plan special surprise home deliveries on holidays. Send cupcakes or treats to employees' homes. Have pizza delivered before supper. Food delivery at home! Free food doesn't have to only be available at the office.
  - The Upshot: It's a myth that @home-preferring workers don't value workplace relationships. In fact, they enjoy and even demand virtual engagement opportunities. Virtual social activities will keep your Avatars aligned and happy. Centrists like them too! In-person relational activities are important for Community-seekers. Bridging activities communicate extra care to all, helping anchor all personas within your social fabric.

Technology Tactics
- Remote-first works only if your technology can support it and if your people embrace technology.
  - Collaboration Technology: Your technology must support synchronous collaboration. Poor whiteboarding tools are a particular concern to remote workers. Also, with so many technologies to choose from, you must have clear guidelines. Do we use Teams or Zoom for videoconferencing? Do I share reports through SharePoint or good old email? How do I set up my home office and my technology for the best videoconferencing experience?[10] Establishing guidelines prevents confusion. Training your workforce on digital skills helps everyone work better.

- Technology Support: Ensure company data is secure outside of the office walls through instituting state-of-the-art cybersecurity. This includes rules on out-of-office printing. Stand ready to provide remote assistance to your remote workforce.
- Technology Etiquette: Establish expectations for appropriate technology-mediated communication. Terse messages come off as angry. Pinging people at all times is not OK. Are cameras on or off? Meetings are remote-first so everyone is equally included.
- The Upshot: Avatars feel at-ease with technology; Centrists mostly do as well. Community-seekers don't love technology-based communication. Clear guidelines and expectations will help all, but especially the Community-seeker persona.

Building Your New Workplace with an Office-Forward Strategy

Why Do Office-Forward: The Good and The Bad

As the pendulum continues to swing back to the office-forward vision of the new workplace, more organizations are going back to the office. The reason? Culture (and other related C's, like connectivity, collaboration, commitment, community, communication). Culture is the spoken why of office-forward. The unspoken why? Another C—control.

But do these why's work? Does office-forward help you (re)build and maintain your culture? Does it help you control your workforce?

In terms of culture, this is a tricky question to answer. It requires distinguishing between return-to-office and office-forward. You see, return-to-office is an implementation tactic; office-forward is a strategy. We know return-to-office does culture no favors. It leads to plummeting employee satisfaction ratings, and consequently—plummeting perceptions of company culture.[11] To boot, employees—particularly the top performers—head to the door.[12],[13]

However, looking at the effects of RTO—a temporary implementation tactic, is different than looking at the effects of office-forward—a long-term strategy. What do we know about how the office impacts culture and related outcomes like collaboration and communication?

Well, we know that good things happen when human beings are in close proximity and can interact spontaneously. In a pre-pandemic study tracking planned *and* serendipitous interactions between Silicon Valley workers, in-person interactions—especially serendipitous ones—were important facilitators of knowledge flow.[14] The more workers ran into each other, the more they exchanged ideas that informed product development and innovation. Researchers also estimated that if half of Silicon Valley's workforce were to work-from-home—making serendipitous meetings unlikely—knowledge flow will fall by over 10%. Fast forward to lockdown when close to 100% of the workforce worked from home, and you see this concerning prediction borne out in lockdown data. For example, in a study of Microsoft employees, collaboration networks became siloed or hyper-localized. Intrateam communication increased but inter-team communication dropped significantly.[15] In a study of MBA students, participants reported fewer instances of "spontaneous collaboration" when they did not work in their colleagues' physical proximity.[16] In a study of a Fortune 500 company, coworkers gave each other less peer feedback. This especially affected female engineers and young engineers.[17] The latter is particularly concerning because it does not appear to be a fluke. Other research has also reported that when employees are out of sight, those in disadvantaged positions (women, racial minorities) are the first to become out of mind.[18] So, office-forward makes a lot of sense from a culture perspective (read: collaboration, communication, connection, community … all important C's). The office brings people in each other's proximity, and there's power in that.

In terms of control, it is undeniable that the office encourages hawkish management. This gives managers the illusion of control, but de-motivates workers who feel watched and micromanaged.[19] The office also amplifies the illusion that physical presence equals performance. It does not. It simply equals presenteeism.[20] And yet, managers—who are tasked with establishing order and control by the organization, and are held to often impossible standards of productivity and efficiency—fall for this illusion. In research, managers admit they feel they have greater control when everyone's in close proximity.[21] So, office-forward makes sense from a control perspective only if you believe that control and the illusion of control are the same thing. (Hint: they are not.)

If your "why" for office-forward is culture and the like, go for it. If your "why" is control, you're fooling yourself.

But here again, we warn that the research above is about general trends. It does not take into account persona diversity. What we shared with you in Chapter 5 and Chapter 6 does account for how the different personas in the office-forward workplace—the Officers, the Progressives, and the Producers—experience office-forward work. Remember, Officers—the fully aligned persona—embrace the positives of office-forward, and discount its negatives. So, if you moved the other two personas closer to alignment, you might be able to implement an office-forward strategy successfully.

Let's focus, then, on how to implement office-forward in a way that aligns more of your workforce.

How To Do Office-Forward: Aligning Your People to Your Strategy

When implementing office-forward, choose tactics that will:

- Keep Officers aligned

Officers—an @office-preferring persona who represent about 50% of your workforce—have a great work experience. Yes, they acknowledge the costs to freedom, but they love their company's culture and they believe that culture happens in a building. Because culture trumps the disadvantages of office-forward for Officers, in-office culture must remain a strong aspect of your office-forward strategy.

- Align the half-aligned Progressives

Progressives—an @hybrid-preferring persona who represent about 30% of your workforce—have a bit of a paradoxical work experience. They appreciate that the office is most conducive to relationship-building and career advancement, but they miss the home. Because being able to enjoy their home is a top concern for Progressives, providing flexibility must become a top priority of your office-forward strategy.

- Re-evaluate Producers

Producers—an @home-preferring persona who represent about 20% of your workforce—have a poor work experience. They feel forced to comply with a strategy they disapprove, and for no good reason, too. Because Producers are fully misaligned in the office-forward workplace, they present a challenge you must address strategically.

The tactics we suggest below speak to these three priorities.

Office Space Tactics: The Office, What Happens in the Office
- Under office-forward, the office space itself is a prized possession. But not all spaces are created equal. Design a space that shows concern for people, and let them use it.
  - Office Design: Is your physical work space able to support the needs of all personas? Some prefer collaboration areas; some prefer quiet heads-down spaces; some enjoy a gym, a café, a bar right in the office. Think about the office décor, too. No one likes to work in a drab, dark space. Bright, open spaces attract people more.
  - Workstations: If you do not have personal workstations, office-forward will be a very hard sell. The pick-your-own-desk adventure is universally despised. Expecting people to haul their mouse, cables, and all sorts of other stuff day in and day out is not right. It's a demotivator even for Officers!
  - Office Personalization: If you want people to be in, they must be able to personalize their office space. Rigid rules around office décor won't help. Better yet—encourage people to use the office for personal needs. Could they host a meeting for their club in the office? Could they invite a local student group for an office tour?

- Office Psychology: Nudge employees to see the office in a positive light. Talk about the office with possessive language (such as "our office"). Place a greeter at the door or think of other ways to make employees feel welcome the second they step in. Solicit and implement employees' suggestions for office space improvements. Are you above bribing people with, say, gift cards for coming in?
- The Upshot: When people feel attached to a space, they are more likely to want to be in it. Officers are naturally attached to the office. But other personas need more nudging. Having your own space, utilizing the office for personal purposes, personalizing the space—these are ways to raise people's attachment to the office space, aligning more employees to the Officer persona.

- The office space is important, but what happens in the space is immensely more important.
  - Social Events: Host fun events in the office. The sky's the limit here—a hot salsa contest, jukebox Fridays, an Oscars party, trick-or-treat for the kids, a movie night with popcorn, cooking classes. Encourage employees to dream up events, too. And don't forget—free food!
  - Social Budget: Provide departments with a social budget. They can order pizza for their weekly meeting. They can throw a birthday party, or a baby shower, or a wedding shower, for a teammate.
  - Foot the Bill: Fun is expensive! Be prepared to pay for this.
  - Leadership Presence: Building a lively office is hard work. Leaders must be present, must mingle and engage with employees during social events, must smile and create a positive atmosphere.
  - The Upshot: Officers demand fun in the office. Progressives want relationship-building opportunities. Social events of different scales and sizes will cement Officers' attachment to the workplace, and will move Progressives closer to alignment, too. Producers?... Some will hate this. But some will get more connected with coworkers during these events, moving to a more aligned persona.

Flexibility Tactics
- In the new workplace, flexibility is a must. Office-forward must evolve toward office-with-flexibility.
  - Flexibility for All: Every persona appreciates workplace flexibility. Even Officers, who rarely use it, like to have it available. Progressives appreciate flexibility as it allows them to enjoy their home at least some days. Producers appreciate flexibility as it gives them time for productive workdays in a quiet setting. No more flexibility disparity based on job type or seniority.

- Flexibility is Not Liability. Avoid falling in the old trap of punishing employees who take advantage of the flexibility you offer. Whether you relax your office-forward policy to allow a work-from-home day (as you should!), or whether you revive some of the old flexibility arrangements such as compressed work week, flextime, and the like, ensure employees can use them without fear of being blacklisted. Every persona appreciates that the pandemic normalized flexibility. Every persona expects it to stay that way.
- Soft Approach. Officers will always support your office-forward strategy. To bring Progressives more on board, go softly. Be flexible with employees. Allow time for half-aligned and misaligned personas to adjust.
- The Upshot: Embracing flexibility helps you remove a core concern of all personas: Will flexibility stay? It also demonstrates you learned a valuable lesson during the pandemic: flexibility does not detract from productivity, and in fact, it makes the work experience of all personas better.

HR Tactics: Recruitment, Selection, and Geographic Dispersion

- Office-forward must be properly communicated during recruitment.

  - Realistic Job Previews: Use the social connectivity office-forward promotes as a selling point. What are the upshots of office-forward? Fun in the office, better mentoring and networking, easier collaboration, clear separation of work and life, a real sense of community, numerous opportunities to meet people and form workplace friendships, clearer career paths. However, in your job ads and during the recruitment process, communicate the full reality of office-forward work. What are the office attendance expectations? How much flexibility is there? Is it OK to actually use flexibility? How do you get ahead in the company?
  - The Upshot: There is a large contingent of applicants who are looking for an office-forward employer. Highlighting the positives of office-forward turns it into a recruitment tool. Painting a realistic picture allows applicants to self-select out of the recruitment process, leaving those with greater potential to be aligned in.

- Office-forward must be an element of your applicant selection processes:

  - Selection Criteria: Individuals differ on their proclivity to be social and outgoing, chatty and gregarious. They differ on their natural comfort level with in-person social interactions. But regardless of these personality differences, some individuals have gained in-person communication and interaction skills which they use as needed; others—not so much. When screening candidates, look for markers of in-person sociability skills.

- The Upshot: Including in-person sociability skills in your selection systems will ensure you are hiring people who are more likely to embed themselves in the social fabric of the organization by using their skills. This is important for alignment.
- Office-forward and geographically dispersed employees:
    - Hiring Patterns: Consider your hiring patterns. Are you hiring across geographies? A geographically spread-out workforce threatens the success of your office-forward strategy. Who will report to your office? Empty offices are an office-forward killer. Consider a geographic re-alignment of your workforce.
    - Dispersed Associates: If you had hired, or will continue to hire, remote workers, do not forget them! Send them little gifts to show appreciation. Hold some of your social events virtually so they can participate. Fly them in periodically for facetime with the team. Ensure clear career growth paths, and quality mentoring and networking opportunities. You hired these remote workers. You must help them feel included and equally valued.
    - Team Composition: What is the geographic composition of your teams? For teams with large numbers of dispersed members, team meetings will have to be virtual. This annoys Officers and even Progressives, and makes Producers strongly question why they are Zooming from the office. Consider re-aligning employees to teams based on geographic location. Teams can also work from home on team meeting days to ensure a level playing field.
    - The Upshot: In today's workplace, you cannot avoid having remote employees. Creating a positive work experience for them in an office-forward company is hard, but is an absolute must. At the same time, accounting for the effects of remote workers on your in-office personas is equally important.

Technology Tactics
- Office-forward does not mean going back in time. It means embracing modern work technology to augment and improve the work experience.
    - Technology Skills: Don't risk your employees getting rusty on technology skills they acquired during the pandemic. Even Officers were amazed at how useful technology was for improving their work performance. And while you may have gone back to office, other companies may have not. Your people will need to be skilled in a variety of interaction methods to do business with other organizations.
    - Technology Boundaries: The clear office-home separation is what drives many Officers and even some Progressives to these personas. Respect work-life boundaries. Don't fall for the temptation of

pinging employees at all times. Establish clear expectations for technology use during work hours only.[22]
- The Virtual Office: Remote meetings, remote social events, and other remote interactions are here to stay. Re-visualize technology as an extension of your office space. Branding helps. When your employees enter your virtual office, they must still feel they are a part of your company.
- Purposeful Technology: Use technology to strengthen your in-office culture. Could your CEO and other top leaders create fun informational videos for your "Culture" Slack channel. Could your company's social media channels feature office happenings or employee testimonials? Communicate your culture through technology.
- The Upshot: Not forgetting the lessons and skills learned during the pandemic assuages concerns of all personas. Branding your virtual space and showcasing your culture to internal and external audiences through technology helps with persona alignment.

Building Your New Workplace with a Hybrid Strategy

Why Do Hybrid: The Good and The Bad

Hybrid sits in-between the remote-first and the office-forward visions for the new workplace. More and more employers are betting that as the pendulum continues to swing between the extremes, it will eventually settle in the middle. Speaking of the middle, that's the why of hybrid—finding middle ground between employee flexibility and company culture. A best-of-both-worlds solution.

But does this "why" work? Does hybrid help you strike a balance between flexibility and culture?

There is some evidence that hybrid might be a best-of-both-worlds solution that capitalizes on the positives of both remote-first (flexibility) and office-forward (culture). Hybrid seems helpful for reducing turnover because employees like the flexibility. In a 2022 controlled experiment where 1600 employees in a technology firm were randomly assigned to a 2-day-a-week hybrid schedule, hybrid reduced employee quit rates by 35 percent relative to office-bound colleagues.[23] This meshes with numerous industry reports that hybrid drives turnover down.[24] Hybrid also seems good for culture and connection. In an internal Atlassian study, scheduling some team meetings in person, while keeping most meetings online, led to a 27% increase in feelings of connection.[25] Similarly, in a representative survey, hybrid workers reported a 15% higher sense of connection to both their company, and their team leader, than fully in-office workers.[26] Taken together, the hybrid workplace may create a best-of-both-worlds experience. Hybrid may be good for both flexibility, and culture.

But, there is also evidence that this best-of-both-worlds workplace might be less attainable than it seems. Because hybrid demands finding balance between true opposites: the office and the home, it can also unravel. Firstly, it is difficult for companies to find the right balance. Should structured hybrid (where the company mandates a home-to-office ratio) be implemented? Would fluid hybrid (where employees get to choose their home-to-office ratio) work better? There are pros and cons to both. Secondly, can employees really find a way to make opposites coexist peacefully? That's difficult. In a McKinsey report, hybrid workers unexpectedly reported more obstacles to effective job performance than both fully remote and fully in-office workers.[27] Among the obstacles were things like inability to be their full self at work, inability to learn new skills, mental health issues, and caregiving demands. McKinsey speculated that this may be due to hybrid workers' experiencing the challenges of both office work and remote work simultaneously. Similarly, in a survey of 10,000 workers conducted by WFH Research, hybrid workers reported the highest levels of burnout symptoms, anxiety, and disappointment with own job performance relative to office-going and fully remote workers.[28] Such data suggest that hybrid workers may be in a vicious spiral, paying the price for constantly switching between both worlds, and bearing the negatives of both.

If your "why" for hybrid is building a best-of-both-worlds workplace, you should brace yourself. This might be harder to accomplish than it seems.

Importantly, the research above reveals general trends, without accounting for persona diversity. What we shared with you in Chapter 7 and Chapter 8 does account for how the different personas in the hybrid workplace—the Integrators, the Traditionalists, and the Rebels—experience hybrid work. Remember, Integrators—the fully aligned persona—embrace the home-office switching and see it as an opportunity to (finally) integrate work and life. So, if you moved the other two personas closer to alignment, you might be able to implement a hybrid strategy successfully.

Let's focus, then, on how to implement hybrid in a way that aligns more of your workforce.

How to Do Hybrid: Aligning Your People to Your Strategy

When implementing hybrid, choose tactics that will:

- Keep Integrators aligned

Integrators—an @hybrid-preferring persona who represent about 45% of your workforce—have a great work experience. They enjoy the flexibility, while also enjoying the opportunities for in-person interaction and collaboration in the office. Because the ability to integrate work into life and life into work is a key selling point of hybrid to Integrators, the office-home mix must remain a strong aspect of your hybrid strategy.

- Align the half-aligned Traditionalists

Traditionalists—an @office-preferring persona who represent about 20% of your workforce—have a mostly positive work experience. They like being around their work colleagues in the office. But Traditionalists mostly value the work-life separation the office creates. Because having a routine is a top concern for Traditionalists, the office must remain a core component of your hybrid strategy.

- Align the half-aligned Rebels

Rebels—an @home-preferring persona who represent about 35% of your workforce—have a poor work experience, despite their half-alignment. Their newfound devotion to life leads Rebels to conclude that work-from-home is the only way. To address Rebels' concerns, work-from-home must be a prominent piece of your hybrid strategy.

The tactics we suggest below speak to these three priorities. Notice, however, that the latter two priorities are contradictory. To bring Traditionalists closer to alignment, playing up the office matters; this is more consistent with the structured approach to hybrid. To bring Rebels closer to alignment, playing up the home is important; this is more consistent with the fluid approach to hybrid. Deciding which brand of hybrid you will go for will inform which persona you must focus more of your alignment efforts on.

Office Space Tactics: The Home Office, The Company Office, The Virtual Office
- In hybrid, there are so many office spaces! Each needs attention.
    - The Home Office: Because hybrid involves some degree of company-sanctioned work-from-home, providing support to employees with setting up their home office may be needed. The dilemma here is that the more employees get attached to the home office, the less they want to work from the company office.
    - The Company Office: Under hybrid, it is crucial that the company office can compete with the home office. To make the company office more attractive, ensure it is not empty. Downsizing the office space may be in order. Create office community by re-assigning employees to areas based on office attendance frequency. Provide personal workstations to those who go in more (Integrators and Traditionalists). Desk sharing is OK for those with lower office attendance (Rebels). The dilemma here is that investing in office

re-design may not be justified if your office attendance is low. But to make the office attractive, you must invest in it.
- The Virtual Office: Don't forget that under hybrid, your office extends to virtual space. Your branding has to be featured there. Thankfully, there's no dilemma here.
- Structured vs. Fluid Hybrid: Paying equal attention to the home office, the company office, and the virtual office is unrealistic. Decide on structured hybrid or fluid hybrid. Under "structured," prioritize investing in the office. Under "fluid," prioritize investing in the home office and in virtual space. Realize the implications for employee alignment. Integrators will be aligned with your hybrid efforts either way. Traditionalists will be more aligned under structured hybrid, and Rebels—under fluid hybrid.

HR Tactics: Recruitment, Selection, and Geographic Dispersion
- Hybrid must be properly communicated during recruitment.
  - Realistic Job Previews: Hybrid is a huge selling point. But because there are different brands of hybrid, communicating what *your* hybrid looks like is key. Is there a home-to-office ratio? How is it enforced? What is the office experience like especially when not everyone is in the office? How dispersed is the workforce? How many of my colleagues are local versus in a different geography?
  - The Upshot: Clarifying what hybrid means in your workplace prevents confusion down the road. Painting a realistic picture allows applicants to self-select out of the recruitment process, leaving those with greater potential to be aligned in.
- Hybrid must be an element of your applicant selection processes:
  - Selection Criteria: Under hybrid, employees must regularly switch between the home and the office. Some people thrive in such change-of-scenery scenarios; others—not so much. When screening candidates, look for markers of blending skills, such as openness to change, flexibility, and adaptability.
  - The Upshot: Including blending skills in your selection systems will ensure you are hiring people who are more likely to thrive, not struggle with, the daily or weekly changes in work location and work styles that hybrid requires. This is important for alignment.
- Hybrid and geographically dispersed employees:
  - Hiring Patterns: The more remote employees you have, the emptier your office is. This may present an alignment barrier for office-valuing personas (Traditionalists and Integrators).
  - Local vs. Dispersed Employees: The greater your numbers of both local and dispersed employees, the more complex your HR processes

get. Onboarding new hires is different when they are local versus dispersed. So is mentoring. So is employee engagement. So is training. So is succession planning. Consequently, aligning diverse personas requires doubling-up your efforts to create HR processes that work for all.
- Team Composition: The more dispersed members on a team, the less sense coming to the office makes. If collaboration and team meetings will happen through technology, they can happen at home. Audit your teams' geographic dispersion, and re-assign individuals to teams accordingly, whenever possible. Office attendance rules could then be based on teams' geographic dispersion, not on employees' distance from the office. For example, employees on mostly co-located teams can be expected to be in the office on some days; employees on mostly dispersed teams can be expected to work-from-home most days. This will help with alignment.
- Career Paths: Establish clear career paths that are irrespective of office attendance. You have decided on hybrid (i.e., flexible) work. Ensure you promote equitably. Don't preference people based on office attendance.
- Structured vs. Fluid: Your brand of hybrid must be consistent with your hiring patterns. Quite literally, everything changes based on where you workforce is—how much office space you need; how much your HR processes and practices must double-up; what office attendance rules or expectations make most sense; what career paths and succession planning you establish. Hiring across geographies is great for fluid hybrid. But a geographically spread-out workforce threatens the success of structured hybrid.

Best-of-Both-Worlds Tactics
- Hybrid strategies are about capitalizing on the positives of both the office (such as company culture and employee connection), and the home (such as employee flexibility and work-life integration). For a best-of-both-worlds experience, you must also try to avoid these opposites' negatives.
  - Relationships: Hybrid solves for the problem of employee disconnectedness and poor collaboration. A few in-office days do the trick! Regardless of your brand of hybrid—structured or fluid—ensure regular in-person activities to keep all personas feeling connected and to ease collaboration. Reminder: these activities cannot occur at the expense of virtual interaction activities. Ensure there are plentiful relationship-building opportunities and social events virtually as well.
  - Leadership: Leadership needs to model expected behaviors and norms. You had chosen hybrid; your top brass has to work hybrid. If

top leaders work mostly from home, this seems unfair to employees asked to come in. If top leaders work mostly from the office, this sends a signal that getting ahead means being in the office. Both are inconsistent with a hybrid strategy. Both complicate your persona alignment efforts.
- The Price Tag: Under hybrid, you still need an office. You must (re)build and maintain a strong office culture. But you also need to continue to invest in technology. You must establish and maintain a strong remote culture. Are you prepared to pay for hybrid?
- Structured vs. Fluid: Adopting a fluid hybrid strategy risks slipping into remote-first. Adopting a structured hybrid strategy risks slipping into office-forward. How do you ensure you stay hybrid in the long-run?
- The Upshot: Under hybrid you have one fully aligned persona (the Integrators), two half-aligned personas (the Traditionalists and the Rebels), and no misaligned personas. Getting hybrid right creates a best-of-both-worlds experience. This keeps your aligned persona aligned, and moves the other two personas close to alignment. In other words, hybrid may be uniquely positioned to lead to almost perfect persona alignment. However, beware that the office and the home both have negatives, too. If you don't get hybrid right, you run the risk of creating a worst-of-both-worlds experience. You'll lose you aligned persona, and you'll push the half-aligned personas close to misalignment. Win it all, or lose it all.

Technology Tactics
- Hybrid depends on technology. Technology and physical space need to blend together under hybrid.

    - Meeting Etiquette: Clarify meeting attendance expectations. When a meeting is scheduled in a conference room, are all attendees who are in the office expected to be in the conference room? Can they attend from their desk? This is a huge annoyance, especially to Traditionalists, and especially when leaders do it. That's a low-hanging fruit in terms of bringing personas closer to alignment.
    - Meeting Protocols: In a hybrid workplace, chances are really, really high that meetings will involve remote team members. Conducting meetings in a remote-first fashion is best. It evens the playing field for all attendees.
    - Hybrid Meeting Rooms: Innovate in blending technology and space. Create hybrid meeting rooms where co-located team members can be together and remote team members feel "right there" through sophisticated technology. This does require an investment in collaboration technology hardware (e.g., digital displays and networking) and software (e.g., groupware and team

tools).²⁹ However, it's a more fitting meeting set-up for a hybrid strategy than remote-first meetings.
- Coordination: Adopt collaboration tools that allow for employees to show when they are in the office and out of the office. Meetings can then be set-up accordingly. This also would minimize the mystery of Who's-In that plagues hybrid workplaces.
- The Upshot: No persona in the hybrid workplace had particular qualms about technology. Hybrid workers had embraced technology. But personas had qualms about poor meeting protocols, etiquette, and coordination. Solving these issues will bring personas closer to alignment.

A Note on Clarity

We have one more tactic we need to share. It is the most important one, and it applies across strategies.

Be clear.

You need to clarify your strategy. Remote-first and office-forward seem straight-forward, but certainly, *your* brand of remote-first or office-forward has nuance. What do you mean by these terms? And hybrid? Hybrid is even more difficult to message because it straddles both worlds, and people hear what they want to hear. Ensure a crystal-clear message—what is the strategy, what are the expectations, and why.

Speaking of why, you need to clarify purpose. Why are you doing remote-first, or office-forward, or hybrid? Avoid flat statements like "we are doing this for culture." Everyone knows your motivation is not just altruistic. Say the quiet part out loud. What about the current strategy is not working? How would that change if the new strategy were adopted? People are much more likely to get on-board if you are being truthful, if they see data, and if they hear a vision.

You need to clarify logistics, too. Here's an example. You might be asking people to come into the office if they live within a certain radius, say 30 miles. But did you consider the geographic dispersion of employees' teams? Logistically, it won't make sense for employees whose teams are dispersed to come into an office. Another example: You might be asking people to come into a desk sharing office. But did you consider that people would compare the convenience of their home office to the huge inconvenience of a pick-your-adventure office? And do you even have enough room for everyone? Logistically, you should create an office arrangement based on attendance frequency before asking people to show up. You want to avoid an Amazon-style fiasco of walking back your office attendance requirements.³⁰ A third example: You might be telling people it is OK to work-from-home full-time, but the top brass might be working solely from the office. Did you consider the mixed signals this sends regarding promotion pathways? Logistically, you should align you leaders' work styles to your company's strategy for appropriate messaging and role-modeling. This works in the reverse, too. Are you offering remote work options to top leaders or top talent to attract them, while requesting your rank-and-file to come in? This will very quickly sour all employees on the office, not to mention it'll make them feel like second-class citizens.[31]

To avoid these and many more pitfalls, involve employees in the strategy crafting process. Start by getting an accurate idea of the persona spread in your company. In the next chapter, you will see a Workplace Persona Assessment tool (also available on our website: https://thenewworkplacebook.com/). You can use the tool to survey your workforce. Find out who your aligned personas are. They are your supporters. Lean on them for both feedback and help with strategy implementation. Know who your half-aligned personas are. Ask for their help, too. By involving them, you bring them closer to alignment. Know who your misaligned personas are, and work with them. Often, the most critical voices are the most helpful.

The bottom line: clarify your company's strategy honestly and fully. Clarity is king. It leads to alignment.

A Note on Productivity

You might notice a glaring gap in our analysis of the benefits of remote-first, office-forward, and hybrid. We never talked about productivity. We want to give this hot topic special attention here. Every company that announces its new workplace strategy—regardless of what they choose—touts productivity as a reason. We are staying remote because we've seen productivity rise! We are going back to the office in the name of productivity! We will do hybrid because this is best for productivity!

The truth is, no strategy trumps the other in terms of productivity.

Let's start with remote-first. Meta-analyses from the pre-pandemic days showed modest gains from virtuality. Remote workers had modestly higher job performance than office-workers,[32] and virtual teams were a tad more productive than face-to-face teams.[33] A very important caveat here, though, is that in the pre-pandemic days, remote work was a privilege reserved for the highest performing employees. That's different than today's landscape where remote work is a mass phenomenon. Data from lockdown, when everyone was remote, is also not very relevant. You see, economists did report that productivity grew during lockdown. In the U.S., productivity picked up in 2020 and 2021 (the lockdown years) relative to 2019 (pre-pandemic).[34] But the caveat here is that in lockdown, everyone worked day and night, scared for their job. That's also different from today's much more settled work landscape. Data based on workers' self-reports is also not very useful. Certainly, remote workers report being more productive at home. But office-preferring workers report being more productive at the office. In either case, self-reports of productivity are not quite the same as actual productivity. So, no clear evidence for productivity advantages under remote-first has emerged. Or for productivity *dis*advantages, for that matter!

Let's move to office-forward. We've all heard loud proclamations in the media about how the office is killing productivity. Indeed, data suggest that return-to-office did the office-forward cause no favors. In a study of S&P 500 companies that implemented return-to-office, stock market performance was flat.[35] Asking employees to return to the office neither helped, nor hurt, these companies' shareholder value. Similarly, an Atlassian study reported that only a third of executives with an in-office mandate think that their return-to-office policy has had any impact on productivity.[36] To sum, return-to-office does not boost productivity, though it doesn't "kill" it either. To wit, productivity did drop a bit in 2022 when most return-to-office mandates were implemented, but went back up in 2023 when even more companies joined the return-to-office bandwagon.[37] And anyways, let us remind you again that return-to-office is a tactic. Office-forward is a strategy. What the data is really telling us is that office mandates are neutral for productivity. Beyond the fact that "neutral" is far from "negative," these data don't speak to the effects of the office itself? Companies are playing the long game, and the focus should be on the effects of the strategy (the office), not the tactic (return-to-office). Referring back to data we reviewed earlier on the positive power of proximity for productivity (and other important outcomes, like creativity), the office seems far from a productivity killer.

Finally, let's look at hybrid. Actually, we can't. Hybrid is a pretty new phenomenon, so data is still accruing. For now, it's probably fair to say that hybrid is not bad for productivity. If it were, companies would not be adopting it as fast.

And so, at best, what we can conclude is that no workplace strategy detracts from productivity. As well, no strategy is a silver bullet. It comes down to execution. Can you pull off your strategy? Well, guess what comes in handy here. Yup—alignment! If you make sure your people are aligned, they'll support you. The rest of it, productivity included, will fall into place.

Reflection on How Organizations Align Workplace Strategies to Employee Work Location Preferences It all comes down to aligning your people to your strategy. For each strategy, we outline a number of tactics related to office space, HR processes, and technology. Whether you adopt remote-first, office-forward, or hybrid, you'll have to think through real estate, human capital, and technology issues.

We also outline tactics unique to each strategy. Don't forget relationship-building in remote-first. Remote-first still requires a human touch. Don't forget flexibility in-office-forward. Office-forward needs to offer flexibility to compete. And don't forget best-of-both-worlds in hybrid. Hybrid must capitalize on the positives of *both* office *and* home, while avoiding their negatives.

Most importantly—be clear. That's the most important tactic. Your people need to understand your strategy, and the *why* behind it. As well, you need to understand your people! Know the persona mix you have in your company. Take the pulse of your workforce with our Workplace Persona Assessment tool to find out how misaligned, half-aligned or fully aligned your people are. Adjust your tactics accordingly.

Knowing your people, clearly communicating your strategy, helping everyone understand the why behind the strategy, and implementing the tactics we suggest, puts you on the road to employee—company alignment. That's the prize. When everyone is all in it together, good things happen.

Notes

1. S. Spiegel, *Fully Remote: How to Set up, Lead, and Manage Your Own Successful All-Remote Company* (Fire Engine RED, Inc., 2019).
2. A. Christian, "US Salaries Are Surging for Fully In-Office Jobs," *BBC*, March 25, 2024, https://www.bbc.com/worklife/article/20240322-us-salaries-higher-in-office-jobs.
3. A. Basiouny, "Can Remote Work Help Diversity Recruitment?," *Knowledge at Wharton*, February 6, 2024, https://knowledge.wharton.upenn.edu/article/can-remote-work-help-diversity-recruitment/.
4. R. Gajendran et al., "A Dual Pathway Model of Remote Work Intensity: A Meta-Analysis of Its Simultaneous Positive and Negative Effects," *Personnel Psychology*, 2024, https://doi.org/10.1111/peps.12641.
5. S. Ren, G. Tang, and D. Chadee, "Digital Connectivity for Work after Hours: Its Curvilinear Relationship with Employee Job Performance," *Personnel Psychology* 76, no. 3 (2023): 731–57, https://doi.org/10.1111/peps.12497.
6. Gajendran et al., "A Dual Pathway Model of Remote Work Intensity: A Meta-Analysis of Its Simultaneous Positive and Negative Effects."
7. A. Niven et al., "Are We Working (Too) Comfortably?: Understanding the Nature of and Factors Associated with Sedentary Behaviour When Working in the Home Environment," *Occupational Health Science* 7 (2023): 71–88, https://doi.org/10.1007/s41542-022-00128-6.
8. M. J. Arena et al., "The Adaptive Hybrid: Innovation with Virtual Work., 2(1), 21–29.," *Management and Business Review* 2, no. 1 (2022): 21–29.

9. M. Juchnowicz and H. Kinowska, "Employee Well-Being and Digital Work during the COVID-19 Pandemic," *Information* 12, no. 8 (2021): 293, https://doi.org/10.3390/info12080293.
10. Salesforce, "Optimize Your Virtual Meeting Setup," *Salesforce Trailhead*, n.d., https://trailhead.salesforce.com/content/learn/modules/virtual-meeting-setup-quick-look/optimize-your-virtual-meeting-setup.
11. K. Tangalakis-Lippert, "The Data Is in: RTO Policies Don't Improve Employee Performance or Company Value, but Controlling Bosses Don't Care," *Business Insider*, January 8, 2024, https://www.businessinsider.com/rto-policies-dont-improve-employee-performance-company-value-controlling-bosses-2024-1.
12. B. Elliott, "Return-to-Office Mandates: How to Lose Your Best Performers," *MIT Sloan Management Review*, March 20, 2024, https://sloanreview.mit.edu/article/return-to-office-mandates-how-to-lose-your-best-performers/#:~:text=RTO%20mandates%20do%20have%20an,declines%20in%20employees'%20job%20satisfaction.
13. Gartner, "Gartner HR Research Finds High-Performers, Women, Millennials Are Greatest Flight Risks When Strict Return to Office Mandates Are Implemented," Gartner, January 30, 2024, https://www.gartner.com/en/newsroom/press-releases/2024-01-30-gartner-hr-research-finds-high-performers-women-millennials-are-greatest-flight-risks.
14. D. Atkin and M. K. Chen, "The Returns to Face-to-Face Interactions: Knowledge Spillovers in Silicon Valley,"," *NBER Working Papers* 30,147 (2022), https://doi.org/10.3386/w30147.
15. L. Yang et al., "The Effects of Remote Work on Collaboration among Information Workers," *Nature Human Behaviour* 6 (2022): 43–54, https://doi.org/10.1038/s41562-021-01196-4.
16. Mitchell, "Collaboration Technology Affordances from Virtual Collaboration in the Time of COVID-19 and Post-Pandemic Strategies."
17. N. Emanuel, E. Harrington, and A. Pallais, "The Power of Proximity to Coworkers: Training for Tomorrow or Productivity Today?," *NBER Working Papers* 31,880 (2023), https://doi.org/10.3386/w31880.
18. I. Villamor et al., "Virtuality at Work: A Doubled-Edged Sword for Women's Career Equality?," *Academy of Management Annals* 17, no. 1 (2023), https://doi.org/10.5465/annals.2020.0384.
19. D. Wilkie, "Let It Go: Teaching a Micromanager How to Chill," *Society for Human Resource Management (SHRM)*, March 31, 2020, https://www.shrm.org/topics-tools/news/employee-relations/let-go-teaching-micromanager-how-to-chill.
20. G. Azmat, L. Hensvik, and O. Rosenqvist, "Workplace Presenteeism, Job Substitutability and Gender Inequality," *The Journal of Human Resources* 59, no. 5 (2024), https://doi.org/10.3368/jhr.1121-12014R2.

21. T. Pianese, L. Errichiello, and J. V. da Cunha, "Organizational Control in the Context of Remote Working: A Synthesis of Empirical Findings and a Research Agenda," *European Management Review* 20, no. 2 (2023): 326–45, https://doi.org/10.1111/emre.12515.
22. V. McKeever, "Portugal Makes It Illegal for Bosses to Contact Employees Outside Working Hours," *CNBC*, November 15, 2021, https://www.cnbc.com/2021/11/15/portugal-bans-bosses-from-contacting-employees-outside-working-hours.html.
23. N. Bloom, R. Han, and J. Liang, "How Hybrid Working from Home Works Out," *NBER Working Papers* 30,292 (2022), https://doi.org/10.3386/w30292.
24. B. Loggins, "Wharton Experts Analyzed This Company's 4-Day Workweek Pilot. Here's What They Learned," *Fast Company*, April 1, 2024, https://www.fastcompany.com/91072238/wharton-experts-4-day-workweek-pilot-results-exos.
25. Atlassian, "Lessons Learned: 1,000 Days of Distributed at Atlassian," *Atlassian*, 2024, https://www.atlassian.com/solutions/distributed/lessons-learned.
26. Future Forum, "Amid Spiking Burnout, Workplace Flexibility Fuels Company Culture and Productivity," *Future Forum* (blog), February 2023, https://futureforum.com/research/future-forum-pulse-winter-2022-2023-snapshot/.
27. A. Dua et al., "Americans Are Embracing Flexible Work—and They Want More of It" (McKinsey, June 23, 2022), https://www.mckinsey.com/industries/real-estate/our-insights/americans-are-embracing-flexible-work-and-they-want-more-of-it.
28. J. M. Barrero, N. Bloom, and S. J. Davis, "Why Working from Home Will Stick," National Bureau of Economic Research Working Paper 28,731, 2021, https://wfhresearch.com/wp-content/uploads/2024/12/WFHResearch_updates_December2024.pdf.
29. C. Clifford, "Google's Plan for the Future of Work: Privacy Robots and Balloon Walls," *The New York Times*, April 30, 2021, https://www.nytimes.com/2021/04/30/technology/google-back-to-office-workers.html.
30. H. Hadero, "Amazon Is Requiring Workers to Be in the Office Five Days a Week Starting next Year," *WBUR (Boston NPR)*, September 17, 2024, https://www.wbur.org/news/2024/09/17/amazon-back-to-office-policy-seaport.
31. R. A. Smith, "Return-to-Office Mandates Apply to Everyone, except a Chosen Few," *The Wall Street Journal*, January 26, 2025, https://www.wsj.com/lifestyle/workplace/return-to-office-mandates-apply-to-everyone-except-a-chosen-few-c77d9559.
32. Gajendran et al., "A Dual Pathway Model of Remote Work Intensity: A Meta-Analysis of Its Simultaneous Positive and Negative Effects."

33. R. Purvanova and R. Kenda, "The Impact of Virtuality on Team Effectiveness in Organizational and Non-Organizational Teams: A Meta-Analysis," *Applied Psychology* 71, no. 3 (2022): 1082–1131, https://doi.org/10.1111/apps.12348.
34. U.S. Bureau of Labor Statistics, "U.S. Bureau of Labor Statistics Productivity and Remote Work," U.S. Bureau of Labor Statistics, 2024, https://www.bls.gov/productivity/notices/2024/productivity-and-remote-work.htm.
35. Tangalakis-Lippert, "The Data Is in: RTO Policies Don't Improve Employee Performance or Company Value, but Controlling Bosses Don't Care."
36. Atlassian, "Lessons Learned: 1,000 Days of Distributed at Atlassian."
37. U.S. Bureau of Labor Statistics, "Economic News Release: Total Factor Productivity, 2023," U.S. Bureau of Labor Statistics, 2023, https://www.bls.gov/news.release/prod3.nr0.htm.

CHAPTER 10

How Do Leaders Align Their Teams

Are you a mid-level manager, charged with leading a team? Regardless of whether you work for a remote-first, office-forward, or hybrid company, we are certain you are being asked to align your team to your company's workplace strategy. At the same time, we are certain you are hearing various, likely contradictory, concerns from your team members. You're feeling pressure from above and pressure from below.

How do you tackle this up-down navigation challenge?

First up: team building. You can't align your team if you don't address the persona diversity on your team head-on. What's your mix of home-preferring, office-preferring, and hybrid-preferring team members? Are your team members aware of each other's work location preferences? Do they understand why teammates' have these preferences? What drives teammates to prefer the home, the office, or a mix of both? Misconceptions of who prefers what work location and why abound. To help your team find common ground, we'll start with an Awareness Raising Primer. We'll share myths versus facts about the different work location preferences employees have developed. We'll then describe a Finding Common Ground team-building activity. We'll show you how to use the Awareness Raising Primer as you lead your team through this activity. This discussion is important to have because misconceptions, if not corrected, quickly turn into fault lines that may split your team apart. If team members fail to appreciate each other's diverse—yet equally valid—points of view, it'd be difficult for you to align your team to your organization's remote-first, office-forward, or hybrid strategy.

Now you're ready to focus on team alignment. The trick is to implement team-wide tactics designed to align the team to your organization's remote-first, office-forward, or hybrid strategy, while also aligning your team internally. The latter requires identifying and addressing a pain point that all personas on your team share, while also getting each persona to make concessions. Striking this trifecta—creating tactics in line with the strategy, rallying personas around a shared goal, and getting personas to each give up something—is how you navigate your up-down challenge to accomplish your mission: aligning your team.

Awareness Raising Primer: Myths Versus Facts

You and your team members are likely aware of the varied work location preferences on your team. You and everyone else surely know that Erica prefers to work from the office, Jermaine prefers to work-from-home, and Arabia is somewhere in the middle, preferring a hybrid approach. But when we talk to companies about persona diversity, we are always struck by how inaccurate, even biased, people's intuitive explanations are regarding who prefers what work location and why. It's always quite eye opening for leaders and employees alike to learn about the different personas' actual points of view.

Part of the reason for these inaccuracies is simply human nature. We all make assumptions, and they are often unconsciously informed by stereotypes. The other part of the reason for these inaccuracies is that the topic of work location preference has become a hot button issue. People don't talk about this topic lest they jeopardize their standing in the organization, or offend a coworker with a different preference. You'd be surprised how often we hear comments like this:

> I feel like it's kind of a sensitive subject sometimes when one person is really strong around wanting to work from home and the other one is strong around wanting to be in the office. So we don't talk about this in too much detail but just around the watercooler. (Clara, sales representative)

One must wonder what conclusions are reached around the watercooler.

Fortunately, both stereotypical assumptions and lack of information could be corrected with intentional discussions aimed at dispelling assumptions, recognizing differences, and finding common ground. This could be a great team-building activity for your next team meeting or retreat.

As a team leader, you'll need two tools: knowledge of myths versus facts, and discussion prompts to help steer the team toward a productive, alignment-seeking discussion.

Let's start with knowledge. Here's an at a glance view—we call it Awareness Raising Primer—that highlights what people assume about the various personas versus what our research reveals about them. First, the home-preferring personas:

Table 10.1. focuses on myths about demographics (who). Notice how some common assumptions are fully incorrect. For example, it's entirely untrue that "young people" prefer @home. In fact, as we showed in Chapter 2 older individuals are much more prone to develop the @home preference. Same thing for "women in general." It's both men *and* women, and it's mostly *married* men and women. Some common assumptions may be on the right track, but need careful nuance. For example, "moms" are seen as @home preferers. This may be true in cases of moms with *young* children, whether single or married. Finally, some "who" factors are not even on people's radar. Race actually predicts the @home preference—racial minority employees prefer to work from home more than racial majority employees, and this needs to be recognized as a factor.

Table 10.1 The home-preferring personas: Who are the @home preferers?

Who Are the Home-Preferring Personas? *(Avatars, Rebels, and Producers)*	
Myths (What People Think)	Facts (What Research Shows)
Young people	Older people (35 and up)
Women in general	Married Men and Women
Women with Children	Single or married women with young children
Rank-and-file employees	Employees across the hierarchy: - Rank-and-file employees - Team leads - Executives (especially male)
–	Racially diverse

The myths that need debunking go beyond demographics (who) and into character traits (why):

As Table 10.2. shows, the common assumption that home-preferring personas "do not care about work" is false. As we showed in Chapter 3, Chapter 5, and Chapter 7, all home-preferring personas care about their work output. They may prioritize family and life, but this is very different from de-prioritizing work. In all, there are six "why" myths that need debunking.

Table 10.2 The home-preferring personas: Why do they prefer @home?

Why Do Home-Preferring Personas Prefer @Home? *(Avatars, Rebels, and Producers)*	
Myths (What People Think)	Facts (What Research Shows)
Don't care about work	Prioritize family & life, but care about their work output
Lazy	Focused on productivity, not presenteeism
Not interested in career advancement	Understand remote work may make it harder to advance

(continued)

Table 10.2 (continued)

Why Do Home-Preferring Personas Prefer @Home? (Avatars, Rebels, and Producers)	
Myths (What People Think)	Facts (What Research Shows)
Introverted, almost anti-social	Do not look to the office for social relationships
Think of work-from-home as free daycare	Kids (if any) in daycare or school
Disconnected from work and from the employer	Disconnected in cases of misalignment (i.e., Producers, Rebels). Fully connected in cases of alignment (i.e., Avatars).

Additionally, our research uncovered a number of new "why's" about our home-preferring friends. You and your team should become aware of those factors, too (Table 10.3).

Table 10.3 The home-preferring personas: New research-based findings about "why"

Why Do Home-Preferring Personas Prefer @Home? (Avatars, Rebels, and Producers)	
What Research Reveals	
1	Value independence and autonomy.
2	Feel work-from-home allows them to be their own person, not just a hired gun.
3	Find remote work authentic, and office work—performative.
4	Find the social stimulation in the office distracting to focus and job performance.
5	Do not miss the office, especially if desk sharing or hoteling is implemented.
6	Do not identify with the office; the office is not a source of identity.
7	Attached to the home office.
8	Feel more productive in quiet spaces with no interruptions (like the home office).
9	Prioritize the flexibility and convenience of work-from-home over other considerations (e.g., workplace relationships).
10	Find work-from-home better for mental health; less stressful.
11	Have developed comfort and skills with using technology for social purposes.
12	Prefer technology-mediated collaboration (can hide nerves when presenting; can quickly IM someone with a question).
13	Feel comfortable, welcome, and at home in the virtual office.
14	Do not miss in-office social happenings as they can happen virtually just as well.
15	Find occasional in-person social interactions sufficient for feeling connected to coworkers & the organization.

(continued)

Table 10.3 (continued)

Why Do Home-Preferring Personas Prefer @Home?
(Avatars, Rebels, and Producers)

What Research Reveals	
16	Proactively seek or happily participate in virtual engagement and networking opportunities.
17	Share positive memories of work-from-home days—either personal (working from a friend's house) or team-related (fun virtual team activities).
18	Able to create work-life boundaries without an external structuring tool (e.g., the commute).
19	Find company nudges to get people back in the office disingenuous.
20	Would look for new employment if remote work is not an option.

Wow, right? Look at this wealth of information! Doesn't it paint a much, much fuller picture of our @home-preferring colleagues? You'd definitely want your team members to add accurate "who's" and "why's" to their thinking about @home-preferring teammates.

Later on in the chapter, we will discuss how you can use these Awareness Raising Primers about the @home personas as you engage your team in a Finding Common Ground team-building activity.

Now, let's move into our Awareness Raising Primers for office-preferring personas.

Similar to Tables 10.1., 10.4. focuses on myths about demographics (who). It points to three fully or partially incorrect common assumptions. For example, it's not "older people" who prefer @office; it's actually less experienced, younger employees. It also points to a who factor that is not on people's radar: race.

Table 10.4 The office-preferring personas: Who are the @office preferers?

Who Are the Office-Preferring Personas?
(Officers, Traditionalists, and Community-seekers)

Myths (What People Think)	Facts (What Research Shows)
Older people	People with less work experience (5 yrs or less)
Men	Single Men and Women (except single women with children)
Bosses (especially male)	Employees across the hierarchy: - Rank-and-file employees - Team leads - Executives (especially female)
–	Racial majority

Next, let's go beyond myths about demographics (who) and into myths about character traits (why):

As Table 10.5. shows, there are five "why" myths about office-preferring personas that need debunking. For example, it is incorrect to assume that @office preferers are "company loyalists." They may believe that "culture happens in a building" but this is a clue to office-preferers' preference for in-person interactions, not some sign of blind followership of the powers-that-be.

Table 10.5 The office-preferring personas: Why do they prefer @office?

Why Do Office-Preferring Personas Prefer the Office?
(Officers, Traditionalists, and Community-seekers)

Myths (What People Think)	Facts (What Research Shows)
Career-obsessed workaholics	Prioritize work-in-office but expect flexibility for better work-life balance
Old-fashioned, not hip with the times	Need the structure and clear work-life separation that "going to work" (i.e., office work) provides
Over-the-top sociable	Value work relationships and see coworkers as friends
Techno-phobic	Believe technology-mediated collaboration and interactions are "not the same," but see technology as integral to innovation in the modern workplace
Company loyalist	Love their company culture and believe culture happens in a building

Let's now look at the additional "why's" about @office personas our research uncovered:

Another wow, right? The information in Table 10.6. really builds out the @office persona.

Table 10.6 The office-preferring personas: New research-based findings about "why"

Why Do Office-Preferring Personas Prefer the Office?
(Officers, Traditionalists, and Community-seekers)

What Research Reveals	
1	Feel pride in, identify with, and feel attached to the office/building.
2	Feel a sense of nostalgia for the days when the office was full of life and energy.
3	Describe vivid memories from the office (e.g., company-wide events; fun team activities, meaningful interactions with coworkers).
4	Go to the office even when optional.

(continued)

Table 10.6 (continued)

Why Do Office-Preferring Personas Prefer the Office?
(Officers, Traditionalists, and Community-seekers)

What Research Reveals	
5	Prefer working in in-person environments for stimulation and energy.
6	Feel more productive and creative in the office due to serendipitous interactions and spontaneous collaboration.
7	Lose sense of work meaning, work enjoyment, self-identity, purpose, and pride when working from home.
8	Feel disconnected from company/team/colleagues at home.
9	Mental health affected when working from home due to loneliness and/or lack of structure.
10	Home office inadequate or non-existent.
11	Distracted by house chores at home and feel less productive. Can focus better in the office.
12	Dislike the physical toll of at home work (e.g., more sitting; Zoom fatigue; headache from headsets).
13	Strongly prefer face-to-face communication and interactions over technology-mediated communication and interactions.
14	Experience technology-mediated communication and interactions as scripted, sterile, unreal, and inauthentic.
15	Wish more peers would come back to work (may hope for stricter mandates; may try to role-model office attendance).
16	Would look for new employment if office work is not an option.

Overall, many "who" and "why" assumptions about @office preferers are wrong and hurtful. As well, much is missing from the public's understanding of our office-preferring friends. You want your team members to correct their "who" and "why" assumptions, as well as to add accurate "who's" and "why's" to their thinking about @office-preferring teammates.

We'll get back to the topic of how to use these Awareness Raising Primers about @office-preferring personas later on.

For now, we'll move into our final Awareness Raising Primer set, the one focused on hybrid-preferring personas:

Table 10.7. focuses on myths about demographics (who). It points to three common assumptions about @hybrid preferers. For example, many tend to assume that women with children have an outsized preference for hybrid work. But, as you may recall from Chapter 2 no clear demographic pattern emerges for the @hybrid preferers.

Table 10.7 The hybrid-preferring personas: Who are the @hybrid preferers?

Who Are the Hybrid-Preferring Personas? (Integrators, Progressives, and Centrists)	
Myths (What People Think)	Facts (What Research Shows)
Young people Women in general Women with Children	No clear demographic profile

Next, let's go beyond myths about demographics (who) and into myths about character traits (why):

Table 10.8. shows three "why" myths about hybrid-preferring personas that need debunking. For example, it is incorrect to assume that @hybrid preferers simply "value flexibility." They may value it for themselves, but they are some of the loudest advocates of the idea that flexibility means different things to different people.

Table 10.8 The hybrid-preferring personas: Why do they prefer @hybrid?

Why Do Hybrid-Preferring Personas Prefer Hybrid? (Integrators, Progressives, and Centrists)	
Myths (What People Think)	Facts (What Research Shows)
Use hybrid as an excuse to get away from the office as much as possible	Believe work no longer needs to happen on a 9-5, five-days-a-week schedule
Overly agreeable, can be pushed either way	Best-of-both-worlds thinking; value a middle ground approach
Value flexibility	Value flexibility but advocate that flexibility means different things to different people

There are also additional "why's" about @hybrid personas that our research uncovered (Table 10.9).

Table 10.9 The hybrid-preferring personas: New research-based findings about "why"

Why Do Hybrid-Preferring Personas Prefer Hybrid? (Integrators, Progressives, and Centrists)	
What Research Reveals	
1	See value in both the office, and the home.

(continued)

Table 10.9 (continued)

Why Do Hybrid-Preferring Personas Prefer Hybrid?
(Integrators, Progressives, and Centrists)

What Research Reveals	
2	Enjoy the office perks (e.g., gym, cafeteria), but mostly value the office for its ability to bring people together.
3	Enjoy the home office; miss their home office on at-office days.
4	Vivid memories of both at-office, and at home workdays and experiences.
5	Enjoy the flexibility to do quiet work at home, and collaborative work at the office.
6	Value work relationships and enjoy interactions with work colleagues.
7	Like to engage in social interactions, but also like alone days.
8	Miss work colleagues, but get enough "social juice" from a few in-office days.
9	Comfortable collaborating and interacting in person, or through technology. See value in both.
10	Believe technology is a good substitute for face-to-face communication if used intentionally and purposefully.
11	Comfortable working in a personal workstation office, or in a hoteling arrangement office.
12	Concerned about visibility, so go to the office to be seen.
13	Lament empty offices; the empty office makes them feel nostalgic.
14	Concerned about work organizations forgetting lessons learned during the pandemic about work, life, productivity, technology, and others.
15	Concerned about the pendulum swinging too hard back to office, or too hard toward remote work.

Clearly, team members should be aware of these research-based why's about @hybrid employees. And, though the incorrect "who" and "why" assumptions about @hybrid preferers are significantly fewer and significantly less controversial, they still need to be clarified.

Now, let's turn to how you lead your team through this possibly challenging conversation Our Finding Common Ground team-building activity should help.

FINDING COMMON GROUND: A TEAM-BUILDING ACTIVITY

To lead your team through a meaningful discussion on persona diversity, we suggest you follow a bit of a script.

Start broad, with a general discussion about pro's and con's of different work modalities. This will make the team-building session feel like a safe space, and most importantly—it will bring out team members' different perspectives. Next, time to dispel myths with our Awareness Raising Primers. This will help your team members feel seen and heard. Finally, steer the discussion toward how your team can find better alignment—both internally, and to your company's strategy. Now that team members understand the diversity of viewpoints on the team, how could they work together, as a collective? What might the different personas be willing to give up for better team alignment? What would the different personas most wish others would respect about them?

Step One: A General Discussion

To get the ball rolling, we recommend you pose the three starter questions listed below. As you can see, they are meant to elicit general thoughts and feelings about work-from-home, work-from-office, and hybrid work—the whole gamut. Everyone has thoughts on each. Invite everyone to chime in, or better yet—call on people to ensure that everyone speaks.

> 1. What are some benefits to work-from-office that we have seen over the years, or even personally experienced?
> 2. How about work-from-home? What are some benefits of work-from-home that we can think based on what we've seen or even personally experienced?
> 3. And how about hybrid work? What benefits have we seen or experienced with that approach?

Once people have warmed up and shared some general thoughts, you can move the discussion into deeper waters. Make the questions a bit more personal. You've already asked what your team members think generally about the different work modalities. Now, ask team members to share what they personally like *and* dislike about *each*.

Here are some questions you can use. Notice how they use the word "you" (whereas the general starter questions used the word "we"). At the same time, notice that each question asks about each work modality. This makes questions feel safer.

> 1. What do you like about working from the office? Dislike? How about working from home? What do you like, and what do you dislike? And working hybrid? What are your likes and dislikes?
> 2. What do you find easier to do from the office? More difficult? How about from home? What do you find easier to do or accomplish, and what is harder? Are there any tasks or activities that are best accomplished through hybrid work? How about any that do not work with hybrid work?

3. What would make you feel included or welcome in the office? What would make you feel included or welcome or give you a sense of belonging when working from home? And when you work hybrid, how is your sense of welcome and inclusion impacted?
4. When you are at the office, how do you feel? What are some feelings or emotions or thoughts that you experience or think about when you are at the office? How about when you are at home? And when you work hybrid?
5. What words come to mind when you think of the office? And when you think of your home office? What words come to mind to describe hybrid work?

It might be a good idea to whiteboard what people share, whether using a physical whiteboard (if holding the team-building session in person), or a virtual whiteboard (if holding the session remotely or hybrid). This makes the personal pro's and con's visible and easier to keep in mind as the discussion continues.

As you listen to people speak, pay special attention to what we call "counter viewpoints." Counter viewpoints are contradictory to the person's underlying work location preference.

For example, team members with a strong @home preference may talk about the benefits of office work:

> I just think that when you're not in the office, it's harder to buy into the company culture. I think working from home, it's more, you just kind of want to be and do things on your own (Graham, account manager)

> It's the camaraderie and time with my other teammates where we can enjoy, you know, just general banter or going to the gym, just seeing other human beings, having talked to someone besides someone in my family unit... That's what really drives wanting to go in. Just, you know, being around other human beings and not just staring at my screen and talking to everybody with my ear buds on. (Vera, senior treasury manager)

These same team members, the @home preferers, may talk about the disadvantages of remote work:

> I think it [work-from-home] kind of just lends this more professional perspective, there's nothing really personal about it. I think if you personally know someone, you're willing to do X, Y, and Z. But if you don't personally know someone, maybe you're not willing to go the extra mile so much, or you don't sympathize with them as much, or you know, all sorts of different things. And so, I'm sure it does affect the way that we work. (Katherine, assistant project manager)

Counter viewpoints can also be expressed by office preferers. For example, team members with a strong @office preference may talk about the benefits of work-from-home:

> It's easy to be home, you know. Like, you don't have to drive to the office and have lunch in the office, you know. It's just really easy. (Andrew, division vice president)
>
> I would say convenient, that's probably a good word. It's more convenient for me as a mom of 3 and a husband who travels. (Emily, assistant division vice president)
>
> I get more done. If I'm at home, I can get through stuff without interruptions. If I'm in the office, there are a lot of interruptions, just people stopping by, or you get up to go get a drink and you stand and talk to somebody. So it's less interrupted time at home. (Maria, division vice president)

These same @office preferers may talk about the disadvantages of office work, too:

> If we want to be competitive and we want to recruit and retain our employees, we'd have to be flexible. I think that's the new world. And now that employees have tasted what this means for family--to be at home sometimes, to be more accessible to your kids, to be able to just do your house chores during the day and not have to pile it all to the evening or on the weekend? I really, I think it would be a disservice if we ever went back to "you have to be in the office eight to five." Who even thought that you have to be in the office eight to five to get your work done? Like, somebody measured that? You could sit down and get something done in two hours. So I think the flexibility, it really was needed and I'm glad that it's here. (Elena, division vice president)

Finally, team members with a strong @hybrid preference may talk about the disadvantages of hybrid work:

> When I was going in five days a week, it was the normalcy, like, that's just what you did every day and you just got in the routine. Now, as I'm going in usually three days a week, there's not as much consistency in routine. So, I feel like, you know, I got to adapt back and forth a little bit more, too. (Henry, director of consulting)
>
> I will say, I have a harder time letting go of work when I'm at home versus when I'm at the office. I know when I get up from my desk and pack up, I'm done for the day. But at home, I feel like I have to check my phone or go back to my remote desk and take a look at what's going on. (Patrick, treasury analyst)

After everyone had spoken, you should summarize the discussion, taking special care to call out any counter viewpoints you heard. You can say something like:

> So interesting to hear we can all see benefits and disadvantages of office and remote work! Totally agree with Graham, Vera, and Katherine that the office might be more conducive to relationship-building. And yes, as they said, work-from-home can make you feel sort of siloed and disconnected a little bit. But also, such great points from Andrew, Emily, Maria and Elena! True, the office can be a zoo—too many distractions, right? And work-from-home, its flexibility is definitely such a plus! It's also super interesting to hear that even hybrid work, which everyone keeps on saying is the way of the future, is not immune to issues, just like Henry and Patrick pointed out. Great stuff, team!

Trust us, it's not going to go unnoticed—especially after your summary—that @office preferers sometimes sound like @home preferers, that @home preferers sometimes sound like @office preferers, and even that @hybrid prefers see problems with hybrid. Hearing counter viewpoints will make it clear that the different personas have a shared belief: office work, remote work, and hybrid work each have benefits *and* disadvantages. That's a great foundation for finding common ground.

It's now time to raise awareness of inaccurate assumptions and dispel some myths.

Step Two: Dispel Myths and Raise Awareness

We recommend that you have printed copies of our Awareness Raising Primers (or downloaded PDFs if holding the team-building virtually). These tools can be found on our website: https://thenewworkplacebook.com/. Go ahead and distribute the Primers to your team. Start with the "who" myths-vs-facts factsheet (Tables 10.1., 10.4., and 10.7.). You can say:

> OK, we've learned about everyone's personal likes and dislikes. It's clear that although we each have a preference for one work modality over others, we see advantages and disadvantages to each. That's great. Now, let's dig deeper.

> Here's some information about who we THINK people with different work preferences are versus what is ACTUALLY true. Let's look at the

> lists with myths versus facts about demographics. I'd like us to share one thing that resonates with each of us about these lists. I'll start. Since I am an @home (or @office, or @hybrid) preferer, I'll pick something from that sheet. Like the sheet here says, I often feel misunderstood because… OR Like the sheet here says, I feel validated because… .

Once you've shared your truth, invite your team members to share theirs. Let's work out some possible If-Then scenarios to give you some ideas of how you may lead this discussion:

- If a young employee shared something like this:
    - "I'm unhappy at home, working from home, and I want to see you people and feel a part of something" (Hannah, senior analyst). Or like this:
    - "With work-from-home, I feel like I haven't been my entire person for the last three years. The way I've phrased it is, I'm like a soulless husk" (Grant, senior data analyst).
- Then, use this as an opportunity to talk about the myth that…
    - …young people prefer @home. Point to Table 10.4. which shows that in fact, young employees prefer @office (or at most @hybrid). Try to specifically engage the more experienced members of your team. In our research, experienced employees were most likely to be under the misconception that young people want @home. They kept on telling us this: "Younger folks, for them, remote work is what they're looking for" (Katie, associate vice president of sales). Seek commitments about how team members will more actively engage, in person, with the younger members of the team going forward. Make a commitment of your own.
- If a mom shared something like this:
    - "I have two kids, two dogs, and a husband and it's a lot, even though the kids are at school. So the positives from the office are that I can separate myself from home" (Jessica, area director).
- Then, use this as an opportunity to talk about the myth that…
    - …women, and especially moms, prefer @home. Point to Table 10.1. which shows that women are just as likely as men to prefer @home, @office, or @hybrid. That table also shows that moms *are* more likely to prefer @home but only if their kids are very young.
    - Apropos, this is also an opportunity to point to Table 10.2. which shows a related myth—that people with children prefer @home

because it's like free day care. This is far from true. People with kids do have their kids in daycare, as your team member will surely attest to.
- Lead the team into a reflection on what we tend to assume about women in the workplace, especially about moms. Make concrete commitments to support moms on your team.

- If a dad, who also happens to be a high-ranking team member, shared something like this:
  - "My father identified himself as his career. He retired, immediately had health problems, and passed. Seeing that, I decided to place value aside from my career. And while this happened because of my dad, virtual work absolutely made it possible. In fact, when my mom had some health issues, I was able to go down and help her. I was able to make this choice because of my son-first-career-second attitude, but also because of my remote position" (Mike, product development director).
- Then, use this as an opportunity to talk about the myth that…
  - …men, and especially men in executive roles, prefer @office. Point to Table 10.4. which shows that in fact, men are just as likely as women to prefer @office, @home, or @hybrid. You can also point to Table 10.1. which shows that executive men are more likely to prefer @home than executive women. Lead the team into another much-needed reflection: this time, a reflection on what we assume about men in the workplace, especially higher-ranking men, and how we forget that men who are dads do have a father identity, too. Make concrete commitments to support men with caregiving obligations on your team.

Imagine the impact of this sharing session for breaking down assumptions and stereotypes about who prefers what work modality.

You should also stimulate discussion around the lists of "why" myths-vs-facts (Tables 10.2., 10.5., and 10.8.). You can say:

> I think that what we've learned thus far is, definitely don't judge a book by its cover! This is great, team. Let's look at the other myths-vs-facts lists, the ones that talk about WHY different people have different work preferences. I'll start again and share something that resonates with me from this list.

Once you've shared, invite others to join. Let's again work out some possible If-Then scenarios:

- If an @home-preferring team member shared something like this:
    - "Remote work probably is keeping me here. That's one of the holds the company now has on me" (Paul, claims manager). Or like this:
    - "I think remote is something that I would want to pursue long term but then I think that would hinder my moving up. Because, if I'm being honest, you don't see any of the upper management or higher-level leaders working remote; they're always in office" (Karen, financial analyst intern).
- Then, use this as an opportunity to talk about the myth that…
    - …@home preferers are "not interested in career advancement." Point to Table 10.2. which shows that in fact, @home preferring teammates "understand remote work may make it harder to advance." Remember the "golden handcuffs" analogy we discussed in Chapter 4? Use that to clarify that @home preferring teammates choose remote work over career advancement, and that they don't love having to make this choice. Seek commitments about how team members will more intentionally include @home preferring teammates in challenging and high-visibility projects versus just assume these teammates don't care. Make a commitment to overcome any "out-of-sight-out-of-mind" bias you may subconsciously harbor.
- If an @office-preferring team member shared something like this:
    - "Moving to in-person, it was a lot easier to become friends with my coworkers" (Ying, assistant analyst). Or like this:
    - "It's random things, like grabbing lunch with some friends" (Jake, client analyst).
- Then, use this as an opportunity to talk about the myth that…
    - …@office preferers are "over-the-top sociable." Point to Table 10.5. which shows that in fact, @office preferring teammates "value work relationships and see coworkers as friends." Ask you team, what important keyword stands out when our @office preferring teammates talk about office relationships? It's the word "friend." Use this ah-ha to clarify that @office preferers don't just like to talk (though that's certainly a bonus for them). Rather, they are interested in building relationships. Brainstorm ideas about how the team can capitalize on @office teammates' relational skills. Better yet, ask those teammates to put their relational skills to work and help the team become more cohesive!
- If an @hybrid-preferring team member shared something like this:
    - "You have more agency over your own time. I like being able to, you know, do chores in the middle of the day, or take off early to go run.

But then, if I need to hop on and do something on a Saturday for work, I can do that. So, I think it's less about the routine for me, less about the time commitment, and more about the flow" (Kevin, junior analyst).

- Then, use this as an opportunity to talk about the myth that…
  - …@hybrid preferers are "using hybrid as an excuse to get away from the office." Point to Table 10.8. which shows that in fact, @hybrid-preferring teammates "believe work no longer needs to happen on a 9-5, five-days-a-week schedule." Challenge your team to look at @hybrid-preferring teammates' workstyle from a new angle. Perhaps these teammates are onto something—a new "work-life flow " that capitalizes on hybrid's flexibility to achieve better work-life integration. Could the rest of the team benefit from learning about and even adopting this new workstyle? Could @hybrid teammates share their recipe for that?

To wrap up the myths-vs-facts part of the discussion, you can say:

> Wow, team, I'm so proud of our open discussion to break down incorrect WHO and WHY assumptions! My lesson-learned is that even though I may have a certain work modality preference, I now have a deeper appreciation for others' viewpoints. I also feel you're better understanding me now. And so, I hope all of us are feeling seen and heard. I'm also glad we were able to make some specific commitments. As a final part of our discussion, let's expand on how we could use our strengths to become a better-aligned team.

Step Three: Team Alignment

You're now only one step away from reaching your ultimate goal with the Finding Common Ground team-building activity: aligning your team to your company's remote-first, office-forward, or hybrid strategy. That's the most challenging part. As a team leader, you do have some leeway in what alignment for your team looks like. At the same time, your company's overall strategy does present limitations. The trick is to agree on team-wide practices that are (a) in line with the company strategy, (b) satisfy an important need for each persona, but (c) require that each persona gives up something. It's a trifecta!

We recommend you utilize the "New Research-Based Findings" factsheets (Tables 10.3., 10.6., and 10.9.) to steer this discussion. Because this looks differently depending on your organization's strategy, we outline ideas for remote-first, office-forward, and hybrid contexts in separate sections next.

Team Alignment in Remote-First Companies
Remember, in remote-first organizations, the predominant persona are the fully aligned Avatars (@home-preferring persona). There are also smaller but still significant numbers of half-aligned Centrists (@hybrid-preferring persona) and fully misaligned Community-seekers (@office-preferring persona). The specific spread of personas on your team should have become clear through the Awareness Raising discussion you just completed.

To align your team to your company's remote-first strategy, it makes sense to keep the Avatars aligned, move Centrists closer to alignment, and move Community-seekers closer to half-alignment. We recommend you are very clear in your communication that to align the team, everyone has to compromise a little. You can say:

> Team, our challenge is to find a way to function as a cohesive team within the boundaries of our remote-first workplace. How could we do this in a way that respects our personal preferences? I suggest finding common ground and a way to compromise. What is it that we have in common? And what are some differences that we would have to live with? Let's look at these lists of New Research-Based Findings here. They identify our differences, but also point to some characteristics we may share.

Then, steer the discussion to an important shared characteristic—all personas care about workplace relationships. Avatars "proactively seek or happily participate in virtual engagement and networking opportunities" (Table 10.3.); Centrists "value work relationships and enjoy interactions with work colleagues" (Table 10.9.); Community-seekers "value work relationships and see coworkers as friends" (Table 10.5.). So, the common ground is that all personas in remote-first organizations want to engage with coworkers.

Next, you must surface the differences among the personas on the issue of workplace relationships. Avatars prioritize productivity versus being social, and they prefer technology-mediated interactions over in-person interactions (Table 10.3.); Centrists care about both productivity and the social stuff, and they feel comfortable in both "real" reality and virtual reality (Table 10.9.); Community-seekers place high value on social interactions at work, and prefer in-person over technology-mediated interactions (Table 10.6.). So, compromises will have to be made around the issues of **relational frequency** and **relational media**.

Summarize these important Ah-ha's by saying this:

> Team, it seems to me we all care about the relationships we have with each other. We want to engage with one another. But, we do differ quite a bit in how much engagement we prefer, as well as in how we prefer to engage. We also must consider our ecosystem: our company values remote work. So, technology would have to be our go-to relational arena. For those who prefer in-person engagement, that's a compromise I hope you can make. But there's nothing about our company's remote approach that prevents us from having more frequent engagements. Those who prefer less of the social stuff, that's a comprise I hope you can make. Can we agree that for our team to be more closely aligned—both internally, and to our company's overall strategy—we should engage more purposefully with each other, using the tech resources available to us?

Once you secure your team's support, brainstorm ideas for as many technology-mediated engagement opportunities as you can. Here are some examples:

- Re-design work tasks to decrease individual work and increase collaborative teamwork. This will create more work-related touchpoints for your team members, which Avatars will like. It may also lead to more natural, unscripted social touchpoints, which Community-seekers will like.
- Implement Agile daily standups. You can have them every morning—a quick 10-minute check-up to start the day, or at least once a week. The teams that told us they do Agile standups absolutely loved them and missed them when they did not occur.
- Fun virtual team socials are another great way to build virtual community. We shared plenty of examples in Chapters 3 and 4—virtual magic shows, motivational speakers, even lama petting. The sky's the limit. Ask your Avatars to help you come up with ideas. Remember, they developed a special new power—the power of projection. They learned how to use technology for social purposes. Use that to engage them, and to help you engage others.
- Start a fun, even silly, channel in Teams (or Slack, or whatever you use). Ensure there is always a little bit of social chat at the top (or bottom) of every team meeting. Work does not have to be—and probably should not be—about work only.
- Blend virtual and "real" reality, such as pizza delivery to everyone's home during the team happy hour. Remember, free food rules! There is no reason to not provide free food even when your team is dispersed.
- Set up regular one-on-ones for your team members. Reach out spontaneously to team members to check in on them. Everyone wants to connect more with the leader!

These and many more relationship-building activities are crucial to bringing Centrists, and especially Community-seekers, closer to alignment.

But—and this is really important—you cannot over-privilege Avatars. It is simply not fair to ask Centrists and especially Community-seekers to flex, while Avatars remain in the comfort zone. And so, schedule some in-person team meetings at the office. If your remote-first company no longer has one—or if the members of your team are quite geographically dispersed—secure a budget to fly the team to an annual retreat. A little bit of facetime from time to time will do the whole team good. It will also bring Avatars down a notch and will show good will toward your Centrists and Community-seekers.

Overall, this solution meets the trifecta challenge. It is (a) aligned to your company's remote-first strategy, (b) aligned to a central shared need among all personas—the need for more relational engagement, and (c) ensures everyone gives up something. It asks Community-seekers (and to an extent, Centrists) to jump on the technology bandwagon; it asks Avatars to more frequently engage with teammates and to accept some in-person engagements. Compromise all around.

Team Alignment in Office-Forward Companies

Remember, in-office-forward organizations, the predominant persona are the fully aligned Officers (@office-preferring persona). There are also decent numbers of half-aligned Progressives (@hybrid-preferring persona) and fully misaligned Producers (@home-preferring persona). The specific spread of personas on your team should have become clear through the Awareness Raising discussion you just completed.

To align your team to your company's office-forward strategy, it makes sense to keep the Officers aligned, move Progressives closer to alignment, and move Producers closer to half-alignment. Again, we recommend you are very clear that team alignment requires everyone to compromise a little. Here's what we suggest you say again:

> Team, our challenge is to find a way to function as a cohesive team within the boundaries of our office-forward workplace. How could we do this in a way that respects our personal preferences? I suggest finding common ground and a way to compromise. What is it that we have in common? And what are some differences that we would have to live with? Let's look at these lists of New Research-Based Findings here. They identify our differences, but also point to some characteristics we may share.

Next, steer the discussion to an important shared characteristic—all personas care about flexibility. Officers "prioritize work-in-office but expect flexibility for better work-life balance" (Table 10.5.); Progressives "value flexibility but advocate that flexibility means different things to different people" (Table 10.9.); Producers "prioritize the flexibility and convenience of work-from-home over other considerations (e.g., workplace relationships)" (Table 10.3.). So, the common ground is that all personas in-office-forward organizations have come to appreciate workplace flexibility.

Next, you must surface the differences among the personas on the issue of flexibility. Officers expect flexibility in the modern workplace, but nothing in Officers' descriptions suggests they demand flexibility (Table 10.6.); Progressives are concerned about the potential loss of flexibility if work organizations swing too far back to pre-pandemic practices, but their concern is mostly about the effects of lost flexibility on others, not necessarily on themselves (Table 10.9.); Producers are also concerned about lost flexibility, but to them, that's a big deal that might motivate them to look for new employment options (Table 10.3.). So, compromises will have to be made on the centrality of **flexibility**.

Summarize these important Ah-ha's by saying this:

> Team, it seems to me we all care about flexibility. It has become important to us all. But, we do differ quite a bit on how much we personally need flexibility. It is a make-or-break for some of us, and not for others. We also must consider our ecosystem: our company values office work. So, the office would have to become our primary work location. For those who associate flexibility with at home work, that's a compromise I hope you can make. But our company's office-forward approach does not prevent us from having more flexibility "locally," meaning—on this team. Those who prefer being together, in person, all the time, that's a comprise I hope you can make. Can we agree that for our team to be more closely aligned—both internally, and to our company's overall strategy—we should infuse flexibility, creatively, in our team's workflow?

Once you secure your team's support, brainstorm ideas to offer as much "local" flexibility as you can. Here are some examples:

- Identify a core set of hours team members are in the office while leaving the rest of the workday to their discretion.
- Set a team rhythm that prescribes some office days but leaves a day or two for individual interpretation.
- Set a team culture of "We are adults." This means people can feel free to take time off when they need to handle personal matters without needing to jump through hoops or feel like they are being micromanaged. Creating this culture of psychological safety within your team would help all team members feel that they are trusted to prioritize

personal matters as needed. Team members will handle their work when they can, like the responsible professionals they are.
- Role-model flexibility by working flexibly yourself. If you do not showcase you mean it when you say that your team will employ "local" flexibility, your team won't buy into this solution. Walk the talk.
- Provide high internal and external visibility to deserving team members regardless of their pattern of office attendance. This will send a clear signal that you value performance, not presenteeism.
- Focus on and reward output and contributions made to the team and organization rather than on how often someone is in the office. Again, this will showcase you value performance, not presenteeism.
- Support individual team members who need more flexibility for personal reasons. This may entail creating individual work arrangement for some team members. Or, this may involve creating job sharing roles on your team. Work with your HR team to explore how flexibility can be supported.

These flexibility-supporting actions are crucial to bringing Progressives, and especially Producers, closer to alignment.

But again, you cannot over-privilege the aligned persona here: the Officers. It's not fair to expect that only some team members flex. Officers have to flex a little too. And so, schedule some team meetings remotely. Maybe shoot for a Friday. Everyone loves an excuse to work from home on a Friday, even Officers. The added bonus of scheduling some remote meetings is that Producers would feel more comfortable. This is because technology-based communication is their preferred communication modality. So, work to infuse more technology-based communication on your team. Maybe start a High-Five channel to call out great work, or a Got-Jokes channel to bring a little virtual laughter to your team. Make it easy for everyone to communicate by normalizing in-person *and* technology-based communication tools. These actions will bring Officers down a notch and will show good will toward your Progressives and Producers.

Overall, this solution meets the trifecta challenge. It is (a) aligned to your company's office-forward strategy, (b) aligned to a central shared need among all personas—the need for more flexibility, and (c) ensures everyone gives up something. It asks Producers (and to an extent, Progressives) to accept that flexibility would not be limitless; it asks Officers to accept that the office might sometimes be less lively, and to accept some technology-based communication and collaboration. Again, compromise all around.

Team Alignment in Hybrid Companies
Remember, in hybrid organizations, the predominant persona are the fully aligned Integrators (@hybrid-preferring persona). There are also quite significant numbers of two half-aligned personas: the Traditionalists (@office-preferring persona) and the Rebels (@home-preferring persona). The specific

spread of personas on your team should have become clear through the Awareness Raising discussion you just completed.

To align your team to your company's hybrid strategy, it makes sense to keep the Integrators aligned, and to move the Traditionalists and Rebels closer to alignment. Notice that under the hybrid strategy, there are no misaligned personas. This is a great advantage of hybrid—everyone is at least halfway where you hope they would be. But we warn: don't assume that moving two half-aligned personas closer to alignment is necessarily easy. Traditionalists and Rebels are the exact opposites of each other. Bringing them closer to your aligned persona—the Integrators—will still take work. Again, we recommend you are very clear that team alignment requires everyone to compromise a little. Here's what we suggest you say again:

> Team, our challenge is to find a way to function as a cohesive team within the boundaries of our hybrid workplace. How could we do this in a way that respects our personal preferences? I suggest finding common ground and a way to compromise. What is it that we have in common? And what are some differences that we would have to live with? Let's look at these lists of New Research-Based Findings here. They identify our differences, but also point to some characteristics we may share.

Next, steer the discussion to an important shared characteristic—all personas care about finding work-life balance. Integrators are all about a "best-of-both-worlds mentality" that equally prioritizes work and life (Table 10.9.); Traditionalists "need the home-office divide for work-life separation" and better mental health (Table 10.6.); Rebels "prioritize family & life, but care about their work output" (Table 10.3.). So, the common ground is that all personas in hybrid organizations have become quite cognizant of the interplay between work and life.

Next, you must surface the differences among the personas on the issue of work-versus-life. Integrators prioritize both equally. They focus on the task that requires the most attention in the moment, whether personal or work-related (Table 10.9.). Traditionalists do value life, but they greatly value work. They use the office as a work-life separator (Table 10.6.). Rebels elevate life. They work as often as possible in their personal space where they can prioritize life (Table 10.3.). So, compromises will have to be made around the issues of **how** to find work-life balance and **what** "balance" looks like.

Summarize these important Ah-ha's by saying this:

> Team, it seems to me we all care about work-life balance. We are more consciously thinking about it now. But, we do differ quite a bit on how we try to find balance, and maybe even on what balance means to each of us to begin with. We also must consider our ecosystem: our company values hybrid work. Fortunately, this means we each have lots of leeway to find the balance that we seek. For those who associate balance with the structure that consistent in-office work provides, that's a compromise I hope you can make. But we also need to be a team, and our company's hybrid approach does not prevent us from having a more coordinated work rhythm on this team. Those who associate balance with complete independence, that's a comprise I hope you can make. Can we agree that for our team to be more closely aligned—both internally, and to our company's overall strategy—we should infuse both autonomy and structure in our team's workflow?

Once you secure your team's support, brainstorm ideas to offer both autonomy and structure on your team. Here are some options:

- Task-Location Fit. We introduced you to this idea in Chapter 7. Pioneered by the Integrators, Task-Location Fit is about deciding where different tasks are executed best. Should idea incubation happen in the office, or could it happen online? How about team meetings? And social activities? What about personnel discussions? And focused work? As a team, agree on a Task-Location scheme. Tweak it to match your team's consensus. If more of your team members need more coordinated office time (for example, you might have a larger number of Traditionalists on your team), then the team can decide to do more tasks in the office. If more of your team members need more autonomy (for example, you have more Rebels on your team), then the team can decide to do more tasks virtually, from home. Regardless, making Task-Location Fit the centerpiece of your team's workflow speaks to the issue of balancing work and life.
- Structured hybrid. To balance the team's needs for autonomy and structure, implement a workflow based on time (versus task). There are several options to explore here:
    - Flextime hybrid: Identify a block of hours each day when the team is in. Here, "hour" is the unit of time you must agree on.
    - Scheduled hybrid: Identify some days where all team members will be in the office. Here, "day" is the unit of time you must agree on.
    - Rotational hybrid: Identify a week each month (or similar) where the team works from the office. Here, "week" (or another larger chunk) is the unit of time you must agree on.

These approaches to squaring the competing needs of the half-aligned personas on your team—the needs for autonomy on the one hand and for structure on the other—bring Rebels and Traditionalists closer to alignment. And, depending on exactly what office-to-home ratio your team agrees on, Integrators will have to adapt a little too. This makes things fairer for all personas.

Overall, this solution meets the trifecta challenge. It is (a) aligned to your company's hybrid strategy, (b) aligned to a central shared need among all personas—the need for work-life balance, and (c) ensures everyone gives up something. It asks Rebels (and to an extent, Integrators) to accept that team-wide coordination of office attendance is needed for the greater good; it asks Traditionalists (and to an extent, Integrators again) to accept that their in-office experience won't be perfectly consistent. So one more time, compromise all around.

> *Reflection on How Leaders Align Their Teams* As a team leader, you have the unenviable task of navigating up and down the chain. You must align your team to your company's strategy. But you also must find internal alignment. Given the persona diversity that exists on every team, threading this needle takes a steady hand!
>
> In this chapter, we gave you tools to help you find internal team alignment. We provided you with state-of-the-art information on the who's and why's of each persona. We provided scripts to lead your team through an Awareness Raising and Finding Common Ground team-building activity. Helping your team members through this almost-taboo conversation is crucial to internal team alignment.
>
> We also outlined tactics designed to align your team to your organization's remote-first, office-forward, or hybrid strategy. These tactics hinge on addressing a core shared need of the personas in each workplace context. For the three personas that reside in remote-first organizations, the shared need is the need for purposeful relationships. For the three personas that reside in office-forward organizations, the shared need is the need for flexibility. And for the three personas that reside in hybrid organizations, the shared need is the need for valuing both work and life. To align your team to your organization's strategy, rally your team members around addressing these shared needs, even if that means that every persona gives up something. That's how you strike the trifecta we discussed: match the company strategy, address a shared pain point, make some compromises along the way.
>
> Note as well that the team alignment tactics we discussed in this chapter (relationship-building tactics for teams in remote-first organizations; flexibility tactics for teams in-office-forward organizations;

work-life balance tactics for teams in hybrid organizations) are perfectly aligned with the organization-wide alignment tactics we discussed in Chapter 9. There, we recommended that remote-first organizations focus on relationships, that office-forward organizations focus on flexibility, and that hybrid organizations focus on a best-of-both-worlds approach. If your company's leadership focuses on these issues from a strategic perspective, and if you focus on these same issues from a team execution perspective, think of how far your organization will go with its chosen strategy!

CHAPTER 11

How Do You Grow into the Persona You Wish to Be

We've learned about the new workplace and the personas that emerge in remote-first, office-forward, and hybrid companies. We've covered how organizations can better align the personas they have in their workplaces to their strategy. We've also talked about how leaders can find alignment for the personas on their teams.

Saving the best for last, it is now finally time to address YOU, our reader. Whether you are an executive, a team leader, an employee, or even an intern, you have come to inhabit a certain persona in your workplace. How can you find personal alignment?

Do you feel some reservations about your current persona? If yes, that may mean that you are half-aligned to your company's strategy. You might be a Centrist (hybrid-preferring employee in a remote-first company), a Progressive (hybrid-preferring employee in an office-forward company), a Traditionalist (office-preferring employee in a hybrid company), or a Rebel (home-preferring employee in a hybrid company).

If you are feeling really unhappy, you may even be a fully misaligned persona. You may be a Community-seeker (office-preferring employee in a remote-first company), or a Producer (home-preferring employee in an office-forward company).

In either case, this chapter will help you visualize the persona you wish to become. What choices can you make to craft the persona you wish to inhabit? We'll help you map out different routes to personal alignment. Some routes keep you in the persona you currently inhabit but suggest ways to improve your work experience. Other routes suggest ways to evolve into a better-aligned persona, improving your work experience even more.

You may also be perfectly happy with the persona you are. This likely means you are aligned to your company's strategy. You are probably an Avatar (home-preferring employee in a remote-first company), an Officer (office-preferring employee in an office-forward company), or an Integrator (hybrid-preferring employee in a hybrid company). That's wonderful! However, there're always ways to take things to the next level. How can you refine your perfect alignment?

What Persona Am I?

As you were reading about the personas on the pages of this book, we are sure you were profiling yourself. However, to more formally "identify" your current persona, please take a minute to complete our Workplace Persona Assessment below. You can also find this assessment on our website: https://thenewworkplacebook.com/. Read each statement below, and circle how much you agree or disagree with each statement. Then, follow the instructions for calculating and interpreting your results (Table 11.1).

Table 11.1 Workplace persona assessment

What Persona Am I?

	Statement	Strongly Agree	Agree	Neutral	Disagree	Strongly Disagree
1	I go to the office even when I am not required to.	1	2	3	4	5
2	I love the physical office space and features of the office (e.g., desk, chair, location, etc.)	1	2	3	4	5
3	I would only consider working for a company that has an office I can go to.	1	2	3	4	5
4	I believe that relationships and culture are best developed and maintained in person.	1	2	3	4	5

(continued)

Table 11.1 (continued)

What Persona Am I?

	Statement	Strongly Agree	Agree	Neutral	Disagree	Strongly Disagree
5	I feel more productive working in an office than I do outside of the office.	1	2	3	4	5
6	When I am in the office, I am happy to be there.	1	2	3	4	5
7	When I work-from-home, I feel distracted and lonely.	1	2	3	4	5
8	I prefer the technology available in the office more than the technology at home.	1	2	3	4	5
9	I prefer in-person collaboration more than technology-mediated interactions.	1	2	3	4	5
10	It is not a priority for me to develop my technology- or remote-work knowledge and skills.	1	2	3	4	5
11	I go to the office to be seen and so that my colleagues have a good impression of my work behavior.	1	2	3	4	5
12	I feel a sense of purpose when working from an office.	1	2	3	4	5
13	I feel more competent interacting with my coworkers face-to-face than I do virtually.	1	2	3	4	5
14	Being in the office never feels like time wasted.	1	2	3	4	5

(continued)

Table 11.1 (continued)

What Persona Am I?

	Statement	Strongly Agree	Agree	Neutral	Disagree	Strongly Disagree
15	Working from an office is best for my mental health.	1	2	3	4	5

To calculate your score, add up the total number of circles in each column. Write the totals under each column.

If you circled "1" and "2" for most of the statements, you are likely an *office-preferring* persona. If you circled "4" or "5" for most of the statements, you are likely a *home-preferring* persona. If you circled a wide variety of statements, ranging between 1 and 5, you are likely a *hybrid-preferring* persona.

Now, combine your preference with your company strategy to determine your specific persona. See the visual below for an illustration.

If your company has a *remote-first approach* (allowing employees to work primarily from home or outside of an office), and you are *home-preferring*, then you are an *Avatar*. If you are *office-preferring*, then you are a *Community-seeker*. If you are *hybrid-preferring*, then you are a *Centrist*.

If your company has an *office-forward approach* (requiring employees to spend most of their work time in an office), and you are *home-preferring*, then you are a *Producer*. If you are *office-preferring*, then you are an *Officer*. If you are *hybrid-preferring*, then you are a *Progressive*.

Finally, if your company has a *hybrid approach* (allowing some balance of in- and out-of-office work), and you are *home-preferring*, then you are a *Rebel*. If you are *office-preferring*, then you are a *Traditionalist*. If you are *hybrid-preferring*, then you are an *Integrator* (Fig. 11.1).

Now that you know for sure what persona you are, it's time to think about alignment.

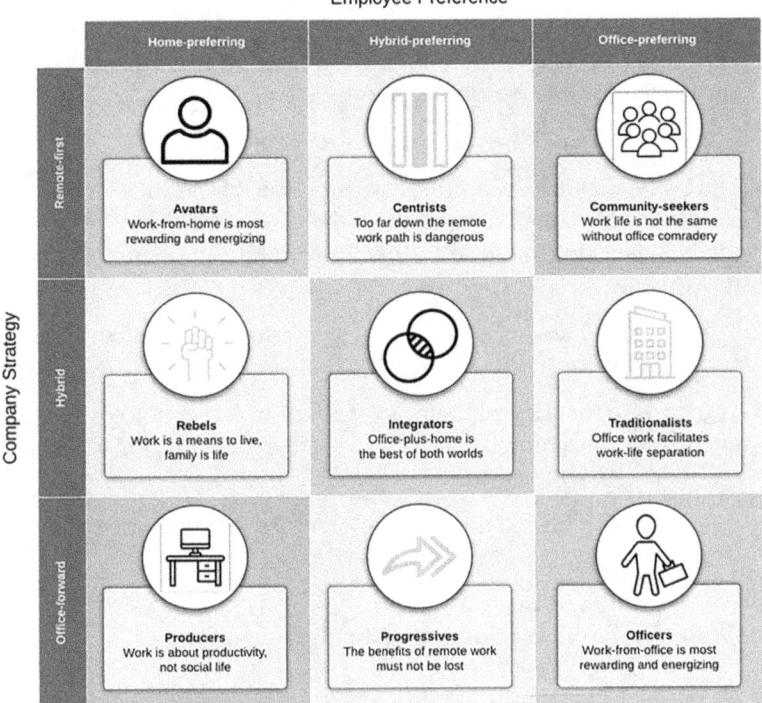

Fig. 11.1 Personas arising at the intersections of company strategy and employee preference

How Alignment Impacts the Home-Preferring Personas

So, you are an @home preferer. If you flip back to Table 10.1., Table 10.2., and Table 10.3. in the previous chapter, you can see all sorts of "who" and "why" factors that likely apply to you.

However, by now you've learned that your @home preference alone does not determine the persona you've come to adopt. Rather, your company's workplace strategy has pushed you into one of three @home personas. Here's a brief summary of the surprisingly stark differences between the @home personas (outlined in detail in Chapter 3 through Chapter 8).

> *Alignment and the @Home Personas* **Avatars: Aligned persona** (@home preferers working in remote-first companies)

- You work for an employer whose strategy perfectly matches your preference. You feel grateful and loyal to your company, and you are fiercely protective of its remote-first strategy.
  - Bonus: You have a great work experience.
- You've developed comfort with using technology for work purposes. You feel at-ease reaching out with questions, asking for help, seeking mentoring, or networking opportunities through technology.
  - Bonus: This helps you come across as an engaged, dedicated employee.
- You've also developed comfort with using technology for social purposes. You enjoy interacting with colleagues from the comfort and safety of your home.
  - Bonus: This helps you come across as a friendly and social colleague.

Rebels: Half-aligned persona
(@home preferers working in hybrid companies)

- You work for an employer whose strategy meets you halfway. You're disaffected with the hybrid strategy because you'd rather work-from-home full-time. You're becoming disaffected with the system as a whole.
  - Penalty: You have a mostly negative work experience.
- You are unconvinced that the office offers value. Annoyed, you express your disapproval overtly (e.g., you question the policy), or covertly (e.g., you go to the office the bare minimum).
  - Penalty: This makes you seem like a troublemaker, or a flight risk, or both.
- You are able to re-charge your social and mental battery on at home workdays. You use your re-charged energy to get through your office workdays.
  - Bonus: This helps you come across as approachable and fun when you do go to the office.

Producers: Misaligned persona
(@home preferers working in-office-forward companies)

- You work for an employer whose strategy meets few if any of your preferences. You feel uncomfortable in the office, like the odd-one-out. You feel misunderstood and not taken care of.
  - Penalty: You have a poor work experience.
- You need quiet to focus, so you stick to your desk for heads-down work. You project an image of a worker bee.
  - Penalty: This makes you seem reliable but unambitious.
- You are unable to regulate social interactions. You are forced into constant social engagements in the office, which takes a toll on you, so you retreat.
  - Penalty: This makes you seem disconnected and almost anti-social.

Clearly, the three @home personas have a very different work experience based on how aligned they are with their company's strategy. The farther a persona moves from full alignment, the fewer bonuses and the more penalties accrue.

Moreover, alignment also impacts how each @home persona is perceived at work on two important factors: work devotion and sociability. Both are highly privileged employee attributes, rightly or not.

Perceived work devotion is important because the "ideal worker" is supposed to demonstrate active engagement at work.[1] Perceived sociability is important because we see sociable people in a significantly more positive light, we privilege them for leadership roles, we gravitate toward them.[2]

Being an @home persona does not mean you are more or less devoted to your work, or that you are more or less social. But, your circumstances make it seem that way. As you see in our summary box above, the aligned persona, the Avatars, functions under ideal circumstances, and come across as ideal workers—devoted and sociable. The half-aligned persona, the Rebels, function under challenging but manageable circumstances, and end up paying a price in terms of perceptions of work devotion. The misaligned persona, the Producers, function under the most unfitting of circumstances, and end

---

[1] Padavic, Ely, and Reid, "Explaining the Persistence of Gender Inequality: The Work–Family Narrative as a Social Defense against the 24/7 Work Culture"; Blair-Loy, "Work Devotion and Work Time."

[2] A. A. Javalagi, D. A. Newman, and M. Li, "Personality and Leadership: Meta-Analytic Review of Cross-Cultural Moderation, Behavioral Mediation, and Honesty-Humility," *Journal of Applied Psychology* 109, no. 9 (2024): 1489–1511; M. P. Wilmot et al., "Extraversion Advantages at Work: A Quantitative Review and Synthesis of the Meta-Analytic Evidence," *Journal of Applied Psychology* 104, no. 12 (2019): 1447–70.

up paying an even heftier price as they are perceived poorly in terms of both work devotion and sociability.

These are all reasons for you to act. We will discuss how you can improve and refine your alignment later in the chapter.

How Alignment Impacts the Office-Preferring Personas

Your turn, @office preferers. Though the media makes you seem like a rare breed, you are not. Our research estimates you represent about a third of the office worker population; others agree.[3] If you flip back to Tables 10.4., 10.5., and 10.6. in the previous chapter, you can see "who" and "why" factors that likely apply to you.

However, again, your @office preference alone does not determine the persona you've adopted. It's your company's workplace strategy that pushes you into one of three @office personas. Here's a summary of the surprisingly stark differences between the @office personas (outlined in detail in Chapter 3 through Chapter 8).

Alignment and the @Office Personas **Officers: Aligned persona (@office preferers working in-office-forward companies)**

- You work for an employer whose strategy perfectly matches your preference. You feel grateful and loyal to your company, and you are fiercely protective of its office-forward strategy.
  - Bonus: You have a great work experience.
- You've developed an attachment to the office itself. Beyond its amenities, you love the energy, the productivity, the opportunity to commiserate with work friends there, the boost of pride the professional environment gives you.
  - Bonus: This makes life feel normal and as it should be. This is good for your mental health.
- You love connecting with work colleagues, stopping by people's desk to ask a work question or just chit-chat, grabbing coffee or going for drinks, doing silly office pranks, getting everyone to come together and have a good time as a team.

---

[3] Zoom, "Navigating the Future of Work: Global Perspectives on Hybrid Models and Technology."

- Bonus: This makes you seem like a team player and even a team builder.

Traditionalists: Half-aligned persona
(@office preferers working in hybrid companies)

- You work for an employer whose strategy meets you halfway. You feel resigned that the office will never truly come back. You take things in your own hands to find community.
  - Penalty: You have an agreeable work experience.
- You are unable to disconnect from work when working from home. You also don't like switching between at home and at-office work; you need more predictability. You choose the lesser evil—going to the office even though it may be empty.
  - Penalty: This takes a toll on your mental health.
- You prefer in-person engagements and collaboration, but you realize how much flexibility means to your coworkers. So, you go along, connecting and working with colleagues across modalities.
  - Bonus: This makes you seem like a team player.

Community-seekers: Misaligned persona
(@office preferers working in remote-first companies)

- You work for an employer whose strategy meets few if any of your preferences. You feel like work has lost its humanity.
  - Penalty: You have a poor work experience.
- You feel forgotten both at home, and in the empty office. You have few work friends, maybe even none, so you have no outlet for sharing emotions. Stress builds up.
  - Penalty: This takes a toll on your mental health.
- You are unable to meaningfully connect with others through technology. You feel that's not real. You keep going to the office, interacting with the few people who are there.
  - Penalty: This limits your internal exposure and social circle. It makes it seem you are not a team player.

Clearly, the three @office personas have a very different work experience based on how aligned they are with their company's strategy. The more misaligned you are, the fewer bonuses and the more penalties accrue.

Moreover, alignment also impacts a very personal outcome: mental health. It goes without saying that mental health is an important outcome. The U.S. Surgeon General recently issued a Framework for Workplace Mental Health and Well-Being, specifically identifying "connection and community" as one of five contributing factors to the deteriorating mental health of the U.S. workforce.[4]

What's more, alignment impacts how each @office persona is perceived at work in terms of collegiality. That's important because modern work is heavily team-based. Employees are expected to collaborate, to be team builders and team players.[5]

Being an @office persona does not mean you are more or less susceptible to mental health issues, or that you are more or less collegial. But, your circumstances may amplify these outcomes. As you see in our summary box above, the aligned persona, the Officers, function under ideal circumstances. Their mental health is good, and they are seen as friendly and collegial. The half-aligned persona, the Traditionalists, function under challenging but manageable circumstances. They end up paying a price in terms of their mental health, but they are seen as team players. The misaligned persona, the Community-seekers, function under the most unfitting of circumstances, and pay the heftiest price. Their mental health suffers, and their collegiality might be questioned.

These are all reasons to act. We will get to that later in the chapter.

How Alignment Impacts the Hybrid-Preferring Personas

We've come to the last preference category—the @hybrid preferers. In Tables 10.7., 10.8., and 10.9. in the previous chapter, you'll see there's no clear demographic characteristic that you share with other @hybrid preferers. But in terms of why you prefer @hybrid, the biggest driver might be that you have a both-and mentality.

However, remember again that it is your company's workplace strategy that pushes you into one of three @hybrid personas. Even though these three @hybrid personas all share the @hybrid work preference, there are stark differences between them based on where they work (outlined in detail in Chapter 3 through Chapter 8).

---

[4] Office of the Surgeon General, "Workplace Mental Health and Well-Being," *U.S. Department of Health and Human Services*, May 30, 2024, https://www.hhs.gov/surgeongeneral/priorities/workplace-well-being/index.html.

[5] Javalagi, Newman, and Li, "Personality and Leadership: Meta-Analytic Review of Cross-Cultural Moderation, Behavioral Mediation, and Honesty-Humility."

Alignment and the @Hybrid Personas **Integrators: Aligned persona
(@hybrid preferers working in hybrid companies)**

- You work for an employer whose strategy perfectly matches your preference. You feel hybrid is the winning philosophy, and you are "Team Hybrid" all the way.
    - Bonus: You have a great work experience.
- You take action to solve issues that hybrid creates. To relieve the stress from the home-office switching, you develop a new skill: Task-Location Fit. To help @home-preferring colleagues feel included, you advocate for them.
    - Bonus: This helps you come across as a flexible and proactive problem-solver.
- You fight a nagging thought that your work contributions are not noticed when you work-from-home. You tend to overwork yourself on at-home days.
    - Penalty: This state of doubt may be psychologically taxing.

**Progressives: Half-aligned persona
(@hybrid preferers working in-office-forward companies)**

- You work for an employer whose strategy meets you halfway. You feel irked that your employer is falling back into an outdated workstyle. You go along, but you wish things were different.
    - Penalty: You have a generally good work experience, but it could be better.
- You complain, mostly quietly, about the at-office requirement. Knowing office presence is expected for career advancement, you go in most days, as expected.
    - Penalty: This makes you seem passive to others, and is bothersome to you internally.
- You do appreciate the office. You believe relationships can be built either way, but there is something to be said about the value of in-person engagements and collaboration.
    - Bonus: This helps you justify going to the office most days.

**Centrists: Half-aligned persona
(@hybrid preferers working in remote-first companies)**

- You work for an employer whose strategy meets you halfway. You feel irked that your employer is going too far down the remote work path. You go along, but you wish things were different.
  - Penalty: You have a generally good work experience, but it could be better.
- You complain about the lack of office culture. You try to go in to find some community, but you quickly give up knowing this train had left the station. Still, this bothers you.
  - Penalty: This makes you seem passive to others, and is bothersome to you internally.
- You do appreciate the freedom and independence of remote work. You believe the office has value, but there is something to be said about having control over your time.
  - Bonus: This helps you justify working from home most days.

Clearly, the three @hybrid personas have a very different work experience based on how aligned they are with their company's strategy. Notice, however, that even the fully aligned @hybrid persona—the Integrators—don't enjoy perfect outcomes. That goes to a point we have repeatedly made throughout this book: hybrid is hard to square. We suppose finding balance between opposites—such as between the office and the home—is objectively hard. And we want to underscore that at the end of the day, it is worth it. But, be ready to have to work to get to balance. Your prize will be positioning yourself as a flexible and proactive problem-solver.

Regarding the two half-aligned @hybrid personas—the Progressives and the Centrists—your tacit endorsement of your company's office-forward or remote-first strategy, respectively, makes you seem passive, which bothers even you. Importantly, being an @hybrid persona does not mean you are more or less of a follower. But, your circumstances may push you into this reaction. Research shows benefits to those who come across as proactive; no such benefits accrue to those perceived as passive.[6]

Let's now switch gears and talk about what the personas can do to find better alignment.

---

[6] S. El Baroudi et al., "Individual and Contextual Predictors of Team Member Proactivity: What Do We Know and Where Do We Go from Here?," *Human Resource Management Review* 29, no. 4 (2019): 1–17.

I AM A HALF-ALIGNED PERSONA. HOW DO I FIND BETTER ALIGNMENT?

What choices can you make to craft the persona you wish to inhabit? We'd like to start with the half-aligned personas.

Half-alignment means that you appreciate some aspects of your company's strategy, but not others. We outline two routes to personal alignment.

Route #1 is to address the thing about your company's strategy that bugs you. This will keep you in the persona that you are, but it will make your overall work experience better.

Route #2 is to play some reverse psychology on yourself to more closely align yourself with your company's strategy. Over time, this may help you evolve into an aligned persona, improving your work experience even more.

Of course, you can also quit and join an employer who has the strategy you are looking for. However, this is rarely as workable as it sounds. And honestly, because you are half-aligned (as opposed to misaligned), you should consider a less disruptive route to better personal alignment.

So, let's flesh out what routes #1 and #2 may look like for each of the four half-aligned personas.

Centrists (Hybrid-Preferring Employees in Remote-First Companies)

You love the freedom your remote-first company affords, but you miss the in-person social interactions.

- Route #1: Address the issue: poor social environment. Advocate for a team day, perhaps once a week, when the whole team goes to the office. If this is not possible, then advocate for periodic team retreats. An ever-easier approach might be seeking out like-minded @hybrid preferers and deciding on an office day or two together. This was one Centrist's solution:

Some of my peers—the other managers, some of them are in the office. And my direct boss is in the office about the same amount that I am, and his boss, who's also sort of my boss, he's in the office occasionally. So I do really look forward to the days that I know we're all gonna be there. Those are good days because we have our meetings in person, or we might all go sit in a conference room, and then other people might join. And like, that's a little bit more of an engaging environment. Or it's at least different than when I'm sitting in front of this monitor. (Noah, risk manager)

> With route #1, you remain a half-aligned Centrist. But, by creating a social circle around you, you smooth over the thing about remote-first that irks you.

- Route #2: Play some reverse psychology on yourself. In a remote-first company, this means convincing yourself that remote work is the way to go. This is what another Centrist was in the process of doing:

I mean, that has been a huge benefit, especially during the summers when my school-aged kid is home a couple of days a week. It's fun to be able to pop out, hang out with him during the lunch hour or even when I have free time. Or the other day, the kids wanted to go do their Valentine's Day party, you know. So there's a lot of flexibility in that for me. (Liam, director of sales)

Telling yourself the complete autonomy of remote work is a "huge benefit" might turn you into more of an @home preferer eventually.

> With route #2, you may evolve into an Avatar, moving to alignment in your remote-first company.

Progressives (Hybrid-Preferring Employees in Office-Forward Companies)

You love the in-person social interactions your office-forward company privileges, but you are upset that getting ahead requires presenteeism.

- Route #1: Address the issue: presenteeism. Schedule one-on-one's focused on career progression. Find tactful, smart ways to remind your leader of your accomplishments. For example, talk about the high-impact project you were able to accomplish on your quiet work-from-home day. In short, make your contributions as visible as possible.
- Also, accentuate your strengths! You are a natural relationship-builder. Offer your help with the company's goal to entice people back to the office. Use your relational skills to give colleagues a reason to be in the office. This helps others feel welcome AND earns you bonus points, increasing your visibility. This is what one Progressive had done:

I try to always be very intentional about planning fun things when people who are remote come back into the office. So when [name] and when [name], when they would come in, it's always like, Oh yeah, [name] and [name] are here now, let's do fun things! It's usually like a happy hour, or we'll go to lunch. Yeah, usually revolves around food. (Zoe, project manager)

> With route #1, you remain a half-aligned Progressive. But, by increasing your visibility, you address your concern that a hybrid preferer like yourself is not seen as promotable in an office-forward environment.

- Route #2: Play some reverse psychology on yourself. In an office-forward company, this means convincing yourself that office work is the way to go. This is what another Progressive was in the process of doing:

When I go into the office, I love it. I love the social interaction, I love that I have my coworkers around me, that I'm able to be back in my space where I, you know, really learned how to do my job. It just kind of feels like we're back to the good old times, so I do like working from my office. (Megan, account manager)

Telling yourself you "love" the office and that working from the office feels like "the good old times" might turn you into more of an @office preferer eventually.

> With route #2, you may evolve into an Officer, moving to alignment in your office-forward company.

Traditionalists (Office-Preferring Employees in Hybrid Companies)

You appreciate the flexibility of your company's hybrid strategy for others, but the half-filled office makes you sad and the home-office switching throws you off.

- Route #1: Address the issue: the empty office. You can actively role-model being in the office to, hopefully, entice colleagues in. Remember, one Traditionalist in Chapter 7, Grant, told us this is what he does,

though he was disillusioned that his efforts had little impact on bringing others in more often.
- There's always the option of finding a group of like-minded office-goers, or even just going to the office regardless, just to be around other people. We heard about this tactic from another Traditionalist:

If I was on a team where the members weren't mostly there, I definitely think that would be a struggle for me. If that were the case, it might be better for me to, like, come into the office, like, just sit in an area where there are people. Even if they were not even my team members, just so there's more of that human interaction. (Ying, assistant analyst)

> With route #1, you remain a half-aligned Traditionalist. But, by finding ways to surround yourself with people, you address your concern that a hybrid workplace is not as lively as you wish it to be.

- Route #2: Play some reverse psychology on yourself. In a hybrid company, this means adopting to the hybrid work rhythm. Take a page from Integrators' playbook, and adopt the task-location fit skill to create structure for yourself. This is what one Traditionalist was in the process of doing:

I go to boxing once a week. It's Friday. So, I've built an [at-home workday] around my workout. I'm usually looking forward to that. So, I go, and I do that in the morning, so I'm excited. When I come home, I'm not as excited because, as I mentioned, my space is not great. But, that's my routine now. (Laura, leadership development manager)

Telling yourself "that's my routine now" might turn you into more of an @hybrid preferer eventually.

> With route #2, you may evolve into an Integrator, moving to alignment in your hybrid company.

11 HOW DO YOU GROW INTO THE PERSONA YOU WISH TO BE   199

Rebels (Home-Preferring Employees in Hybrid Companies)

You are genuinely unsure why the office is still a thing and you resent being told what to do, but you do report you miss socializing.

- Route #1: Address the issue: lack of self-determination. Request an individual work arrangement of remote work. A lot of Rebels expressed they would love to do that; here is an example:

I've had both experiences with the same position. I like the remote-all-the-time. If my situation was different, going in like once a month would be maybe ok 'cause that kind of matters, especially with building relationships on the team. But as a single mom... (Rachel, business analyst)

However, no Rebel that we spoke with had requested an individual arrangement. We do encourage you to make your case. Perhaps you are on a team that is dispersed across different geographies; it wouldn't make sense for you to come into the office if none of your teammates are there. Perhaps you are a parent of a young child or a caregiver of an aging parent; it would be helpful to have a caretaker accommodation.

- Another issue that bugs you at your hybrid employer is that teams don't coordinate office attendance. Many Rebels complained, rightfully, that this defeats the purpose of going to the office. Well, that's an easy solution, then. Influence your team to agree on a team day or two. One Rebel told us this was what he wishes his leader would do:

I mean, they could say, Hey, you have to come in for team meetings, you know. That's fine, being around each other. I'm ok if they came back and put parameters around it, you know, and then we'll try to find a way to meet the parameters because we can see the benefit that it provides. (Raul, sales specialist)

> With route #1, you remain a half-aligned Rebel. But, by exercising some agency on an office attendance compromise, you address your concern that a hybrid workplace is more restrictive than you believe it needs to be.

- Route #2: Play some reverse psychology on yourself. In a hybrid company, this means justifying being in the office some days. Perhaps the office is better for networking. Perhaps there is some boutique project you can involve yourself with if you do go to the office. Perhaps you rekindle old relationships. These are the reasons that helped one Rebel go in sometimes:

> I'm always looking for that kind of deeper project work to forge ties with people. Yesterday I was there for, you know, not very long, but I was able to meet somebody who just started within the last week, and it wouldn't have gone the same way having not been there. I also interacted with a longtime colleague who I didn't realize was still there. And you know, he had done something, this mini project that was a huge help in our work, and for some reason, I had no idea! And so, we were able to just connect and talk about that. Or like, I was able to talk to some other people about the trip we were recently on for this film project in California. Those little things, those moments are ... they wouldn't happen the same way over a Teams chat, you know. And so, those moments of some real connection and personal conversation with colleagues, or meeting a new colleague, make me go in sometimes because they help me feel connected. That's high value chatter to me. (Robbie, senior content strategist)

Telling yourself "those moments are worth it" might turn you into more of an @hybrid preferer eventually.

> With route #2, you may evolve into an Integrator, moving to alignment in your hybrid company.

I am a Misaligned Persona. How Do I Find Better Alignment?

As a misaligned persona, what could you do to craft the persona you wish to inhabit?

Misalignment means that you do not appreciate many (if any) aspects of your company's strategy. And so, your routes to better personal alignment here look a bit different.

Route #1 is to evolve into a half-aligned persona. This may be through a combination of addressing the most pressing concern you have about your company's strategy, and/or playing some reverse psychology on yourself to trick yourself into closer alignment.

Route #2 is to seriously consider other options.

Let's flesh out what routes #1 and #2 may look like for our two misaligned personas.

Community-Seekers (Office-Preferring Employees in Remote-First Companies)

You feel forgotten at home, and forgotten in the empty office. You feel work had lost its humanity. You feel technology-based interactions are not the same. Your work experience is miserable.

- Route #1: Address your most pressing concern: your loneliness.
    - Ask for more opportunities to team-up with others on projects (versus doing solo work). Remember Hannah, the Community-seeker you met in Chapter 3? She had asked to be added to an Engagement Council just to have more interactional opportunities with others, even though they were still remote. At least you are talking to someone!
    - Seek out a group of like-minded office-goers and create a mini community for yourself at the office. This is what we recommended for Centrists and Traditionalists, too, and it is what some Community-seekers are already doing anyways. Remember Max from Chapter 3? He had his group of office buddies to help meet his need for social interactions.
    - Ask your manager to come in. This is what Victoria did: "My manager wasn't coming in before I started reporting to her. I told her it'd be nice to see her sometimes. So now she does come into the office on the same days I do" (Victoria, investment analyst). Daniel (intern) had also done the same thing. Most managers do want to support their team members—so ask!

> With route #1, you may evolve into a Centrist, moving to half-alignment in your remote-first company. That will improve your work experience.

- Route #2: Consider other employment options. Be honest. Is this work arrangement damaging to your happiness at work or your overall mental health? If you are like any of the Community-seekers we spoke with, the answer is a resounding YES. As well, can you accomplish your work- and life objectives at this remote-first employer? Your answer is likely NO. So, switching to an office-forward—or at least a hybrid—employer might be the most prudent course for you.

> With route #2, you evolve into an Officer (if you join an office-forward company), or you evolve into a Traditionalist (if you join a hybrid company). Both are a step up from your current persona of Community-seeker.

Producers (Home-Preferring Employees in Office-Forward Companies)

You just want to get your work done. You don't get what the office fuss is all about. You feel misunderstood and strangely alone in the lively office.

- Route #1: Take action to connect to your company's social fabric.
  - We realize this is not your cup of tea. Remember Chloe from Chapter 6 who prefers to "stick" to herself? Or Katherine who's not "longing" for a connection to her coworkers? Or Abby who wants to avoid the office "drama"? However, realize this—connecting to the company's social fabric doesn't only mean partaking in office chit-chat or parties. It may be work-related things, like volunteering to give the new intern or new hire an office tour, or joining a team project or an employee resource group. Starting small and keeping social interactions work-related might be more your cup of tea.
  - Ask your manager for help. Or better yet, a close work friend whom you trust. As a Producers, you often need extra coaxing to feel comfortable with social situations. Find your advocate, someone to push you a little bit and someone who'll be there to support your evolution.

> With route #1, you may evolve into a Progressive, moving to half-alignment in your office-forward company. Being honest, though: "may" is the key word here.

- Route #2: Consider other options.
  - Ask for a personal work arrangement to work-from-home. One of our Producers, Abby, had done this and she was thriving at home. Be prepared to make your case. For Abby, she needed to follow her husband whose job moved out-of-state. You might be thinking, 'Well, lucky for her, but my spouse is not moving…' Surely though,

your office-forward company does have fully remote employees. Research what it takes to land such an arrangement, and give it a try.
- Switch employers. Your current work arrangement is impacting your feelings about work and may be damaging to your mental health. To shield yourself from the negative effects of misalignment, look for a hybrid company at the least; a remote-first employer would be ideal.

> With route #2, you evolve into an Avatar (if you join a remote-first company), or you evolve into a Rebel (if you join a hybrid company). Both are a step up from your current persona of Producer.

I Am a Fully Aligned Persona. How Do I Refine My Perfect Alignment?

No work experience is absolutely perfect. Even fully aligned personas have some wrinkles they might want to smooth over. So, let's talk about how you can refine your nearly-perfect personal alignment to take it to the next level.

Avatars (Home-Preferring Employees in Remote-First Companies)

You have a great experience in your remote-first company. You absolutely enjoy working from home, and you feel one with life and one with work. But even you feel a little bit of pain. Your main concern is that sometimes, you are just going through motions, and it's just business:

> I feel like everyday is kind of like the same. It's almost like groundhog day where every day is the same day, a little bit, you know. (Travis, division director)
>
> It's like, okay, 8–9—I have a meeting, 9–10—another meeting. And you get in, and it's just business, business, business, the entire day. (Kyle, associate vice president of product)

You feel that way because you lack many of the sources of intrinsic motivation typically found in the office. These are things like the joy of chatting it up with old work friends, the fulfillment of mentoring others, the sense of purpose from seeing how your work fits into the big picture.

To solve this, you need to usher intrinsic motivators back into your work life. This is best accomplished through intentionally stepping back into the office a little. So:

- Be more active in social engagements, and make sure some are in person. One Avatar looked forward to periodic in-person interactions with her team:

It would be nice to see more people sometimes. Like around Thanksgiving, we went into the office for like a little Thanksgiving lunch. So we went, and I did see a couple of other people, even in different departments that I kinda knew virtually, and I actually met them in person. So, yeah, I mean, it's nice because I don't know people just through, you know, a call. (Sophie, senior software engineer)

- Go one step further—organize in-person social engagements for your team. This is what another Avatar wanted to do:

I do still feel the complete virtual misses something, some physical presence. And so, one of the things I've talked with my current leader about is, how can we create a budgetary allowance to get us together at least once a year, and to have specific purpose around that meeting that is very work-related, but at the same time allows us to build those interactive bonds. (Mike, product development director)

- Ask for a mentoring assignment, but make sure in-person interactions are a part of the mix. Many Avatars shared mentoring had suffered in the fully virtual environment. As one Avatar leader put it, "We haven't cracked the code yet" (Travis, division director); another agreed: "Immediate teams are fine, but the next level of acquaintance is taking a hit" (Nabil, senior product manager). One Avatar leader had already gone back to in-person mentoring ... well, in-person onboarding, at least:

When new team members come, it's very hard to connect and onboard and establish that trust. If it had taken two weeks to establish that trust, now it takes two years for them to see us and to feel connected. So I ask them to cut a day where I can meet up personally with them, to give a feel of who I am. And I get a feel of who they are. (Helen, IT applications manager)

- A surprisingly large number of Avatars shared working in the building makes it seem more professional and important. Here's an example: "In the first thirtyish seconds that I come into the office, it definitely is, 'You're coming into work, and you're ready to work'" (Kara, associate vice president of division). So, to reconnect to the big picture, to get your sense of purpose back, go back to the building sometimes. One Avatar attested to the effectiveness of this tactic:

> So when you go, you feel like I'm a part of something bigger, I'm a part of this organization that's trying to do all these things. That's the feeling I get when I go into the building. Versus, like, when I walk into my basement, it's like, I'm just doing my job. I'm not necessarily connected to the broader picture. (Kyle, associate vice president of product)

By creating different sources of intrinsic motivation for yourself, your work experience will turn from great to excellent. But importantly, to maximize the impact of these tactics, make sure you re-embrace the office as much as your home-preferring heart would let you. Note that this advice to you triangulates perfectly with our advice to company leaders (Chapter 9) and team leaders (Chapter 10) in remote-first companies to not shun the office completely. In remote-first organizations, bringing back an element of "real" human interaction is crucially important for everyone's experiences, including the most avid supporters of remote work, the Avatars.

> The office is a source of intrinsic motivation even for Avatars. So Avatars, to improve your already great work experience, re-engage in person and with the office with some frequency.

Officers (Office-Preferring Employees in Office-Forward Companies)

You have a great experience in your office-forward company. You absolutely enjoy working from the office where you feel energized and engaged. But even you feel a little bit of pain. Your main concern is that the flexibility associated with other work modalities, such as hybrid and remote work, should also be a feature of the office-forward modality.

> I do think flexibility almost has to stay. One of the issues that we are running into is recruitment. Or even our employees are being recruited and being offered 100% remote work, and more pay. So, it's kind of hard to compete without flexibility. (Maria, division vice president)
>
> I think in today's climate where it's really hard to get good employees, a lot of people look for that flexibility. So to be able to offer that is a huge advantage when you're trying to recruit people. Personally, I like having the option. I do think that it's good to at least come in a couple times a week. But I think it's nice to be able to also have that option to stay at home, and I know a lot of people will look for that in jobs now. (David, client services consultant)

And so, you need flexibility for business purposes—you understand you can't recruit and retain without it. But also, you realized flexibility brings personal benefits:

- A big benefit is more time for family. Ethan, an avid Officer who had started going back to the office full-time as soon as the company decided on its office-forward approach, reflected:

It was during COVID, and my kids were five and three, and they'd just run around and play with each other like little hooligans. You could hear them in the other room. I really liked that sound, like, the idea of them having fun. I was doing what I wanted to be doing and what I needed to be doing--working. And I just felt really comfortable. I felt really comfortable, and I knew that they were happy. And I felt like I was around them. And just as I'm saying this, it feels it's contrary to my separation preference that we talked about earlier. But maybe there's room for both, maybe they're not—these ideas—are not mutually exclusive. Like, I liked, I liked that feeling. (Ethan, sales representative)

Yes, maybe these ideas are not mutually exclusive indeed. Another Officer, Emily, passionately talked about the benefits of flexibility for managing her family:

I love it. I love the flexibility. I love…like last week, I had a really rough week, so I was like, I'm just gonna work from home this week, get some stuff done. My husband was traveling all week. It was just super nice to have that flexibility to do that. In the past, that would have been looked at like 'she's lazy and not doing her job'. Now, that perception has changed. (Emily, associate division vice president)

This is the same Officer who was fiercely protective of the office earlier in the interview, telling us: "I love this building, I'm very passionate about it!" (Emily, associate division vice president).

- Another benefit of flexibility Officers discovered was the restorative effects of work-from-home on mental health. One Officer shared:

Mental health days and time. It's not that you're sick, that you don't come into work. You really just mentally aren't there. And if I do experience one of those days, then yes, I will work from home because, you know, Apollonian allows us to do that. I just cannot do it [work-from-home] five days a week. (Clara, sales representative)

This is the same Clara you met in Chapter 6 who shared that work-from-home was detrimental to her mental health. Another Officer agreed on the mental health benefits of some at-home workdays:

We have the flexibility of if you wake up and you're having one of those days, you know, you could stay home if you want to. I will certainly work from home a day here and a day there. (Sara, division vice president)

- A third benefit of flexibility Officers discovered was simply the convenience of the occasional work-from-home day.

For me, I like the flexibility. Although I'm not a fan of work-from-home as I do feel it's not getting as much production done, I'm still working Friday's at home, you know. It's nice to put sweatpants on in the morning, or it's nice to do a load of laundry during the day, or clean up the kitchen while you have some time, or if I have light meetings, it's nice to have this on a Friday where I can stay home rather than having to do that in the office. (Christopher, account manager)

By pushing to normalize and even institutionalize flexibility in your company's office-forward culture, your work experience will turn from great to excellent. But importantly, to maximize the impact of flexibility, make sure you embrace work-from-home as much as your office-preferring heart would let you. Note that this advice to you triangulates perfectly with our advice to company leaders (Chapter 9) and team leaders (Chapter 10) in office-forward companies to not shun remote work completely. In office-forward organizations, encoding an appreciation for flexibility in the culture's DNA is crucially important for everyone's experiences, including the most avid supporters of office work, the Officers.

> Flexibility, as facilitated by work-from-home, is important even for Officers. So Officers, to improve your already great work experience further, insist on your company embracing flexibility as part of its office-forward strategy.

Integrators (Hybrid-Preferring Employees in Hybrid Companies)

You have a great experience in your hybrid company. You absolutely enjoy mixing and matching office and home; in person and virtual; work and life. You feel you are maximizing productivity. You feel you have balance. But even you feel a little bit of pain. Your main concern is that your efforts might not be visible enough because you are not always in the office:

I will say, though, I am a little more apprehensive and anxious when I do work from home that I'm going to miss something, and it's not because I'm not working. I just feel like I'm better off in the office than at home. (Patrick, treasury analyst)

When I'm at home, I'm so concerned about my Microsoft Teams status because I want people to know I'm at my desk, I'm working. I don't want them wondering what I'm doing. When I'm in the office, you kind of have permission to take a breather because you're in the office, and people know you're in the office, so they just kind of assume you're working, right, even if that's not true. Like, if someone stops by your desk and talks to you, it might start work related, but it could turn into personal stuff, and you're not really thinking much of your status because you're in the office. When I'm at home, I am concerned about my Teams status from 8 am to 5 pm. Like, even if I were to be in the office and wasting more time, it doesn't concern me as much as if I'm at home and, you know, yeah, I don't know... I just, I feel like when I'm at home, I'm constantly fighting that perception. (Mindy, assistant director of client services)

To solve this, you need to do two things.

- One, this state of doubt is psychologically taxing for you. So, go to the office as often as you feel you need to. You like being in the office anyways. Here's how you talk about the office:

It rejuvenates me. It helps me connect. It's cool. (Oliva, junior analyst)

I love it. I honestly get energized. (Maggie, operations manager)

Our offices are really nice. I'm really grateful for the office we have. We even have our own Starbucks. (Mindy, assistant director of client services)

It's a huge draw. I love the facility. It's a big reason why I want to continue to go down there. (Henry, director of consulting)

Our campus is pretty grand. I think to myself, They did all of this so that I can enjoy. (Eva, assistant director of communications)

Boy, who's sounding like an Officer working in an office-forward company? But listen closer. This is *really* why you like to go to the office.

I do kind of correlate my in-office days with when I maybe have bigger meetings or maybe more formal meetings with people who are a little bit higher up. And also, the things that I tend to work on when I come into the office are of greater importance. I feel like, when I'm in the office, I'm trying to put my best foot forward because there's people that can see you, there's people that can just randomly talk to you, but it is exciting. (Olivia, junior analyst)

I also notice—this doesn't necessarily feel just—but I notice more opportunities in person. I sit really close to our chief data officer and because nobody goes in, he gets lunch with me or chats with me more often. Which isn't necessarily fair, but is something that I notice. (Tina, data governance specialist)

I just, you know, eavesdrop on what's going on in the world around me, right? Leaders are always going in and out of meetings, and you hear those conversations that happen after the meeting, right? And sometimes, I hear that they're struggling with something, and then, I can try to create something and save it. And then I say, 'Oh, hey, I heard about that, I can tell you this, this will help your problem'. So it's easier to make some of those inroads in the office. When you're home, you're grasping for straws. (Alex, senior financial analyst)

What this means is that you *really* go to the office because you're good at impression management. Going to the office is one way for you to assuage your concern that you are not being noticed. So keep on going in, and being intentional about it. It works for you!

However...

- Two, while making yourself physically visible is a solution you are naturally good at, we warn you that it might take a psychological toll on you. It might make the office experience feel performative. Plus, you do like working from home, too. So, don't deny that part of yourself. Learn to make yourself visible virtually as well. You care about balance. Adding virtual impression management skills to your already good in-person impression management skills will give you balance in this area.

This is what Olivia told us she does to stay visible virtually: "I have monthly touch bases set up with my leader where I'm still having, like, virtual lunches with them or things like that." Here's what another Integrator, Connor, told us he does:

I make an intentional effort to keep connections, keep the people on my calendar once a quarter, you know. That's really huge for me. Like, when I meet with someone and think it was really valuable, I know I have to be on top of it. If I can't have lunch with them, I better put something on their Outlook calendar, like a 30 min chat. And then, it's the optional things, like listening to our earnings calls, right, making sure that I'm listening to the town halls, right, if I'm not in person for them, little things like that. Because you know, from home, it's pretty easy to say 'decline' and hang out with roommates. But like for me, it's important to kind of keep that presence at least. (Connor, consultant manager)

Scheduling purposeful chats or virtual coffees and lunches with your leader, following up with people you believe are important for you to connect with, maintaining a virtual presence at company-wide remote events—these are all great techniques you can add to your impression management repertoire. Here's another easy suggestion—complete your online profile (in Teams or whatever system your company uses). Fill in details about you—the person and the employee. What would help people know you better? Add a good picture. Put your schedule and availability on there. Make it easy for others to know you, virtually.

By sharpening your impression management skills, your work experience will turn from great to excellent. But importantly, to maximize impact, make sure you balance in-person with virtual visibility and presence. Note that this advice to you triangulates perfectly with our advice to company leaders (Chapter 9) and team leaders (Chapter 10) in hybrid companies to adopt a best-of-both-worlds mindset. In hybrid organizations, finding balance between the office and the home, between in-person and technology-mediated interactions, between work and life is crucially important for everyone's experiences, including the most avid supporters of hybrid work, the Integrators.

> Visibility and presence are important for Integrators. So Integrators, add virtual impression management skills to your already great in-person impression management skills for a balanced approach to building your presence.

A Note on Persona Change

Personas are not static—as detailed above, you can change your persona to achieve better personal alignment.

Beyond initiating a change process specifically for alignment, people also change over the course of the lifespan. For example, you may become a parent, your significant other may need to move to a different city/state for a job, your aging parents may need care. These life events may necessitate a persona change.

To wit, some of our interviewees anticipated their persona will change from an office-preferring persona to more of a hybrid- or even home-preferring persona once when they become parents. Victoria (investment analyst) shared: "I think as I personally grow, and you know, if I have a family or anything, I think that flexibility will be very nice." Nicole (data analyst) had very similar thoughts:

> In terms of the stage of life that I'm in right now, it makes a lot of sense, and I thoroughly enjoy going into the office every day. But I know that that may change. So I appreciate that while I love working in the office now, and I love being around a lot of people, I don't want to be naive to the fact that, hey, that may change as life changes.

Other interviewees anticipated that their persona will change from a home-preferring persona to more of a hybrid- or even office-preferring one when their kids grow up. Pattie (risk manager) shared: "I have young kids, they're one-and-a-half and three-and-a-half. But if I decide in five years I want to go back to an office, I want to have that option."

This speaks not only to the point that personas are fluid. It speaks to the importance of self-awareness. To achieve better alignment for yourself—whether now or in the future as your circumstances change—you have to know yourself.

Reflection on How You Can Grow into the Persona You Wish to Be A truly important message we hope you take away from this chapter—and in fact, from our book—is that you are not stuck in the persona you currently inhabit. You can evolve in a better-aligned persona. Think about it. If you like work-from-home, you don't have to be stuck in the Producer persona, or even the Rebel persona. You can take a variety of steps to evolve into an Avatar. Similarly, if you like work-from-office, you don't have to be miserable as a Community-seeker, or only somewhat happy as a Traditionalist. You can do a number of things to evolve into an Officer. And, if you like hybrid work, you can be a somewhat happy Centrist or a somewhat happy Progressive, or you can take steps to evolve into an Integrator. It is empowering to know that persona evolution is possible, and that it is something we can control or at least affect. However, persona evolution is impossible without self-awareness. Being aware of your current needs and values, as well as anticipating your future needs and values, is crucial to your ability to evolve into a better-aligned persona.

Another important message to carry with you is that no persona is perfectly happy, even the "perfectly" aligned personas. Avatars, Officers, and Integrators all have a wish list. What's interesting is that their wish lists are best fulfilled via the same tactics we recommended companies utilize to better align their workforce-at-large to their strategy (Chapter 9) and leaders utilize to align their teams internally (Chapter 10). These tactics focus on in-person relationship-building (for Avatars), demanding more flexibility (for Officers), and finding a balance (for Integrators). And so, by implementing these tactics to refine your perfect alignment further, you help your leader and your company with their alignment efforts. Alignment all around.

CHAPTER 12

Alignment and the New Workplace

At the beginning of this book, we made two claims. We argued that:

1. In the post-pandemic workplace, there's not one new normal.
2. The way to get to your "new normal"—whether you are a professional employee or a work organization—is to find alignment.

As we close this book, we'd like to revisit these claims.

NOT ONE NEW NORMAL

In the new workplace, there's not one right way to be a worker. Employees have developed different work location preferences: @home, @office, @hybrid. As we discussed, no preference reigns supreme. Instead, employees appear relatively evenly split across these three workstyles.

There's also not one right approach to build a workplace. Work organizations and their leaders have adopted different workplace strategies: remote-first, office-forward, hybrid. And, just as no employee preference reigns supreme, no organizational workplace strategy reigns supreme either.

However, as we argued on the pages of this book, employees' work location preferences and companies' workplace strategies do not exist in isolation. Rather, these diverse employee preferences and diverse company strategies combine to produce even more diversity: persona diversity. Specifically, the various combinations of employee preferences and companies' strategies yield nine workplace personas. You can imagine this as a multiplicative formula:

*Employee Workplace Preference Diversity*_(Three Employee Preferences)
× *Company Workplace Strategy Diversity*_(Three Company Strategies)
= *Persona Diversity*$^2_{(Nine\ Workplace\ Personas)}$

This is interesting, but what's important is the big discovery of our research, our Ah-ha: Of the nine personas in the new workplace, only three are fully aligned to their company's strategy. This means that six personas exist at some degree of misalignment.

In remote-first companies, there are the fully aligned Avatars who prefer to work from home. But there also are the half-aligned Centrists who would rather their company adopt a hybrid strategy, as well as the completely misaligned Community-seekers who would love an office-forward approach. Avatars are perfectly happy and loyal to their remote-first employer, but Centrists' and especially Community-seekers' work experience is not that great; both personas have issues with the remote-first approach.

In office-forward companies, there are the fully aligned Officers who prefer to work in the office. But there also are the half-aligned Progressives who would rather their company adopt a hybrid strategy, as well as the completely misaligned Producers who would love a remote-first approach. Officers are perfectly happy and loyal to their office-forward employer, but Progressives' and especially Producers' work experience is not that great; both personas have issues with the office-forward approach.

In hybrid companies, there are the fully aligned Integrators who prefer to work in a hybrid fashion. But there also are two half-aligned personas: the Rebels who prefer to work from home, and the Traditionalists who prefer to work from the office. Integrators are perfectly happy and loyal to their hybrid employer. But Rebels are upset that their hybrid employer is not a remote-first company, and Traditionalists are upset that their hybrid employer is not an office-forward company.

And so, every work organization has to deal with a persona mix where one persona supports the current strategy, but two other personas wish for different strategies.

To get a taste of this challenge, hear the differing visions for the "new normal" the different personas offer. Home-preferring personas—your Avatars, Rebels, and Producers—hope work-from-home is here to stay. They're cheering for remote-first:

> Pre-pandemic, I feel like the workplace was filled with a lot of people who were tired and stressed, and that could translate into their work and them not, you know, putting in their best foot, or working to the best of their ability because they're just mentally drained. And yes, the pandemic sucked, but we all got to work from home, and based on what people said, people were happier, people were relaxed. So I hope that we don't try to go back to that lifestyle where

everyone's just tired and drained and it was work, work, work. I hope we can still enjoy our lives and we can still put in our best foot at work at the same time. (Karen, financial analyst intern)

In sharp contrast, office-preferring personas—the Officers, Traditionalists, and Community-seekers—hope the office becomes primary again. They're cheering for office-forward:

> I'm glad I can provide a different side of work-from-home because I think that people talk so much about its positives, but I'm definitely a huge advocate for work-from-office. I'm thankful I have a job, and I'm thankful my job is flexible and has given people those opportunities. I just, I am definitely ready for it to go back to normal, to say the least. What I would like to see happen is people open their minds up a little bit to coming back to office, especially the older people who have families and stuff. I hope they start to see, Okay, we are really missing a big chunk of our jobs by working from home, and we're not getting things done in the way we were, you know. We're kind of plateauing. (Hannah, senior analyst)

And, hybrid-preferring personas—your Integrators, Centrists, and Progressives—hope for a mix of office and home, with a dash of structure. They are cheering for hybrid:

> I hope that [the flexibility] stays. I definitely think we need maybe a little bit more structure. Like, there's being flexible, right, but there's having some sort of guidelines or structure. Like my father's company, for example, sets standards: 'We are going to be in Tuesday through Thursday, and then Monday and Friday, you can do what you want.' So like I said, there should be some structure. There should be, you know, some kind of rules in place, right? (Olivia, junior analyst)

These differing visions are why it is important that the new workplace continues to offer options. As we said at the beginning of the book, in the new workplace, sameness is out, choice is in. At the same time, however, it is unrealistic to expect that employees would just sort themselves into the company strategy that works best for them. Persona diversity won't just disappear. So, what are employees, leaders, and companies to do? The logical answer—one we laid out on the pages of this book—is finding alignment.

Finding Alignment

The idea that the new workplace is about **finding alignment** is why we wrote this book. You no longer have to fit into some mold, some right way to build a workplace or to be a worker. Finding alignment means you get to figure out what works for YOU! We find this inspiring. We believe it is liberating.

But finding alignment takes some serious work. Where to start? We find unpacking definitions to be a useful start.

"To align" means "to bring into line; to get or fall into line."1 In the context of building the new workplace, the pieces that need to "fall into line" are the three levels of the organization—macro, meso, and micro. How do organizational decision makers (macro), team leaders (meso), and employees (micro) come together—or fall in line—to create a holistic strategy for the new workplace they want to build?

You know we love visuals, so of course, we have a visual for that (Fig. 12.1).

Look at the figure above. It represents the puzzle of the new workplace, with its beautiful diversity of workplace strategies: remote-first, office-forward, hybrid. Each of these strategies can (and probably should) look a bit different

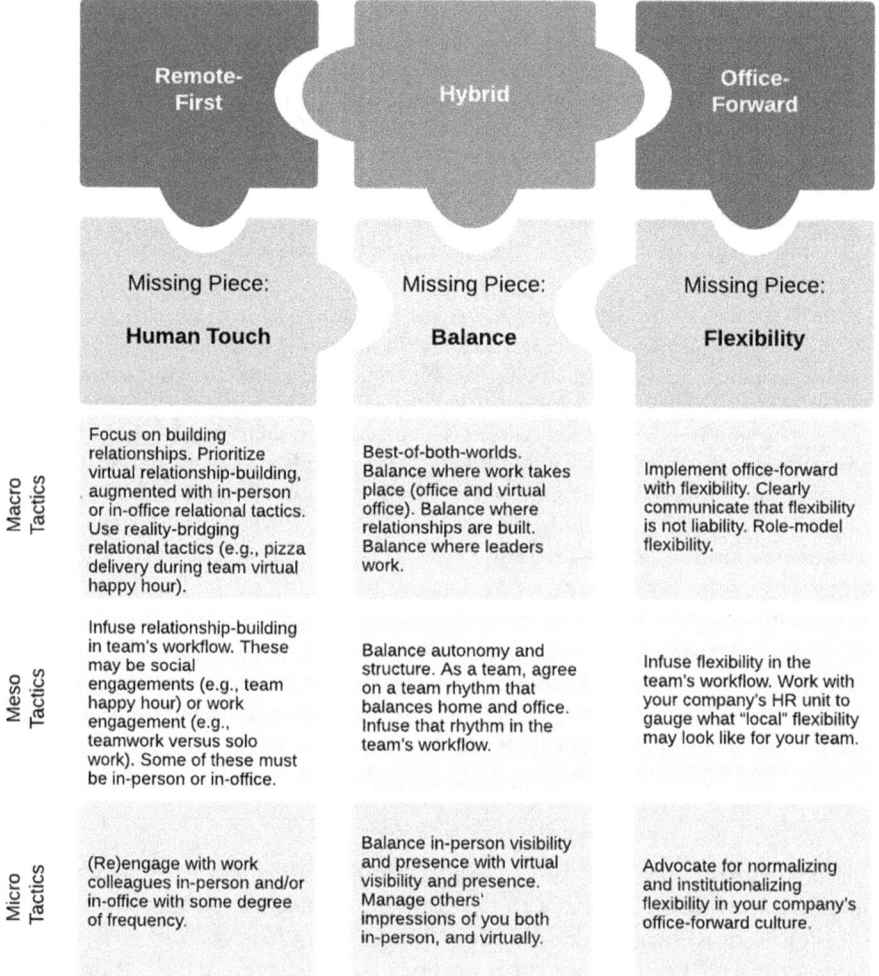

Fig. 12.1 The new workplace

from one work organization to the next. That's the beauty of it—employers and employees have choices.

But that's the thing—you must choose. You must put together your puzzle. That starts from the top. As one of our interviewees eloquently put it,

> Companies need to do a really good job of defining what their culture is now. Before, you could rely on people being together and understanding the culture from being together. A lot was implicit, but when everyone was together, you would get the vibe from being together. Seems to me that now, it might have to be made explicit. We might have to actually say, What exactly is our culture? Who are we? Why is this important? And then, how do you embed this into how we actually interact with each other? I don't think any of that's easy, but I do think that companies have to take a stand because it's dwindling. (Ryan, director of supplier management)

This perfectly aligns (pun intended) with our call for clarity earlier in the book. What do you choose? Remote-first? Great! How are you going to implement that, what would that look like at your organization. Or maybe it's office-forward? Super. Again, what does that look like in your company? Or is it going to be hybrid? Amazing. But what does that mean, what is your version of hybrid? Regardless of which strategy you choose, you must know your "why" and you must explain the "why" to your people. You have years of data on what works and what does not work for you; you also have intimate knowledge of your organization's DNA. Put these data-based and emotional pieces together into a comprehensive vision for what your workplace is going to be. Communicate that vision clearly and with conviction.

By making your choice, you have put the top row of the new workplace puzzle together. Let's move on to the second row: Figuring out the missing piece to your chosen strategy. Arguably, this is the key to successfully piecing together the puzzle.

The reason we suggest that figuring out your missing piece is the key to the puzzle goes back to the persona diversity we systematically described for you on the pages of this book. As we explained, you will face a mix of aligned, half-aligned, and misaligned personas regardless of the strategy you choose. If you choose remote-first, you'll have Avatars who would love your choice, but you'll also have Centrists who would want you to put the brakes on remote-first a little bit, and you'll have Community-seekers who would really want you to slam on those brakes and reverse course. If you choose office-forward, you'll have Officers who would be thrilled with your choice, but you'll also have Progressives who would wonder whether your choice might be a bit old-fashioned, and you'll have Producers who would go as far as thinking your choice is toxic. And, if you choose hybrid, you'll have Integrators who would quickly come to appreciate your choice, but you'll also have Traditionalists who would wish you just took a more straight-forward stance and chose the office, and you'll have Rebels who would wish you took a braver stance and stayed remote. So, your choice will always have detractors. Importantly, even your supporters are not blind to the negatives of your choice.

Well, this is the key! To successfully implement your chosen strategy, rally everyone around solving for its negative! Align the macro, meso, and micro pieces to fill the void left by the missing piece.

The Missing Piece in the Remote-First Strategy

As the Figure above shows, the missing piece in the **remote-first strategy** is the human touch. All personas that inhabit remote-first organizations acknowledge that. Community-seekers are really upset that work has lost its meaning because it has become so impersonal, leaving them feeling like "soulless husks." Centrists miss seeing more of their colleagues and they worry about acclimating newcomers to the organization and about "the little guy in the mailroom" who may lose their job. And even Avatars, who feel perfectly happy dwelling in virtual reality, confess that they sometimes feel lonely and even "forget who you work for."

As the Figure advises, to successfully build out your remote-first strategy once you've chosen it, focus your macro, meso, and micro alignment tactics on infusing humanity back into your workplace. At the organizational level (macro), decision makers should prioritize relationship-building via technology, but should also push for augmenting those efforts with in-person relationship-building activities and events. At the mid-level (meso), team leaders should purposefully infuse relationship-building in their teams' workflow, ensuring that some activities are in person. And, at the employee level (micro), employees should be encouraged and enabled to (re)engage with colleagues in person with some degree of frequency. This triangulation aligns your tactics along one clear axis: bringing humanity back in the remote-first workplace via building relationships. This, coupled with a clear, and clearly communicated, vision for what remote-first means to you is how you complete your new workplace puzzle successfully.

The Missing Piece in the Office-Forward Strategy

In the Figure above, the missing piece in the **office-forward strategy** is flexibility. All personas who reside in-office-forward organizations wish that flexibility be a prominent aspect of office-forward. Producers are fearful that the flexibility they found during lockdown might completely vanish, and they don't love "feeling required" to be at the office at all times. Progressives feel flexibility represents trust, and they warn that removing flexibility would make people wonder "you do trust us, right?" And even Officers, who feel perfectly happy dwelling in the office, confess that they "love the flexibility" and believe that "these ideas [of flexibility and being in the office] are not mutually exclusive."

And so, as the Figure above advises, to successfully build out your office-forward strategy once you've chosen it, focus your macro, meso, and micro alignment tactics on infusing flexibility back into your workplace. At the organizational level (macro), decision makers should communicate flexibility is valued and should prominently role-model what we call office-forward with flexibility. At the mid-level (meso), team leaders should infuse flexibility in the team's workflow, and should ensure such "local" flexibility is sanctioned by the organization. And, at the employee level (micro), employees should advocate for normalizing and institutionalizing flexibility in the organization. This triangulation aligns your tactics along one clear axis: making room for flexibility in the modern office-forward workplace. This, coupled with a clear, and clearly communicated, vision for what office-forward means to you is how you complete your new workplace puzzle successfully.

The Missing Piece in the Hybrid Strategy

Finally, in the Figure above, the missing piece in the **hybrid strategy** is balance. All personas who arise in hybrid organizations are looking for a better balance between work and life, home and office, in-person and technology-mediated interactions, task accomplishment, and relationship-building. Rebels may prioritize family and life and may prefer technology-mediated interactions, but they also seek out "high-value chatter" and want to be around "other human beings." Traditionalists may prioritize relationship-building and may believe work is best done in the office, but they also seek out ways to separate work and life for better structure and mental health. And Integrators, who feel perfectly happy switching between the home and the office, confess that it took them a hot second to figure out how to "flip my mind" to embrace the constant home-office switching and find balance.

As the Figure above advises, to successfully build out your hybrid strategy once you've chosen it, focus your macro, meso, and micro alignment tactics on bringing balance into your workplace. At the organizational level (macro), decision makers should embrace a best-of-both-worlds mentality, showcasing the benefits of balancing work and life, home and office, in-person and technology-based interactions through the hybrid approach. At the mid-level (meso), team leaders should create a team rhythm that balances autonomy and structure. And, at the employee level (micro), employees should balance their in-person visibility building skills with new skills to increase their virtual visibility. This triangulation aligns your tactics along one clear axis: finding balance between opposites in the hybrid workplace. This, coupled with a clear, and clearly communicated, vision for what hybrid means to you is how you complete your new workplace puzzle successfully.

In Closing

The beauty of the new workplace is its diversity of approaches. Prior to the global COVID-19 pandemic, there was one workplace model. And it was old! It dated back to the days of the Industrial Revolution. And as far as employees' work location preferences? What preferences? That wasn't even a thing!

Some might say the old days were simpler. But sameness is boring and uninspiring. We're glad it is out. Choice can be scary and confusing, but it's also exciting and full of potential. We're glad choice is in.

We hear the loud, competing voices screaming over each other.

> Back to the office! Remote work is an abomination!
>
> No! We want freedom! No more being shackled to the office chair in the service of the powers-that-be!

We know passions are running high. We are aware the issue has even become politically divisive.

But we hope that the new workplace continues to offer a diversity of options. We hope that there continues to be not one new normal, not one right way to be a worker, not one right approach to build a workplace. Yes, making workplace diversity work is hard work, but it's worth it. It stands the chance of providing organizations with competitive advantage. It stands the chance of allowing workers to customize the work experience and tailor it to their wants and needs.

We hope that after reading this book, you come to see the new workplace not as a field to wage battle on, but as a field of opportunities.

Notes

1. "Align," in *Merriam-Webster.Com Dictionary* (Merriam-Webster, n.d.), https://www.merriam-webster.com/dictionary/align.

Appendix

Additional Book Resources

Additional research findings and resources from this book, including the Awareness Raising Primer (from Chapter 10), Finding Common Ground team-building activity (from Chapter 10), Workplace Persona Assessment (from Chapter 11:), and other tools can be found on our website: https://thenewworkplacebook.com/ (Fig. A.1).

Fig. A.1 QR code for the new workplace book website with additional resources

INDEX

A
Agile, 46, 137, 175
Airbnb, 35
alignment, 1, 4, 7, 9, 37, 59, 64, 69, 81, 86, 91, 97, 115, 126, 129, 131, 133, 139, 145, 151, 152, 186, 189, 192, 211, 216
  company, 153, 166
  full alignment, 8, 119, 189, 217
  half-alignment, 8, 61, 89, 119, 121, 125–127, 195, 217
  misalignment, 7, 8, 61, 63, 64, 91, 92, 200, 214, 217
  personal, 183, 190, 195, 200, 203, 210
  team, 157, 166, 173, 181
Allstate, 36
Amazon, 150
Apollonian, 5, 68, 69, 71, 97, 206
Atlassian, 152
attachment, 14, 40, 74, 75, 79, 141, 146
autonomy, 58, 180
Avatars
  consequences, 55, 64
  definition, 7, 37, 39, 55, 133, 184, 214, 217
  psychological factors, 40, 44, 50, 52, 73, 187
awareness, 37, 69, 97, 169, 211

Awareness Raising Primer, 157, 158, 161, 163, 165, 169, 174, 176, 179, 181, 221

B
balance, 112, 115, 117, 119, 144, 180, 194, 207, 209–211, 219
bandage, 124, 125
BBC, 16
best-of-both-worlds, 32, 144, 145, 148, 149, 152, 179, 182, 210
Blair-Loy, Mary, 125
boring, 85, 121, 126

C
Centrists
  consequences, 59, 64
  definition, 8, 37, 39, 59, 133, 183, 214, 217
  psychological factors, 41, 47, 51, 52, 193
character traits, 159, 161, 164
Chesky, Brian, 35
Chipotle, 67
Christmas, 47
clarity, 108, 131, 143, 148, 150, 153, 174, 176, 179, 217
CNBC, 16
collaboration, 68, 87, 95, 109, 119, 138–140, 142, 145, 148, 175

collegiality, 192
commitment, 56, 60, 64, 132, 138, 170–172
Community-seekers
  consequences, 61, 64
  definition, 8, 37, 39, 61, 134, 183, 214, 217
  psychological factors, 42, 48, 51, 53, 191
connection, 68, 78, 79, 84, 87, 91, 101, 105, 106, 133, 135, 136, 139, 144, 148, 202
control, 79, 138, 139
convenience, 50–52, 90, 133, 135, 150, 207
  inconvenience, 51, 52
cost-benefit analysis, 50, 51, 53
cost-savings, 132
counter viewpoints, 167, 169
COVID-19, 3, 4, 16, 24, 37, 68, 71, 97, 132, 213, 220
crafting, 4, 8, 9, 115–117, 151, 183, 195, 200
creativity, 36, 67, 68, 75, 152
culture, 3, 24, 30, 36, 37, 50, 68, 73, 79, 92, 96, 107, 115, 118, 133, 138, 140, 144, 148
cynicism, 125

D
defiance, 90
demographics, 11, 22, 31, 32, 136, 158, 159, 161, 163
desk sharing, 39, 95, 121, 134, 146, 150
disconnectedness, 61, 62, 64, 90, 105, 110, 134, 148
Disney, 67
dispersed teams, 36, 37, 41, 100, 106, 143, 147, 148, 150, 175, 176, 199
Diwali, 45
Dropbox, 36

E
employee resource groups, 136, 202
empty office, 43, 104, 121, 134, 143, 146, 147, 197, 201

energy, 83, 84, 87, 205
engagement, 37, 44, 46, 47, 91, 112, 132, 136, 137, 148, 174, 176, 189, 204
  disengagement, 61, 62, 64
ethnographic study, 3
executive status, 13, 17, 22, 97, 104, 183

F
fairness, 72, 79, 149, 176, 178, 181
fear, 43, 90, 118, 125, 126, 142
feedback, 83, 108, 139, 151
finding common ground, 169
  team-building activity, 157, 158, 161, 165, 173, 181, 221
Flash, 43
flexibility
  benefit, 3, 5, 11, 28, 36, 50–52, 64, 67, 68, 71, 79, 115, 118, 126, 132, 140, 141, 144, 148, 173, 176, 207, 211, 218
  illusion of, 125
  personal characteristic, 51, 71, 110, 147, 177
FlexIndex, 36, 69
flextime, 124, 142, 180
Forbes, 16
forgotten, 90, 106, 201
Fortune, 4, 5, 13, 15
freedom, 22, 28, 56–58, 60, 64, 71, 113, 133, 135, 140, 195
fun, 29, 31, 36, 73, 81, 84, 91, 107, 108, 118, 123, 141, 142, 144, 175, 206

G
gender, 11, 22, 25, 31
generational differences, 78
golden handcuffs, 58, 64, 136, 172
Goldman Sachs, 67, 68
Googles, 95
gratitude, 117, 118, 126
Guardian, 16

H

Harmonium, 5, 96, 97, 99, 100, 104, 105, 108, 111, 118, 125
home, 74
hoteling, 39, 41, 42, 52, 74, 96
house, 74
Houston, Drew, 36
HubSpot, 96
human connection, 36, 44
humanistic-concern, 132
humanistic employee experience, 132, 133
human touch, 44, 152, 218
hybrid
  flextime, 180
  fluid, 95, 96, 100, 145–149
  rotational, 180
  scheduled, 180
  structured, 95, 96, 145–149, 180

I

ideal-worker norm, 125, 189
identity, 25, 40, 74, 79
IF-THEN scenarios, 170, 172
Iger, Bob, 67
immersive virtual environments, 45
impression management, 209, 210
Inc. Magazine, 27
Industrial Revolution, 6, 220
Integrators
  consequences, 115, 126
  definition, 7, 97, 99, 115, 145, 184, 214, 217
  psychological factors, 101, 104, 108, 112, 193
interruptions, 77, 108

J

Jassy, Andy, 3
job performance, 58, 132, 145, 151

L

life-first mindset, 117, 118, 123, 126
lonely, 42, 50, 59, 62, 64, 85, 90, 104, 119
loyalty, 56, 64, 132

M

macro, 9, 216, 218
marital status, 17, 21, 22, 25, 31, 136, 159
McKinsey, 95
meetings
  etiquette, 149
  hybrid, 74, 149
  in-person, 6, 46, 101, 138, 144, 176, 195, 199
  protocols, 41, 149
  remote, 44, 106, 135, 136, 138, 143, 144, 178
mental health, 21, 52, 53, 84, 85, 87, 113, 123, 145, 179, 192, 201, 203, 206
mentoring, 91, 136, 142, 143, 148, 203, 204
meso, 9, 216, 218
micro, 9, 216, 218
Microsoft SharePoint, 135, 137
Microsoft Teams, 44, 45, 48, 52, 74, 76, 77, 87, 103, 106, 107, 117, 135–137, 175, 200, 208, 209
middle ground, 64, 144
mid-level manager, 157
Mitchells vs. the Machines, The (film), 75, 78
mommy track, 16, 124
motivation
  extrinsic, 84, 87, 90
  intrinsic, 84–87, 91, 203, 205
  lack of, 120, 121
Musk, Elon, 3, 13

N

need to belong, 29
New York Times, 16
Niccol, Brian, 14

O

office design, 39, 42, 140, 147
Officers
  consequences, 81, 91
  definition, 7, 68, 71, 81, 140, 184, 214, 217
  psychological factors, 71, 75, 79, 190
Office, The (television), 82

oneness, 57, 59

P
paradox, 92, 117, 119, 134, 140
parental status, 15, 26, 210
paternity leave, 124
persona
   breakdown, 37, 69, 97
   definition, 6, 32
   diversity, 8, 37, 68, 69, 97, 129, 133, 139, 145, 157, 158, 165, 181, 213, 215, 217
   evolution, 202, 211
   spread, 8, 9, 151, 153, 174, 176, 179, 214, 215
personal circumstances, 92
Pichai, Sundar, 95
powerlessness, 90
pragmatic, 92
preference
   hybrid, 1, 9, 11, 31, 99, 163–165, 168, 192, 213
   work-from-home, 9, 11, 13, 15, 17, 19–22, 37, 39, 158, 159, 161, 167, 187, 213
   work-from-office, 1, 9, 11, 13, 22, 25, 30, 71, 161, 162, 168, 190, 213
presenteeism, 139, 178, 196
pride, 82, 84, 91, 117, 120
Producers
   consequences, 89, 92
   definition, 8, 68, 71, 89, 140, 183, 214, 217
   psychological factors, 73, 77, 79, 188
productivity, 77, 79, 91, 119, 142, 151, 152, 174, 207
professionalism, 134
professionalism, 120
Progressives
   consequences, 86, 92
   definition, 8, 71, 86, 140, 183, 214, 217
   psychological factors, 73, 76, 79, 193
projection, 44, 47, 48, 52, 53, 175
Promethean, 4, 37, 39, 52, 55, 58, 64, 68, 97
proximity, 36, 68, 138, 139, 152

Q
quitting, 63, 64
quiet, 56

R
race, 20, 159, 161
realistic job preview, 135, 142, 147
Rebels
   consequences, 122, 126
   definition, 8, 97, 99, 119, 146, 214, 217
   psychological factors, 103, 105, 110, 112, 188
relationally impoverished place, 50
relational poverty, 133
relationships
   building, 28, 112, 115, 136, 140, 141, 148, 152, 172, 176, 196, 200, 211
   high-quality, 47, 48
   meaningful, 19, 22, 87, 91, 181
   positive work, 74, 78, 81, 88, 92, 133, 137, 142, 148, 172, 174
reverse psychology, 195–200
role-model, 102, 104, 108, 151, 178, 197

S
S&P 500, 152
Second Life, 45
selection criteria, 136, 142, 147
serendipitous interactions, 138
Shah, Dharmesh, 96
Slack, 20, 144, 175
sociability, 142, 189, 190
social engagement, 37
social fabric, 61, 62, 64, 136, 137, 143, 202
solidarity, 68
Solomon, David, 67
spiral, 64, 145
Starbucks, 14
strategic leadership, 108, 134, 140, 182
structure, 35, 69, 111–113, 121, 136, 146, 180, 181, 198
Supergirl, 43
switching scenery, 3, 108, 110, 112, 115, 145, 147, 191, 193, 197, 201

T

tactics, 52, 96, 129, 131, 133, 134, 139, 140, 145, 146, 152, 157, 181, 205, 211, 218, 219
task-location fit, 108, 111, 112, 115, 180
  workflow, 109
team-building, 129, 157, 165
team composition, 143, 148
technology
  collaboration, 89, 136, 137, 148, 149, 174, 175, 178, 201, 210
  etiquette, 138, 143
  purpose, 144, 149, 175
  skills, 143
  support, 138, 149, 152
  tools, 119, 135
telecommuting, 11, 124
Tesla, 67, 68
touchy-feely, 74, 77
Traditionalists
  consequences, 121, 126
  definition, 8, 97, 99, 121, 146, 183, 214, 217
  psychological factors, 101, 107, 111, 113, 191
triangulation, 205, 207, 210, 218, 219
trifecta, 158, 173, 176, 178, 181
trust, 35, 72, 204
turnover, 144

U

United Way, 82
U.S. Census Bureau, 30
U.S. Surgeon General, 192

V

virtual coffee, 77, 136, 137, 209
virtual office, 45–50, 52, 135, 144, 147

W

Wall Street Journal, 14, 15, 27
well-being, 21, 84, 123, 125, 132
WeWork, 36
Wharton, 132
Wilson, Tom, 36
Wolf of Wall Street (film), 56
work devotion, 125, 127, 146, 189, 190
work-life
  balance, 43, 50, 104, 108, 116, 117, 126, 145, 179, 181, 182
  boundaries, 143
  flow, 173
  integration, 123, 145, 148, 173
  oneness, 57
  policies, 124
  separation, 108, 112, 142, 146, 179
work meaningfulness, 63, 64, 82, 91, 120, 150
Workplace Persona Assessment, 9, 129, 151, 153, 184, 221
workplace strategy
  hybrid, 3–5, 95, 99, 115, 126, 131, 144, 152, 178, 186, 213
  office-forward, 3–5, 67, 71, 81, 91, 131, 138, 152, 176, 186, 213
  remote-first, 3, 4, 35, 39, 55, 64, 131, 132, 151, 174, 186, 213
workstations, 4, 5, 40, 68, 75, 119, 126, 140, 146
worries, 60, 64, 112, 118
worst-of-both-worlds, 149

Z

Zen, 57, 59, 64, 133
Zoom, 4, 44, 45, 47, 48, 52, 62, 74–79, 85, 87, 103, 106, 112, 132, 135, 137, 143
Zoom-fatigue, 132

GPSR Compliance

The European Union's (EU) General Product Safety Regulation (GPSR) is a set of rules that requires consumer products to be safe and our obligations to ensure this.

If you have any concerns about our products, you can contact us on

ProductSafety@springernature.com

In case Publisher is established outside the EU, the EU authorized representative is:

Springer Nature Customer Service Center GmbH
Europaplatz 3
69115 Heidelberg, Germany

www.ingramcontent.com/pod-product-compliance
Lightning Source LLC
LaVergne TN
LVHW011008250326
834688LV00004B/140